YUKON
ANTICS

Dedication

To my wife, Laura, for her constant support and encouragement of my writing, both in good and adverse times and to those members of my family, who have had to share the "paying of the dues," in order for me to become a full-time writer.

YUKON ANTICS

HAROLD R. HINE, Q.C.

hancock
house

ISBN 0-88839-195-1
Copyright © 1987 Harold R. Hine, Q. C.

Canadian Cataloging in Publication Data

Hine, Harold R.,   1925-
Yukon Antics
ISBN 0-88839-195-1

1. Hine, Harold R., Q. C. 2. Lawyers - Yukon Territory -
Biography. 3. Air pilots - Yukon Territory - Biography. 4. Yukon
Territory - Biography.
I. Title

KE416.H55A3 1987   349.719'1'0924   C86-091588-3

Edited by Diane Brown
Design by Herb Bryce
Printed in Canada by Friesen Printers

Cover: Photo of Beechcraft Staggerwing by Ken Holmberg
Courtesy of Dr. J. V. W. Johnston

Photos: From author and publisher's file,
except where noted

Published simultaneously in Canada and the United States by

HANCOCK HOUSE PUBLISHERS LTD.
19313 Zero Ave., Surrey, B.C. V3S 5J9

HANCOCK HOUSE PUBLISHERS
1431 Harrison Avenue, Blaine, WA 98230

Table of Contents

Introduction

The Yukon! Just to utter that word conjures up no end of images of excitement, raw existence, the struggle of mankind to make his fortune by sheer will alone. The word connotes challenging, unforgiving wilderness. The last frontier.

Congregation of the people in the Yukon into communities might consume a combined total of fifteen square miles. The rest of the Yukon is left for occupation by what it is that your mind conjures up about vastness and the wild frontier.

Streams teem with energetic, fighting fish. The mountains nestle virgin lakes which are often not much more than liquid ice. The summer season is too short to permit the water the comfort of warming up. Those same mountains harbor dynamic animals who have never had to contend with the inhumanity of man. They have never had the misfortune to meet one.

The nature of the terrain fluctuates from barren tundra to lush green valleys; from 2,000 feet above sea level up to 19,500 feet and just about everywhere in between.

The Yukon radiates an open invitation to the explorer, the wanderer, the unjaded personality. It inflames the imagination of the hunter about the big game which is still in abundance there. Mention a moose in West Germany and if you are talking to a huntsman you will get a long dissertation about the fact that they do not have any such animals left. What you will hear is a disconsolate treatise, inherent with concepts of utter inanity and creature extermination. Such stories should caution and guide us in the proper management of our own wildlife, much of which is now concentrated in the Yukon. For example, the Yukon is home to the largest known concentration of Dall sheep.

To insure that I am not misunderstood, I hasten to add that in this wilderness there is boundless beauty. There is constant gorgeous scenery which defies the imagination. It isn't only the visual beauty which is ever present, there is another sensation which is an integral part of that picture. It is difficult to define. The stillness, the sense of space and time, the continuum of divers colors, changing terrain, and all of those art works of God; all of this and more must be seen to be truly felt and comprehended in a personal quotient.

The people who seek out the Yukon are a hardy lot. They sense the adventure of the place, the historical significance. Yet, unless they are prepared to vegetate on some government sinecure, there is only constant challenge to survive that awaits them. This engenders more than average community spirit in the population. Esoterically they share unusual objectives, comaraderie, lifestyle, and situations unthinkable in the big cities. Facade is unacceptable. Only the genuine is eligible. There is no time for the fast buck artist, the flim flam, or the insincere. Sometimes the continuity of a life depends upon the dependability and reliability of a neighbor. Born out of all of this interdependance comes a sociability and forgiveness of human foibles and weaknesses which is unmatched on the "outside." Yukoners have a designation for all places, people, and things which are not within their immediate purview. They are all on the "outside" because they have no applicability to the realities of the last frontier.

Chapter One

We drove that long and dusty trail
Pushed through our last frontier,
A residual road from wartime zest,
Constructed out of fear.

It united neighbors at terminal ends
But side effects were legion,
The mostly virgin Yukon vast
Became a sought out region.

Our personal trek, amid some qualms
To acquire a new life stanza,
No gold rush in that certain sense
Yet sought as our bonanza.

Off to Whitehorse

There we were, hanging by the propeller, the plane heading straight up into the blue. I knew that at any second the plane would, with distressful notice, shake, quiver and with a dramatic shudder or two, pitch forward and we would be plunging down toward the unfriendly earth below. It was agonizing to wait for that flutter, that moment of hesitation when the plane could no longer climb. There was the first shudder, then the next, then over the hump we went.

Suddenly, alarmingly I was no longer looking up into the heavens; I was plummeting into a headlong dive, straight for the ground. The wind whistled by the outside airfoils. The plane started spiraling through the air. The trees, mountain walls, earth, and lake merged into a rotating blur.

From the rear seat came gasps of anguish and cries of

alarm. Most of my passengers had never before experienced such an exhibition of aerodynamics. A whole litany of expressions involving the deity was heard. "My God!" ... "Jesus Christ," were but a few of the milder ones.

Another time I had been immersed in the frigid water of a glacier-fed lake. I was forced into a position where I had to, most reluctantly, volunteer to become a packer of duffel bags, tents, groceries, men, and a bloody dog. Packing such things under normal conditions is not that upsetting. Packing such things through waist-deep liquid ice is uncommonly agonizing.

At yet another date, I had been intimidated by a jet fighter over Alaska. Thank God he didn't shoot! Just having him dive at me was frightening enough. He wanted me to land, so land I did, only to find myself under arrest and incarcerated by an arrogant, pompous, demanding, military paragon ... for an offense which I did not commit.

What the hell was I doing? I didn't need these harrowing experiences. The practice of law is also harrowing, at times, but not in the same fashion. The courtrooms are warm and comfortable. The people with whom I dealt, as the city solicitor for Whitehorse, were all exceptionally nice and sociable. As a crown prosecutor in the Yukon Territory, I had a respected place in the community. Occassionally, I would have to deal with the undesirables, but that was really a predictable task in comfortable surroundings. I belonged to the military Mess of both the air force and the army. There was always plenty of excitement in those; all the parties and sociability that one could ask for.

So why did I find it necessary to involve myself with flying, when I had all these other things going for me? I can't answer that; maybe it was, and still is, my karma.

Perhaps, before I get carried away with my Yukon antics, it would be best to give you some background on my decision to leave "civilization" for the "north."

In 1953, I was practicing law in Nanaimo, British Columbia, Canada. I had been there for three years, and was enjoying a good practice and a burgeoning clientele, but there were two major factors, of primary importance to me, which were sadly missing. Firstly, I dearly wanted to become a courtroom lawyer. Secondly, I wanted to learn to fly an airplane and, if possible, to use that newfound skill in my practice. Due to the way in which my business was developing, I found that I was doing a lot of solicitor work as opposed to doing barrister's

9

work.

I was active in the courts but I recognized that in order to become skilled at this specific work, I needed more in depth experience. I needed the challenge of "meatier" cases. There were in Nanaimo, in those days, too many senior members of the Bar. They jealously guarded the status which they had achieved and had little time to train "juniors." I do not criticize, I merely state the fact. They had worked hard to acquire their lucrative and esteemed bailiwicks and could hardly be expected to gratuitously train a junior, who would most certainly branch out on his own in open competition, once trained. In a nutshell, if I wanted courtroom experience, I had to go elsewhere and get it on my own.

So there was the dilemma. While my practice was growing, it was in the wrong direction. Therefore, the longer I stayed in Nanaimo, the dimmer was the prospect of having a career in the courts.

The solution was patent. If I wanted to settle into a life style which was not totally to my liking then I could do nothing; alternatively, if there was to be change, I would have to be the instrument of that change. Looking back on my life, I realized that I had always been the maker of my own destiny.

I had graduated from the law school at the University of British Columbia in 1950 when I was only 25 years of age. I had spent four years and three months in the Royal Canadian Naval Volunteer Reserve during World War II. Like so many other youths of the war era, I had lied about my age in order to enlist. How the recruiting officer could believe that this peach fuzzed boy of barely fifteen years was old enough, is still a conundrum to me. My record of service states that I served honorably, in "Canada, on the High Seas, and Britain."

Upon my discharge from the navy, I went back to school in Regina, Saskatchewan. I had not completed my education before enlisting, so I thought it better if I did it now. I completed the four years of high school in nine months and thereby qualified to enter second year arts at UBC. My objective was the law school in Vancouver.

Before leaving for Vancouver, I married my childhood sweetheart, Laura Davis. We had seen one another only three times during the war but the letters must have kept the connection alive and well. We will have celebrated forty years of marriage before this book is published.

Now back to Nanaimo days.

I let it be known in and around Vancouver that I was interested in different circumstances and soon I received a telephone call inviting me to an interview there.

The person I met was George C. van Roggen, now the Honorable Senator van Roggen of the Canadian Senate. He had a partner in a law firm located in Whitehorse, Yukon Territory. They were looking for a third member to assist in handling the heavy work load, which the two of them had developed. The other partner was Erik H. Nielsen who is now, and has been for more than twenty-five years, the sitting member in the Canadian House of Commons, representing the Yukon. He has also held the title of Deputy Prime Minister of Canada.

During the interview I learned that Erik had distinguished himself as a pilot during the recent war. Hhhmmm!

The law firm had a large court practice. They handled the briefs for the federal government, and were the office of the city prosecutor for Whitehorse. Hhhmmm!

Neither partner had any particular bent in the direction of court work, although both were competent in that field if necessary. Hhhmmm!

The die was cast!

That night, on the ferry carrying me home across the Gulf of Georgia, I had about three and one half hours to ponder the rationale of my resolve. The logistics of such a move were enormous; not to mention the emotional impact. We had just purchased a new home in Nanaimo. In fact we had not completed decorating it. Maybe this was a plus? Could we reasonably expect to sell it without taking a loss? What about my clients? Would they be charitable and understand? Would they accept the change to dealing with my associates readily, or grudgingly? The children were still young enough that they had not had time to form any permanent, or even strong, peer relationships. Cathy, our daughter, was then only five years of age. Art, our son, was only two. (Our third child, a son, Laurence, was not born until 1955, in Whitehorse).

Although Laura, my wife, and I had been in Nanaimo only three years, we had managed to acquire some strong ties with new friends. Laura's aunt and uncle lived there, so there was a small family connection as well. These were some of the challenging problems manifest in undertaking this new venture.

As was my habit and professional training, I withdrew a blue-lined, legal pad from my brief case and listed the pros and cons of the entire concept.

So preoccupied was I with these deliberations, that I was surprised when I heard the familiar sounds of the ships engines altering revolutions, mingled with the sounds of the ships whistle, announcing our arrival in Nanaimo. It was then about 10:30 in the evening.

I located my car and drove the few miles to our home. With every turn of the wheels, the burden grew heavier. I sensed a futility in my quest. Did this whole scheme arise out of some personal selfishness of mine? Had I evaluated the proper, applicable factors ... with genuine objectivity? Was I about to propose a disservice to my family, friends, clients, to the community clubs to which I belonged? Was the actual impetus only the furthering of my career? Did I have nomadic tendencies? What were my true, supportable motives? I had to be certain about these, before making any abortive proposals or announcements. The range of analysis was interminable. Suddenly, I awoke from my esoteric wanderings to find myself turning into our driveway.

I had probably driven home "without due care and attention." I was a lucky one, I had not been apprehended.

As was her custom, Laura was waiting up for me. I often thought about how considerate, thoughtful, and sharing she was to do this. Notwithstanding the often lateness of the hour, coupled with the fact that she would frequently have to get up for the children during the night, she would always wait up unless we both understood that I would be away until after midnight.

"Hi there, Big Chief!" I said, as we hugged one another hello.

"How did things go today, dear?" was her customary response.

As I headed for the bedroom to change out of my street clothes into something more comfortable, I heard Laura behind me. She was carrying two glasses which she had kept cooling in the fridge. One had Canadian Club in it for me, the other contained ginger ale for Laura. She had resolved that she would not ingest any artificial stimulant, other than coffee, until she had passed the stage of being responsible for bearing and rearing children.

I have always admired her for this strength of character.

"Well, Laura, it has been a very interesting ... yet monumentally disturbing day," I answered.

"What's the problem, dear?" she asked as she hung the

clothes, which I had carelessly tossed across the bed, into the closet.

"Well ... there is no problem ... not really," I hedged.

"No problem, eh? ... not really, eh? ... then why are you putting your house-coat over your shirt? ... come on into the living room and tell me all about what is not bothering you."

She gently took me by the arm and ushered me into the living room.

Once seated in my favorite chair and after a sip or two from my drink, I struggled with how to launch the subject. How to make the presentation in a palatable, comfortable, and effective manner.

Laura recognized my mental gymnastics. She had watched me function in the courtroom on several, probably many occasions. She sat on the edge of her favorite chair, legs crossed at the knees, with her left hand supporting her chin and the other holding a swaying glass. Her eyes were steadfastly focused upon me. She waited, and waited. Then, impatient with my hesitancy, she said in a stage whisper, "Harold, come on, you're not facing a jury. You may be facing the ultimate judge, maybe, but you needn't prepare your case with such obvious agony. Just tell it to me the way it is, SIR!" she said with a big, encouraging smile.

As I continued to patently agonize, Laura rose and walked over towards me saying, "There can be no problem involving us, which is insurmountable. Why not just start talking about it? I'll let you know if I can't keep up."

"Ok, guy, it's like this. I have been offered a chance to do court work for a small, but aggressive law firm. The partners are very effective in getting business and have a good practice. The money is good, more than I make here. The senior partner, whom I met, seems to be a fine person—a novelty really— he is what one characterizes as a true gentleman. The other partner, whom I did not meet, has a distinguished record with the RCAF ...."

I stopped and took a large swig from my glass. I looked about surreptitiously ... I hoped surreptitiously, over its rim as I drank. I thought that my eyes must be vacillating, like those of spectators at a ping-pong match. My training in body language made me hate such personal disclosures.

"Ok, Harold, out with it. What's bothering you? You're in appalling shape."

My left hand rushed to my forehead and scratched a nonexistent itch, it then coursed down over my brow, then across my mouth, ending up on the lobe of my left ear.

"Uh huh! ... I know that move ... you're trying to tell me something which you think will be repugnant to me and you're stalling while you think up a sweet coating for the unpalatable pill ... right? ... come on you fink ... out with it ... what is it?" she insisted.

Like a person jolted by a cattle prod, I started to get up.

"Sit down there ... you fink ... sit ... and start talking," she said, with solicitous overtones and a faint smile.

"Well," I began, without confidence, "Well, I'm not just sure how to put this so that you will ... I mean ... so that we can ... that is we ... the whole family ... will have to move ... if I take that position offered ... we will have to leave Nanaimo, of course ... "

"Well, dear, I'm sure that I assumed, that if we move, we would all move and if the law firm is not in Nanaimo then we will have to move elsewhere. Where is it, that we will 'all' move to?"

"Well ... I understand that we will be provided with a new ... no ... a modern house ... fairly new ... not far from the office, and ... "

"But where, dear? ... is it Chilliwack ... Vancouver ... either of them has nice schools, libraries, theaters, curling ... all the amenities ... which is it?"

"Well, it's a bit further north, guy," I stammered. I wasn't ready for this. Yet, I just could not drag out this agony another minute. I ejaculated the statement, almost in a shout, "It's Whitehorse, you know, in the Yukon Territory!"

Laura recoiled in shock. There was disbelief written all over her face. Her head shook an involuntary negative. She stared at me incredulously. She started several different times to say something ... I don't know what ... she stopped short of articulation. Then finally she blurted, "In the Yukon? ... that's in the Arctic ... in all the ice and snow ... isn't it? ... do they have courts up there? ... do they? ... that's no man's land. I'm not even sure that I really know where it is ... where is it, Harold? ... do you know? how far away is it? ... why there? ... you say that they have courts there ... where? ... in an igloo? Harold, you're joking aren't you ... you fink ... if you're joking ... "

"Laura, I'm not joking. I'm serious. I may be crazy, but I'm serious. If we go on this job, it will be to the Yukon. It isn't the Arctic. It isn't all ice and snow. They do have some long winters, just like in Regina, where we both came from ... but they have some nice summers, too. What they do have is court work galore and I can fly there. I'm not exactly sure where Whitehorse is. I think it is just north of Dawson Creek in northern British Columbia."

"Yeah ... how far north? ... isn't that the place where Robert Service wrote about the "land of the midnight sun." Let's get out a map ... do they have streets there? ... sidewalks? ... telephones? ... paved roads? ... street lights? ... WOW, Harold, you really have done it this time! ... Whitehorse and the land of the midnight sun! ... who will the children play with? ... polar bears? ... do they have schools? ... restaurants? ... auditoriums? ... shops? ... Oh boy! ... "

It didn't take a genius to recognize that Laura was in a high state of agitation. Now was not the proper time to pursue the subject. It was time to retreat and present the case another day, in a better way, if that was possible.

"Let's call it a night, guy. Let's get some sleep, maybe we will feel better about it in the morning," I suggested, as I rose from my chair.

"Yeah ... 'maybe' is certainly the correct word, dear ... maybe, but not likely," she said, with a hug for me, accompanied by a weak smile, a very weak smile.

Two months later we, the whole family, including Laura's mother, were driving the Alaska Highway on our way to Whitehorse. We had severed our ties in Nanaimo with much less furor than anticipated. Research into the status of Whitehorse had not been entirely encouraging, but it certainly was a long way from being the Arctic. It did contain almost all of the items which Laura specified as essential. Not new, nor modern, necessarily, but they were mostly all there in whole, or in part. There were, in fact, very few sidewalks, paved, wooden, or otherwise; but she settled for the other, more meaningful requirements on her list.

The Alaska Highway is, in reality, a long, seemingly endless, twisting, ribbon of dust. It was, and I understand continues to be, mostly unpaved. It was built often on muskeg and more often, on a type of powdered clay which waits at rest, eager to be bestirred, so that it may retaliate by lavishing its omnipresent cloud upon its antagonist. There was mile after mile of "washboard" in the gravel surface. This insured a slow trip or a nerve wracking ride. The trees were stultified

15

from the arid soil, in which there was insufficient nourishment. The topography varied from undulating, rolling hills to sheer, craggy mountains. There were many streams and rivers. Lakes were plentiful but shallow. There was little vegetation except the fireweed, which is the Yukon symbol.

Whenever we stopped, which was frequently with two young restless children aboard, we had to wait for what seemed to be an interminable period, to allow the ubiquitous dust to settle. Just to breath at all, in that maelstrom, was a serious challenge. Once at rest the dust may have given some form of communication to the other permeating presence that a feast was available. The moment that we opened the car door, we were infested with the largest, most voracious, blood-thirsty mosquitoes I have ever seen. They descended upon us like a black cloud. They were unrelenting in their pursuit of blood. They were huge. Could one really mistake these for humming birds?

Poor kids. Once they uncovered themselves to squat, they were immediately covered by ravenous insects. It was an experience to remember, and we have.

Our arrival in Whitehorse was most inauspicious. A stinging, blinding dust storm was in progress. I kept a cautious eye (whenever it was free of dust) upon Laura's reaction to this situation and her first impressions of the town ... of the old shacks ... the sidewalkless, unpaved streets ... the junked autos and parts thereof, which cluttered the lanes ... the patina of gray dust which covered everything in sight ... the broken, unmended fences ... the irregularity of the streets, which meandered like trails ... the fact that our house was far from ready and further away from being modern. It was a "wartime" house which had been acquired in a different location and hauled to its present resting place ... directly across the street from the city graveyard.

If Laura then, or ever, had any misgivings about going to Whitehorse, she has kept them to herself, even to this day.

The other side of the coin is that we learned to love Whitehorse and many of the people there. It was a highlight of our life.

Chapter Two

Call to the Bar, that was the plan
A really simple task,
But soon we had an entourage,
Far more than we did ask.

The majestic judge with regal flair
Informed those near and far
That his pronouncements, made that day
Called Harold to Yukon Bar.

Call to the Bar

That first year in Whitehorse passed quickly. I was much busier than anticipated. A new courthouse had been constructed, which meant beautiful new facilities, with the usual lovely finished oak paneling, elevated judge's bench, red shining leather on the judge's chair and likewise on the chairs for the jurors. The lawyer's work desks were large and designed to contain and hold many reference books. They were also large enough for a small lectern, which could be used to elevate the reading material being used at any given time. It was also a convenient item to lean upon when addressing judge or jury.

I was "living" in the courtrooms. It was great! I loved every moment of it.

Laura and the children had settled in well. Laura had the capacity to make friends easily, but selectively. Her mother stayed on with us, which was of great help to all the family, but to Laura in particular. Mother and daughter both loved to knit, sew, and in general do a lot of craft work with their hands. They both enjoyed cooking. This didn't mean that every meal was gourmet, but they were consistently interesting and appetizing.

Laura's mother is a gem. She is 89 years of age today and still going strong. At the time we went to Whitehorse, she had been a widow for many years. She had four children. Belle, about whom you will read more in this book. Arthur, who is a close friend of mine. We had played hockey together in Regina and had spent some time together overseas. Frank, who had died at an early age. Then Laura. Her life has not been an easy one, yet she continues to accept what life has to provide with the stoicism of a saint. She has been "Mom" to many, many people, all of whom love her dearly.

In order to practice law in the Yukon, it had been necessary for me to become called to the Bar of that particular jurisdiction. The uninitiated may find it of interest to learn that each and every separate province, territory, and state has a distinct, diverse, and sometimes totally unique, legal system. Many jurisdictions have exceptionally similar laws. There is, and has been for many years, a movement afoot to make the laws uniform in the various jurisdictions, where it is at all possible. Yet, for example, a judge for the Province of British Columbia has no authority in, say, the Province of Alberta, unless he is specifically so authorized by a federal government mandate. A provincial court judge (same as state judge) has no authority outside of the province in which he was appointed.

Thus it becomes mandatory that when a lawyer transfers from one jurisdiction, where he has already been called to the Bar, to practice the laws in some different jurisdiction, he must be called again to the Bar of that new place.

It was sheer coincidence that my particular "call" was to be a first of sorts.

For many years there had been no superior court judge resident in the Yukon Territory. If a trial, at that level of the judicial system, was to be tried in Whitehorse, then the federal government sent in a Justice of such a court from another jurisdiction. In most cases it was from the Province of British Columbia, which Province contained the established Court of Appeal for the Yukon Territory. Lawyers conducting an appeal of a case originating in the Yukon had to travel to Vancouver to be heard. There, the Court of Appeal Justices heard the facts and applied the law of the Yukon Territory to those facts. In most instances, the law was the same as that in British Columbia but I can think of times when such was not the case.

In any event, back to the "call." As I was saying, there had been no resident Justice in the Yukon before whom an applicant for admission to the Bar could appear. The result was that in the past such an applicant would proceed through government channels instead and would receive a document which recorded that he or she could indeed practice law in the Yukon. It could be likened to appearing before the clerk at the marriage bureau to become married, instead of having a large church wedding. Just prior to my arrival in Whitehorse Mr. Justice J. (Jack) Gibben, had been appointed the sole Justice of the Territorial Court of the Yukon Territory. He had studied law in Manitoba, possibly just after the first World War. He had practiced law at Dawson, in the Yukon Territory. Just before his elevation to the Bench, he had been the Commissioner of the Yukon Territory. (Much the same office as that of a Lieutenant Governor of a Province.) He was a short, dapper man with a unique appreciation of human nature. While he was into his early fifties at that time, he was young at heart and enjoyed the company of younger people. He had been away from the practice of law in the court system for many years but he tried gamely to get caught up.

It was before him that I appeared, to become called to the Bar of the Yukon Territory.

Due to the fact that there had not been a resident Justice in the Yukon for many, many years, a "call" of this particular nature became a "cause celebre."

The longer I lived in Whitehorse, the more I learned that almost any event, of any nature, type or description, could spontaneously, be turned into a "cause celebre."

The net result was that what might have been a singular, novel inauspicious, private occurrence suddenly became a public, omnipan, large, exciting, cosmopolitan, flamboyant, tour de force.

At that time, the presence of the military was large. The Royal Canadian Air Force had a sizable complement of personnel, located on the ridge overlooking the city. The air base and the air strip were both there. The commanding officer of the air base was one Squadron Leader "Chuck" Olsen, about whom the reader will learn more, herein. He was a well-decorated and highly respected member of the military. He was tall, handsome, slim, and muscular. He wore an Errol Flynn mustache. He was a picturesque individual and full of the devil. His military bearing and sense of humor were both epic. His capacity

19

to entertain was of historical proportions. His beautiful wife, Sasha, was truly his helpmate. She was always there in the wings to insure that all plans, of a social nature of course, went according to objective. She was tall, lithe, with well-defined features. She had the face of a classic beauty supported by dark hair and piercing dark eyes. She always made me think of the Spanish aristocracy because of her proud bearing and esoteric smile.

The commanding officer of the army, Brigadier Love, was known to me, but for some reason I never got to know him as well as I did "Chuck." The army supplied the medical and dental personnel for the military and, I believe, for the civil servants who operated the North West Highway System. They maintained the Canadian portion of the Alaska Highway.

There was a detachment of the Royal Canadian Mounted Police present in Whitehorse as well. The commanding officer was Inspector (later Assistant Commissioner) Richard Steinhauer, who became a particular friend of mine. He was huge. No other word would do him justice. I believe he stood about six feet four, very broad shoulders, slim waist, and weighed maybe two hundred and twenty pounds. All muscle. He also had a great sense of humor, which he governed closely because of his responsibilities and his need to maintain a military countenance. No one ever looked quite as striking as "Dick," when he wore his uniform. His mere presence manifested an aura of majesty and justice. His wife was a nurse. She was the daughter of a senior officer of the RCMP. A lovely lady. They had two daughters, if I remember correctly.

The mayor of Whitehorse, who was to become a staunch friend of mine, was also the local butcher. He, too, was huge. Almost the size of Dick. He was jovial, infectious when he laughed, which was often; wise, a go-getter; always considerate of others; polite, and a family man. Like so many others in Whitehorse, he had a well-earned reputation for enjoying a good party. I should know, 1 went on many with him. His name was Gordie Armstrong. His loving, patient wife was Peggie. She was always the gracious hostess. She was a tall, slender brunette. She always left me with the impression that she was inherently a shy, retiring person. The exact opposite of her husband. They had one daughter, Pat, who was just slightly younger than I.

There was then no equivalent, in the Yukon, to what we know in the provinces as a provincial government. The federal government was all pervasive, in almost anything of an official nature. The senior responsible individual was the commissioner who had direct communication with Ottawa and took his instructions therefrom. All the other various departments had counterparts in Ottawa and would react to directions from that source as filtered through the commissioner. There were hundreds of such civil servants. There was a municipal government of elected officials who had a small staff to carry out the restricted responsibilities not already controlled by the federal arena.

Both the air force and the army had Officers' Messes. This, of course, was the normal practice in military establishments. They invited selected members of the community to become honorary members. Such individuals were at liberty to frequent the Mess at will and to run a "tab" for drinks, meals, and entertainment.

I had the honor to be so invited to both the Army and the Air Force Officer's Mess. Consequently, I got to know a goodly number of the personnel and members of each. Another person with whom I became friendly was a Colonel Brown. He and I were in the drama club together and several times took parts in the same plays.

Well now, back to the "call."

Several weeks before my actual arrival in Whitehorse, George and/or Erik had established a date upon which the "call" was to take place. Mr. Justice Gibben had agreed, excitedly and with uncommon interest, to preside.

In an unlikely move, some formal invitations were sent out to various and sundry senior members of the two governments, the military, and to certain civilian members of the community.

The courtroom to be used was not the new one to which I referred earlier. That one was not, at this particular time, completed. We would, therefore, use the older, smaller courtroom, which was located over the Post Office cum Federal Building. It was aged. It probably had been constructed at or about the time of the great gold rush of the Klondike. It was painted the usual government battleship gray, built of wood and complained, squeaked, and creaked with every footstep applied to the floor. It did so with probable cause. Whitehorse, per se, was built upon a beach of permafrost, which froze, thawed, and shifted with the regularity of the seasons. Naturally, this activity undermined the base for this, and every other building, in the city.

The courtroom itself was on the second floor level. To get there, one had to climb up a flight of steep, narrow, creaky stairs. They angled twice in order to get to the landing which formed the hallway in front of the courtroom entrance door. The floor consisted of heavy, thick, brown battleship linoleum, scratched from the many, heavy booted attendees at court proceedings. The courtroom, per se, consisted of the judge's "bench" which rose above the linoleum some six or more feet. There it leveled off at a right angle to form the surface upon which rested the judge's water jug and his Bench Book. It was in this book that he would record his notes made during trials. A tired, old wooden chair was located behind the bench. A barrier, or fence, divided the courtroom roughly into two equal parts. On the one side, the populace could sit in the carved, wooden pews. There were, possibly, four rows. From this vantage point they could sit and watch the proceedings. On the other side of that fence the members of the court and the judiciary performed their appointed functions. This fence then, was tokenly known as the Bar, beyond which a person could pass, when "called."

It is an historic and symbolic ritual.

The judge had private chambers to the right, (east) of the bench. He could walk down a short flight of stairs and in a few strides would be through a door into his judicial quarters, known as his "chambers." Therein he changed garb, studied law, wrote or otherwise prepared his judgments and performed his ablutions.

From the gossip about town it soon became apparent that the occasion was to be replete with ladies in new dresses, hats, gloves, bonnets, and shoes. The dresses would be decollete, long with fringed base. The finest jewelry would be taken from its customary hiding place. This would not necessarily call for formal attire, probably more like an Easter parade. The officers of the various military and quasi-military divisions prepared to wear dress uniforms. They had been spurred on, reluctantly I'm sure, by the ladies who needed an excuse to dress up. This, perforce, called for the extracting of those uniforms from the trunks where they reposed, then trying them on. I heard that the local tailor did a booming business in alterations at that time. The ladies ordered fabric shipped up from the "outside." (The generic reference to any place not in the Yukon proper). I understand that some even traveled "outside" to attend at their favorite milliner and/or seamstress.

For the military men it was pea jackets, braided seams, epaulets, and shoulder boards containing distinction of rank. Even the occasional sword and scabbard was prepared for active duty.

To think that a mere "call" to the Bar was to occasion all of this.

The evening and night preceding the happening was to be a marathon party which concluded at a hurried breakfast, just in time for a quick shower, a change of clothes, and a race to the courthouse.

My associate, George, felt that it was his solemn obligation and duty to take me to every bar in town and there to introduce me to any of the firm's many clients we might find therein. They in turn, thought that it was mandatory for them to buy us a drink. Up to that point I had no idea that there were, or even could be, that many bars in such a small community. When we escaped from the last bar, we "had" to make a courtesy call at each of the military Messes. Thereafter, we visited the mayor, who decided to tag along as we went on to visit many others. This included the judge who was to admit me to the Bar in but a few hours. He decided to join our entourage.

Finally, for reasons known only to George, we ended up at the home of John Rowan, the executive secretary to the Whitehorse Chamber of Commerce (of which body I was later to become the vice president). The poor fellow had been in bed, fast asleep for hours, when this unruly, boisterous gang descended upon him just before dawn.

True to the spirit of the Yukon (where no one in need shall be turned away from any door) John got up, put on his bathrobe and invited all of us in. He was a man of stout heart and charitable nature. He would have to be, to passively permit, nay, invite this motley, loud, ebullient, noisy, roisterous crew into the sanctity of his home. I assumed that his wife, Elsie, saw the better part of common sense and remained hidden.

While we were all (I had no idea where many of those present joined us, nor when) standing or milling around in the kitchen, the host shooed us off into the living room. I stayed behind for some reason ... maybe I had been invited to do so. To my utter amazement, John lifted a scatter rug from the floor and a trap door was exposed. He raised the lid and went down a ladder, then disappeared into the bowels of the earth.

Soon he reappeared carrying many bottles of booze, together with some plates containing foodstuffs which had been covered with kitchen towels.

Had he expected us? I never found out.

The cavity beneath his house was his refrigerator. The perma-frost was his coolant. He had tapped nature's icebox.

As the light of day became more obvious, various attendees slipped away. Some went to prepare for the event. Others to repent.

When we were narrowed down to the host, George, and me, a breakfast was prepared. I called Laura, to apprise her of my whereabouts and relate what had happened. I hung up to the sound of her chiding laughter.

"Try to get there on time, dear. Remember, you're the main event," she teased.

When George and I finally arrived, on time, at the judge's chambers, we were a sorry lot to behold. Although we had all been home in time to shower, shave, and change clothes, we looked bleary-eyed and bedraggled. The judge struggled with his winged collar button. He claimed that his fingers were numb. George helped him get it all together. The judge couldn't find his written speech, he decided to wing it. Knowing him, we thought it best to discourage an extemporaneous speech. It would be better, under the circumstances, for him to read something, anything applicable. An urgent, rapid search found the somewhat dilapidated sheets of paper in the breast pocket of the suit he had worn the night before and out of which he had just changed to put on his vest and gown.

We were ready, as ready as we were going to be that day.

George and I entered the courtroom first using the judge's chamber door. This bestirred the crowd. Quietly we stalked a seat. Had my eyes betrayed me? There was a huge crowd present in the courtroom. Standing room only. How beautiful they all looked. It was like a Hollywood musical. Rows of people sitting perched on those uncomfortable pews. They looked like a ferrotype picture, which I had seen, of royalty at the opera. All these wonderful people turning out in exceptional attire for what was essentially a rather mundane event. Was it for me, or the event, or did it matter? My brain would not compute.

Only once before, I had felt this elevated. It was when I was a youth in Regina. I had watched a parade of Scottish Highlanders marching down the street, with their pipes bawling, the kettle drums rattling, and the plaid swirling. So stirred was I by the entire scene that I fell in behind them as they collected volunteers for the navy.

Suddenly, I was yanked out of my reverie. The clerk of the court appeared at the judge's door and sang out, "Order in Court." In strode Mr. Justice Gibben. All five feet five of him bristled with military bearing. After all, he was here as the monarch's representative. How admirable, how commendable, considering the way he might feel today. Regardless of circumstances, he was to uphold the dignity of the court, which he did in grand style.

All in the courtroom rose as one, including George and me. They stood at attention, or at least in orderly fashion, until the judge was on the bench. He acknowledged the tribute paid to his station, then said preemptorily, "Be seated please."

With a nod of his head the judge directed the proceedings to begin.

George rose solemnly, bowed courteously to the judge, then began his address. "My Lord, Mr. Commissioner, Mr. Mayor, Officers, distinguished guests, ladies and gentlemen, it is my distinct honor and privilege today to present to this honorable court, Harold R. Hine, Esquire, a member of the Bar of the Province of British Columbia, who seeks admission, as a solicitor, and a call to the Bar, as a barrister, of the Law Society of the Yukon Territory."

With that I rose and gave what I believed was a courtly bow in the direction of the bench. The judge responded with a gentle nod of his head.

All of this was followed by a series of speeches, mostly salutary and congratulatory. I do not remember all of what actually followed. Naturally, reference to my chronology, my military service, my graduation in law from UBC, my qualifications entitling me to be called, and other matters which George thought to be applicable, were submitted to the court. Suffice to say, that at the end of it all Mr. Justice Gibben directed me to stand again, at which time he pronounced that I was indeed, that day, called to the Bar of the Yukon Territory.

Chapter Three

Soaring free of tethered bonds
Which earth and life impose,
A much sought state of many men
Permits no languid pose.

To venture forth and gain your wings
You must have strong desire,
No inert, listless dreams suffice
There must be hearts of fire.

And when, at last, you break those bonds
And without them travel free,
Up in the air ... across the skies
Truly liberated you will be.

Flying at Last

During that same first year in Whitehorse another event of monumental proportions, for me, occurred.

I got my pilot's license!

The flight training course had been exciting and interesting, from beginning to end. Particularly my first solo flight. I had been assured by all the "old timers," i.e. fellow students who had just a few more hours' flight time than me, that the first flight alone in the aircraft is a horrendous, nerve wracking experience. They emphasized that once off the ground there would be no one to turn to if a goof occurred. They solemnly recounted numerous horrifying events about which they swore they had first hand knowledge, pertaining to the drastic consequences of an error which happened on the first solo flight of some former, close friend. I heard what they said but I would not let myself focus on the possibility of failure. I loved flying and felt good about my skills.

After about ten hours of flying dual with my instructor, Lloyd Romfo, he and I had been up doing "circuits and bumps" (take off, make prescribed turns to place you in the proper position to land, then land with as little impact upon the runway as possible) when at the end of one landing run he asked me to taxi over to the flight school ramp. This was the usual directive but had I detected something dissimilar in the way he said it today? Was there something novel in his demeanor today? I couldn't pin down what that difference was, if it existed at all, but I had a feeling of excitement, that this might be the big moment that all would-be pilots wait for. He had not really said anything new or unusual. Maybe it was just the way he had said what he did say. Maybe it was just my over anxious imagination, or maybe it was just wishful thinking. I continued to taxi to the apron, exactly as I had done for those ten previous hours. Usually he made some comment, some observation about the way in which I had handled the plane while flying those circuits. Not today. We sat in the aircraft, on the apron, saying nothing and with the engine idling. I wanted to reach over and shut it down, but hesitated. He usually told me to do that. I had been particularly proud of the way in which I had handled the plane this day. Yet he said nothing. He sat there making entries into the aircraft logbook. He normally did this after we left the plane and went into the school room to discuss the performance of the past hour. I had really felt expansive about my accomplishments that day. The "high" which I had experienced following the last landing was now being replaced by a sense of uncertainty, of misgiving. Did he not feel confident about my abilities? What had I overlooked or forgotten to do? Was I lacking in the mechanical art of flying? Was he not satisfied with some of my skills? I had received top marks in all the written tests. Why this delay? What did he have in mind?

We sat on the ramp for what seemed to be an interminable time. The instructor said nothing, he just kept making entries in that damn logbook. The engine idled and I fidgeted. He still had said nothing about performing my close down check which he would usually have done by this time, he said nothing. Then, he slammed the logbook shut and opened his door. With a big smile he said, "Sorry to tease you that way, Harold, but we instructors have to get something out of this, too. Take it up on your own ... let's see what you can do independently. Take her around on one complete circuit, then bring her back here, OK?"

The cat had my tongue. I stared at him, as though I had not really heard those magical words. My head was nodding an affirmative to him. I extended my hand for a hand shake. Silly damn thing to do. The situation did not call for congratulatory activity, not yet anyway.

The best I was able to do was to say, "You bet I will," with patent enthusiasm.

"I'll be watching you. I'll be right here when you return," he said as he closed his passenger door.

There I was, alone at last. God what delight! What exhilaration! How magnificent! I was going to achieve that second goal today!

I was going to solo!

As I had been trained to do, I first contacted the White-horse Tower by radio, before making any overt maneuvers. I picked up the "mike" and said, "Whitehorse Tower this is CF-HSK ... catch me at the flight school ramp ... taxi instructions please." (Here I hasten to point out to the reader that I have now forgotten the actual call letters of the plane which I flew that day. I have lost my pilot's logbook. For this chapter I'll use those letters which actually belong to another aircraft about which I have written in this book, those being, HSK.)

Immediately, the response from the tower was, "HSK ... Whitehorse Tower ... the live runway is one eight (180 degrees or due south on the compass) ... wind is from the south at 8 knots ... taxi to position and hold ... short."

"Runway one eight ... taxi and hold short," I repeated. (This practice is designed to prevent error in both transmission and reception.)

From that moment when I took singular control of the aircraft, until I completed my first solo circuit, I experienced an escape from all earthly burdens, the likes of which I had never experienced before. This mechanical marvel was going to react to my every whim ... my least directive, administered through the control system of the plane. It would lift off, climb, bank, fly straight and level, descend and land, in perfect synchronization with my mind and hands. It became an extension of my being, my very self. If I treated the plane with respect and proper guidance, it in turn would carry me up and away from the toils and troubles of earthbound humans. It could not only transport me from point A to point B in accordance with my desires, it could do so in a way that made life more interesting, more challenging. I would see North America in a way in which few people do. I would see the marvelous works of God from the air yet not so high that they would be remote and unappreciable. I could fly above, around, through and about those phenomena thus truly absorbing their essential beauty and import.

There was a new quotient in my life. It was the ability to pilot an aircraft. It was a demanding responsibility. Not only was there the requirement to fly well and properly at all times, there were other factors which were of just as much importance as the mechanical skill of piloting the plane, per se. There was the constant obligation to insure that the plane was properly fueled for the particular usage on every given flight. In addition to merely flying the plane, there was the one other essential element which meant survival or otherwise, and that was competence at accurate navigation. Without this ability a pilot should not enter his plane.

In summary, what happened that day was that I was introduced to a new world, a new existence. Flying, becoming a pilot, brought to my life a new dimension, without which I cannot imagine my life having been as fulfilled as it has. What the practice of law lacked in challenge, flying supplied in balancing factors.

When I landed the plane that day I entered a new world. I have never had a lasting regret about that event. There have been times during my years of flying that I wondered what had made me get into that sphere, but those situations were always temporary and few and far between. I have been flying from that day until now. My pilot's license now reads that I am licensed to fly "all types of airplanes, single and multi-engine, land and sea."

True to his word, my instructor, who had been joined by a group of students, was standing on the apron as I taxied up and shut down the engine. As I climbed out of the cabin, they all charged the plane like a herd of bellowing elephants. My inbred reservation or my conditioned resistance to any outward display of emotions collapsed. I jumped around like a leprechaun. I had flown an airplane "solo" and by God I was going to revel in that accomplishment!

There is a tradition among fliers that when one of them "solos" he or she is expected to foot the bill for a party. My case was no exception. We had one monstrous wing-ding. If someone merely showed up in the bar that night, stranger or not, they were invited to join our party for a drink. The cost was huge but the sensation and satisfaction of the cause for the event was bigger by far. I was thankful that I had no serious commitments for the following day.

But this is not the end of this story, not by a long shot.

Following that memorable day, I put in the required minimum flying hours in order to receive my actual license. Although getting the license is the culmination of learning to fly, it does not have the same sense of accomplishment and is not, therefore, as ostentatious an event as the first solo flight. Therefore, I celebrated this fact with a quiet family dinner.

There were, however, other plans afoot, of which I was not yet aware.

It was not uncommon to receive a specific invitation to join a group of officers at the Mess. The usual objective was to enjoy lunch together, discuss the weeks events, then play a round or two of bridge. At that time, I considered bridge to be an interesting and challenging game.

When I was asked by the army's senior medical officer to attend on a particular Saturday at the Army Officer's Mess, I thought nothing special about it. The invitation was for lunch, following which there was to be a film. It was to be a showing of the new procedures which had been developed in medical treatment of auto incurred injuries. I accepted with anticipated pleasure. I could enjoy a good meal and at the same function learn things which would help me in my practice of law.

When I entered the Mess I noticed that the folding chairs had been set up in the anteroom, immediately adjoining the Mess hall. It looked like a revival hall. In the dining area, the usual tables were set up around its perimeter. Was there an inordinate amount of foodstuff set out, or was it my imagination? There was a podium at the far end of the anteroom, but nothing else of note. I might have been early. There was nobody present, as yet.

I walked across the dining room floor and went through the door which led into the bar. There I found my host. He was sitting with a few other army officers, with whom I was more or less acquainted. I ordered a round of drinks, sat down, and joined into the conversation. There didn't seem to be as many members present that day. They usually lolled around the bar and gossiped together. Not today. Strange, when there was such an interesting program organized.

Soon, as it neared one o'clock, I noticed that those members who had shown up had wandered out into the Mess hall. There were now only three of us in the bar. Me, my host, and an air force officer whom I knew. He had joined us when some of the others had left the table.

At exactly one o'clock, the door to the bar burst open. Come to think of it, I had never seen it closed before. In stepped an air force warrant officer, 1st class. He was wearing full Mess Kit uniform and, by God, he was carrying a sword!

What was going on? ... an air force warrant officer in the Army Officer's Mess? ... in formal military attire? ... and with a sword?

The two men who had been with me disappeared, drinks abandoned.

The warrant officer snapped to attention and bellowed in such a voice as would awake the dead, "HAROLD HINE ... front and center ... follow me ... SIR!"

To say that I was astonished, shocked, surprised, and amazed would not accurately report my feelings at that moment. Like a robot I stood and passively followed the WO1 through the doorway and into the Mess hall. He took a few strides forward, then made a snappy left turn to head into the anteroom, bearing his sword before him.

What I saw in the anteroom electrified my mind. If I had been astonished a few moments ago, I was now astounded, flabbergasted, and aghast. The room was full of people in varying stances. Down the aisleway, between the blocks of chairs, stood a sentinal-like row of RCAF officers holding their swords aloft to create an archway of ornamented, shining metal. They wore their dress caps (usually taboo in the Mess). The swords dangled golden tassels. I saw that the finely pressed trousers, which ended at shining black boots, were adorned with gold stripes.

At each side of this avenue of sky blue, black, and gold, there were people standing. People dressed in finery. Ladies wearing hats, and men in their Sunday best. There was a padre with a white collar in evidence. Lawyers, doctors, accountants, a druggist whom I had come to know, an optometrist with whom I played cards, the officer-in-charge of the RCMP, the ubiquitous mayor, Mr. Justice Gibben, Judge A. H. Gibson, and many others whom I cannot now identify specifically, were present. Many, to whom I refer, were accompanied by ladies, some of whom I knew or had met.

My head was spinning. What was this all about?

The warrant officer must have anticipated my dilemma, he hesitated for a moment or two at the beginning of the "Arch of Swords," then whispered, "Follow me, Sir."

He then proceeded to slow march down the aisle toward the lectern. When my head stopped swiveling in its assessment of the scenario before me, I looked forward and there, at the focal point of the tunnel, I saw Squadron Leader "Chuck" Olsen. He, too, was wearing full regalia. Was he the precipitator of this phenomenon?

When we reached the end of the tunnel, my conductor wheeled smoothly to his right and disappeared. This left me standing alone, directly in front of "Chuck." He stood dispassionately, without any apparent participation in the activities. His eyes did not meet mine. He was at attention, as though he was on parade. Then he nodded, almost imperceptibly. I heard the swish of the swords cutting through the air as they were brought to rest. Another nod and I heard people stirring and chairs creaking as they assumed the weight of their occupants. There was a lot of coughing and a general hubbub. I had not, previously, noticed how quiet it had been.

Another nod and the warrant officer reappeared. He was carrying a sky blue velvet pillow in his extended right hand. The pillow was trimmed with gold and dripped miniature, golden tassels.

At this point, the squadron leader stepped down from the podium onto the floor directly in front of me. The pillow was extended to his breast level and when I saw what rested upon it, I nearly broke into tears. "Chuck" was speaking but I heard nothing that he said, so overwhelmed was I by emotion. I was having a very difficult time controlling my mouth. I gulped air in quick, short breaths, and seemed to need to sniff a lot. I needed my handkerchief but couldn't unbend enough to reach for it. The back of my neck hurt. My throat was tight and sore. It was difficult to swallow, yet I had to, repeatedly.

"Chuck" reached to the pillow. He lifted a set of RCAF wings, into the center of which his wife Sasha had sewn a small plastic cameo of the head of a white horse. He took one step forward and pinned those wings upon the lapel of my suit jacket.

32

All those wonderful people present had staged a "Wings Parade" for me. For me!

I shall never forget the feelings I experienced at that moment. Not until the day I die.

Chapter Four

Come fly with me in my flying machine
We'll get into postures that you've never seen
We'll dance through the sky like a mosquito hawk flits
I'll guarantee one thing, you'll have no time to knit.

Laura Goes Flying

Some months after my wings parade Laura asked about going up flying with me. She thought it would be nice to have a look around at the countryside from the air. She had never flown in a small plane before and was curious to learn why I loved it so much.

I had been up flying at every given opportunity. I wanted to build up my hours and thereby gain more and better experience. Many of my friends and associates would go with me upon a moments notice. There appears to be a universal curiosity about flying which incites people of all walks of life to try it. Even if only once.

For the day established for Laura's flight I arranged to get a Fleet Canuck. It is a high wing monoplane with fabric covering. In this plane the pilot and the passenger sit side by side as opposed to tandem, the way it is in many other craft, like the Fairchild Cornell, which our law firm owned and which I flew often. The Fleet was a trainer, which was fully aerobatic. I liked this particular plane for many reasons, one of which was its wide range of visibility. It even had a Plexiglas insert in the ceiling of the cabin, much like the sun roof in some of today's sleek automobiles.

The Fleet had good power and exceptionally fine aerodynamics. She climbed strongly and reacted instantly to both the throttle and the airfoil controls. She could glide, in very slow

34

descent, for unusually long distances. There was no aerobatic maneuver which she could not do, and do well. She would not equate with the performance or responsiveness of today's jet fighter but then she did not have the power, speed or modern engineering features either.

For that day and age, she was almost "top-o-the-line" for private flying and more than adequate for our purposes.

As Laura and I drove towards the airport, I stopped at the Tourist Services Market where I bought a half dozen rolls of toilet paper. Laura sat, knitting as usual, while I was absent. When I returned with the rolls she gave them a quizzical glance, but said nothing. She had to finish the sweater she was working on by the following day. It was someone's birthday gift. She was engrossed in counting stitches so her mind was thereby, as usual, totally preoccupied.

Some might say that knitting was a boon to man. Whoops!

We continued to drive up the four-mile hill which leads to the airport turn off. Soon, we had arrived at the flight school parking lot. CF-DPM (the identification letters for the Fleet) was parked out on the apron. Laura and I walked out to the plane. She carried her knitting, I carried the toilet paper. She appraised the plane in much the same way as one would glance at a freshly cut lawn. She gave it not much more than a cursory assessment, then with a slight shrug of her shoulders she allowed as to how it was "nice."

I helped Laura into the right hand seat, which is the passenger's seat. I stashed the toilet paper in the carrying net which was slung behind the seats, above the luggage compartment.

I did my customary "walk-around" the aircraft. This is mandatory. Prior to every flight, the pilot must encircle the plane, checking various designated items, as he goes. In this particular case it meant checking to insure that there was adequate fuel and that the oil was topped-up. It included making sure that the airfoils had no dents, holes or other abnormalities and that nothing was loose which should be tight and secure.

Having satisfied myself as to the airworthiness of DPM, I got in alongside Laura who was still knitting furiously. I started up the engine and sat waiting for the oil temperature to rise to the recommended level for power usage. I radioed the tower for taxi instructions, got them, got clearance, and soon we were airborne.

So adept at knitting was Laura that I saw those needles dashing while she deigned to glance out the window to watch the ground and plane separate. She never missed a stitch while we climbed to 9,000 feet. Occasionally, she seemed to slow the ferocity of her attack upon the wool and concentrate on some feature below which had caught her eye. Once she almost slowed to a halt when she recognized historic Marsh Lake, away off to the east. She and her friend, Bette Jorde, and the respective children liked to drive out there for a picnic and a day at the beach.

Having arrived at my desired altitude, I leveled off and throttled back to the proper revolutions per minute (rpm) for level flight. I circled slowly, all the time scanning the entire area for other aircraft. I then radioed the Whitehorse tower and inquired as to whether there were other planes known to be in the vicinity. I was advised that it was "all clear."

"Laura, would you please hand me one of those rolls of toilet paper from out of the net," I asked.

She deposited the knitting onto her lap and turned slightly to accomplish the task. She then held it in her hand, with a quizzical expression on her face, but said nothing.

"OK, now here's what to do," I said, shifting my attention back and forth, so as not to miss any invading aircraft. "When I say 'go', you slide open the glass window beside you, then throw the roll out the window."

"Sure sounds like an exciting experience to me, Harold. Do you think I'll be able to stand it? Or is there more to it?" she teased.

"Well, yes there is. First take the roll out of its wrapping, then be sure to lift up the edge, which is usually stuck down, so that there is nothing holding the roll together."

"Wow, and I get to do this all by myself? How exciting!"

"Well, it gets to be a bit more exciting after you throw the roll out the window," I shouted through my leer.

"Oh, oh, what have I let myself in for? What happens next, dear?"

"We're going to cut the paper into smithereens before it can get to the ground."

"You're kidding, dear. How on earth do you do that?"

"Not on earth, Laura, in the air," I said through gritted exposed teeth, widened eyes, exhibiting my best villainous leer and twisting an imaginary, Simon Legree, mustache.

"But how ... how do you cut it? ... it's gone ... out the window."

"You watch, I'll show you. Are you strapped in?"

I checked her harness and mine one more time, then yelled "OK, let it go!"

Laura slid open the window, pulled up on the toilet paper edge, then threw it out. She watched it fall. It unrolled into a hundred foot streamer, dangling before her eyes.

Laura turned toward me to make some comment, but before she got the words out, I pulled the plane into a tight turn to the left. Our bodies had been in a forward motion, then suddenly with the turn in direction and the natural physical forces being applied, we were thrust deeply into our seats, our facial muscles were pressured to pull down on our eyes and attempt to open our mouths. The wings were at a right angle to the surface of the earth, so that we were laid over to our left, as though curled up in the fetal position on a bed. Laura's body pressed against mine, as she looked past me, directly down to the ground.

She screamed and grabbed my arm.

I dove the Fleet at the streamer and hit it with my left side wing, about ten feet from the tip. Then I pulled the plane up to a climbing attitude and applied full throttle. We climbed rapidly for a few minutes, in as steep an ascent as I knew the plane would handle. All this while the paper was descending leisurely. At the top of the climb I pulled back on the throttle so that the plane stalled. For a few moments we just hung in the air looking up at the sky, bodies pressed into the seat back. Then the craft pitched forward. The sensation is much like going over the hump of a roller coaster. As the plane started to dive, I applied full left rudder and pushed the control stick to the left as well. The plane rolled over. For a few moments we were flying upside down, hanging by our seat straps. Then gravity applied its force and the plane dove for the ground. Down we plunged, spiraling. I pulled back on the control stick, pressed on the right rudder bar in order to stop the volutions, then put the plane at such an angle as would enable me to pull up enough to aim at the paper again.

All this time our bodies had been reacting to the various physical features of nature such as gravity, inertia, centripetal, and centrifugal forces. We experienced most, if not all, of the aerodynamics. We had been exposed to the sensations of acceleration, sudden deceleration, inversion, weightlessness, deviation, and what are now called 'G' forces. In rapid succession our bodies had gone through almost every position assumable by man.

"Haarrooolldd! ... Stop it ... wait a minute ... hold it!" Laura screamed.

Through all of these maneuvers the toilet paper had been dangling lazily, just within the range of my vision. I charged it again and hit it at about its middle, with my right wing tip.

"Haaarrrooolld!" Laura screamed again, digging her nails into my arm. She now had both hands on that arm. Funnily, I wondered what had happened to the omnipresent, knitting paraphernalia.

"Haarroold! ... Hold it! ... Stop! ... How could you? You never told me ... you fink ... I didn't know ... I dropped my knitting. Look at this mess ... ."

I made a sudden move to adjust the throttle, she throttled my arm.

"No you don't! Don't you dare! Not yet anyway! Hold it! Boy ... what an exhibition! Is this what you do when you come up flying? You idiot! ... you fink! ... I ... I ... WOW! That sure gets the heart started doesn't it, dear? Whew! So that is why you enjoy it so much ... crazy thing is that I think I liked it ... frightened as I was. You rat! Maybe I might be able to understand more fully your love of flying ... once I get my breath. Whew! ... now I'm almost back to normal. You fink, why didn't you tell me ... beforehand? I suppose you want to use up the other four rolls now, eh? Just let me get my bearings and settle down a bit ... sure was exciting wasn't it, dear?"

Once I heard the word "dear" I knew that the worst of the tirade was over. Later that afternoon, when we returned to Whitehorse, we had used up all of the toilet paper for target purposes.

Chapter Five

To broadcast was an urgent need,
An entertainment center,
A challenge night was then conceived
So everyone could enter.

I challenge you, you challenge me
To perform upon the stage,
And if you do, I pay the fee
It soon became the rage.

And very soon we had the funds
The sum that we must spend,
But other antics were pursued
With a performer we had attend.

Radio Week in Whitehorse

Within weeks of my arrival in that northern city, I had become a member of the Whitehorse Chamber of Commerce. I believe in the objectives of that worthy body. Its existence was important to the orderly development of the commercial aspects within the community. Through the regular meetings and other functions of the Chamber, I met a lot of very fine, dedicated people.

At this time (1953), Whitehorse had a very inadequate radio station. One was really exaggerating to call it a "station." There was a small group of volunteers who made broadcasts at irregular times and then only for very short periods. We did, on occasion, get tapes sent up to us by the Canadian Broadcasting Corporation, but that was infrequent and the programs were not all that interesting. There was no television of any nature, type, or description. We had one theater which presented two different films each week. There was one newspaper which was published twice per week. The publisher was Harry Boyle, who is now a county court judge sitting in Vancouver, B.C.

We wanted more and better entertainment. "We," being members of the Chamber, members of the drama club, people from the military, and most of the citizenry in general. A committee was struck, with the Chamber being the lead functionary. Guess who became the chairman of that committee? You're right! It would appear that I suffer from a severe case of foot in mouth disease. I am not now sure, but I think I may have volunteered for the job.

Well, OK then ... it had to be organized. What was "it?" First, determine what we required, then interpolate that into dollars. The result was that we appeared to need about $4,000 to purchase some badly needed equipment, i.e., turntables, microphones, instrument panels, and many other items of an electrical nature.

We divided into groups or mini committees. The technical people, those who knew something about the equipment used in broadcasting; the fund raisers extraordinaire, mostly women's auxiliaries and other women's organizations; the project committee, those who would design a means by which we could raise the money; artists; drama freaks (of which I was one); publicists; negotiators; and the laborers with some skills like carpentry, sewing, painting, and the like.

For some years I had been toying with an idea which, if implemented in a small community, could stir up enough interest to involve a large number of the public and simultaneously raise money.

The scheme was simple really. It was a form of challenging, with a "pass-it-on" feature. You may remember a peer sport as a child, when someone would punch you on the arm and say "pass-it-on."

The way I saw it working was as follows. We first of all rent, or better still get donated, the use of the high school auditorium for one or two nights. Then we get, let's say, the mayor, to challenge the commissioner to sing a specific song on what we would call "Challenge Night." The commissioner could accompany himself on the piano, get a pianist, use music from a record, or just sing alone. The challenge would be accompanied by a proposal that if the commissioner did in fact so perform, the mayor would pay into the kitty, say $20. If the commissioner reneged, then he would have to pay the $20. In turn the commissioner could challenge, say, the CO of the Air Base, to recite a poem by Robert Service. The sum involved could be no less than twenty dollars and no more than fifty, unless a group was involved, i.e. four people challenged to sing as a quartet, in which case the maximum was one hundred dollars. All monies were to be paid within four days of the challenge being listed in the newspaper. Proceeds to go to the treasurer of the Radio Committee.

To my utter astonishment, the idea caught on like wildfire! Challenges flew back and forth like tennis balls in a tournament. In a community of about 4,500 souls, I think that there were some 200 people challenged within a week. The bars took up the idea with enthusiasm. Many a challenge was issued over a drink. It was a tremendously fertile source of funds.

What I had planned as Challenge Night turned into Radio Week.

The committee was most efficient and exceptionally effective. We paid for almost nothing. What we required was wrestled, urged, cajoled, pried, and possibly even blackmailed, out of those who had what was needed. We advertised to sell pre-sold tickets to the event. Once again we had a wonderful response. It became mandatory that we start assigning specific dates to the tickets. If the random holders all showed up on the same night, there would have been a stampede. We were sold out of the first several nights in the first twenty-four hours. Names of the challenger(s) and challengee(s) were published, along with the amounts involved. We were amazed at who had actually accepted the challenges. Maybe we had a bunch of latent "hams" in our midst.

The overall response was nothing short of phenomenal. If all went as forecasted, our financial objectives had been achieved and then some.

I contacted Max Ferguson (Mr. Rawhide) of the CBC. Sure, he would come and be glad to perform for such a worthy cause! He agreed to give us one performance per night of his famous characterizations. Max wouldn't hear of him receiving payment for such a gig. He would be content if he received complimentary accommodations at the Whitehorse Inn and his transportation covered, there and back. I forget now who paid his air fare from Toronto to Whitehorse. I have a sneaking hunch that the Air Force gave him a "freebee." From what

I saw, I'm sure that he only got to the hotel a few times for meals and the occasional cat nap. He was a celebrity from the "outside." He was a national figure in the entertainment world. He became the toast of the town, the most sought after guest at cocktail parties and dinners in a community notorious for its competitive soirees, put on by the would be "hostesses with the mostest."

For weeks prior to the actual event, we had to make sets, sew diaphanous drapes for one sequence which was a huge success, arrange and rearrange rehearsal times and dates, test the sound equipment and note the various levels for each act, help with costumes, get makeup artists from the drama club to apply and assess which colors, highlighting, lip cover, etc., etc., to use and then record it for duplication on the all important night. We had to paint backdrops, then arrange them in proper sequence so that changes could be made quickly, efficiently, and above all, accurately, as and when required.

I cannot now remember all of the actual challenges, but I do remember that my partner George had to sing "The Prisoner's Song," wearing appropriate garb. He got a set of long johns, painted black strips around them, and carried a ten pin bowling ball in his arms. From the moment that he walked onto the stage, until he stopped singing (now there is an abuse of the term if ever I heard one) the audience went wild. He was well-known and well-liked. He was also a bachelor and had many friends. They must all have been there at one time.

For the life of me, I cannot remember exactly what it was that I did. I believe it was to sing one of the songs made famous by an entertainer of that day. I think his name was Jorge Jorgenson. In any event, I remember that it was a song and it was in the Swedish dialect. I'm told that it had something to do with being home for Christmas.

The wife of Colonel Brown, a beautiful, sensuous, slender, French Canadian lady, (in the real sense and meaning of that word) had a grand piano brought into the auditorium from somewhere. She wore a low cut, form fitting black dress, with a flounce angled around it from the waist to the knees. Sitting on the top of the piano, which I believe was played by her husband, she dangled her black clad, delicately tapered legs over its edge. She sang "C'est Si Bon" in a husky, throaty, Lauren Bacall type of voice. To make the scenario complete, she had been blessed with a good singing voice. It was a sensational act.

One of the druggists recited "The Cremation of Sam McGee," which was particularly well received.

The turnstiles clicked and the cash register hummed. Radio Week had been a huge success. Talk about the benefits of a community pulling together, instead of polarizing.

On the last night of the week, a dinner for the work crew followed by a trip to the Tahkini Hot Springs was planned.

So as to not mislead the reader, a short description of the hot springs, as they then were, should be inserted here. The hot water bubbled to the surface at a spot about eighteen miles northwest of Whitehorse, just off the Mayo Road. Some enterprising individual had built an enclosure around the fissure in the earth, out of which the heated water disgorged. The walls of the enclosure were of rough boards about four feet from the ground. Above this rested glass for another three feet, completing a seven foot wall. There was adjoined to this enclosure a small building of equally rough construction, which housed an office and changing rooms with lockers. To enjoy the allegedly healing waters, one walked out of the changing room and down a flight of six or seven wooden steps which disappeared directly into the steaming water. One could rent bathing suits and inner tubes. It was a classic example of man's ingenuity and inventiveness.

That, essentially, was it.

By the time we had finished our dinner, concluding with the usual after dinner drinks and speeches, it was almost midnight. Those who had determined that they were going to the springs made their apologies and left before the final speeches were heard. Several cars were loaded with loaded people. I had Max, as well as Laura and two other ladies, in my car. There was much clowning and laughing on the trip out. The caravan stopped several times for either intake or output of liquids. When we arrived at the hot springs, it was locked up tight. Nary a light shone nor a greeting extended. We opened the doors of the many cars and had a round robin of drinks and a few songs. It was a pleasurable evening, with a soft warm breeze and a bright moon. The occasional cloud made its pass over the moon, at which time it was pitch black all around us. There was no street lighting nor other visual assistance, except the car lights.

After half an hour of libation and the music festival, someone (the devil) suggested that a swim was in order. Surely we could scale the fence and enjoy the soothing, healing waters? What about the fact that we did not have bathing suits, someone less bent than the others wanted to know. Would the management be upset? Did anyone have any towels with them? On and on came the questions.

Suddenly, a voice which I recognized as Max's shouted, "To hell with all of that ... turn out the car lights and count to twenty ... last one in is a coward!"

With that, one of the rear doors to our car flew open and a body stood out in the dimming natural light. The car lights were out and providence was shoving a cloud over the face of the moon. A figure streaked by my driver's door. It was dark, but not too dark to realize that the body was without clothes. Just at the count of twenty, when all the lights were pulled on again, that same figure was seen to drop over the fence and into the water on the other side.

That was all that was needed. Once again that voice cried out, "Come on in, the waters fine!" Out went the lights and into the pool fled some twenty or more people. Men and women alike. Mostly without clothes. Some of the ladies were wearing their undies, I think.

For an hour or more we cavorted, splashed, burbled, and thrashed. Some kind soul took it upon herself to be the bartender and was joined by other nonswimmers in supplying totally unrequired drinks to those of us in the pool.

Tiring of the aquatics, we elected to return to the cars. Would some one please turn off all of the car lights? They had been on and off intermittently during the frolic. "Sure," someone yelled. "Same deal?" another voice asked. "Count of twenty," came the response. Out went all the lights. Some of us made it back to our respective cars during the twenty count hiatus. Others were not so fortunate. Some never even got out of the pool, due to the crush of bodies bent on getting over that wall and across the open stretch of ground to their cars in time. Max was one of those left behind. He and two others.

"OK, you clowns ... one more time with the lights, OK?" shouted this well-known voice.

"OK," came a chorus of voices, belonging to latent prevaricators.

The lights went out and three bodies catapulted over the wall. As they dashed over the open ground, on came the lights!

There in shining, dripping color was our special guest and two others all trying to make themselves invisible and running

44

around in tight circles, each wanting to hide behind the other. It was musical chairs in the nude, without chairs.

Finally, Laura leaned over from her seat on the passenger's side and doused my car lights. (How had they come on?) Again a naked body rushed by the side of my car and clambered into the back seat, cursing. In the dark he could not find his clothes and he was wet. Laura, who always thinks of such things, tossed him a towel. She came prepared. We had done this hot springs routine before.

Some time later, one of the CBC tapes, which was sent up especially for the Radio Week Gang, arrived from Toronto. It was one of the "Rawhide" programs. The story line was about the return to "civilization" by Max from the heathen north. He concluded by making reference to a little black widow spider which had pursued him all the time he was up in "pagan country." It had bugged him so much that he had even given to this annoying creature a nickname. He had captured it, put it into a bottle, and when well up into the air, upon flying out of the north to the "outside" at Toronto, he cast it out of the plane, into oblivion. He thought that would be the just desserts for that evil millipede, "Harold."

Chapter Six

Truth or Consequence—a TV game
In truth you've missed the plan
The consequence was a Klondike trip
For nuggets there to pan.

Contestant and a crew arrive
In Whitehorse, one fine day,
A committee hired to welcome him,
In costume do they play.

Then off to Dawson, near the gold
Costumes, crew and all,
When gold is found the play does end,
And we all just had a ball.

Truth or Consequences

Some months after the immense success of Radio Week, I had settled back into business and was preparing for a manslaughter case which I was to prosecute, when my secretary, Phyllis, buzzed me on the intercom. "There is a guy on the line asking if you were the man responsible for the challenge night. He says he wants to hire whoever that was. I told him that it was you. Was that OK?"

"Well, Phyllis, you can't go wrong, when you're telling the truth. Sure, I'll talk with him."

The chap at the other end introduced himself as a senior executive of the Quaker Oats Company. He informed me that the company had an idea in the planning stages, wherein they thought that they might buy some acreage up on the Klondike River, then subdivide it into mini parcels of one square inch

46

each. By purchasing one of that company's products, you could "own a piece of the Klondike." Those who responded would receive a Klondike Big Inch Land Deed. What did I think of the idea?

"Well, it is certainly novel, isn't it?" I replied.

"Do you foresee any legal problems with our doing that? What kind of land law do you have up there?"

"We have a form of the Torren's system. Are you familiar with that?"

"Sure I am. That's great! It should work then. How would you like to be retained by us, for matters pertaining to this promotion?"

"I would like that, of course. You are a well-known and well-respected company. Just the type of client a lawyer seeks. What is it that you have in mind, exactly?" I asked, with growing interest.

"What we have going at the moment, ... uh, ... Harold, isn't it? ... "

"Right, and I don't think I caught your name."

"Roger (not the real name), I'll send you a formal retainer letter, but there are some features of this promotion that I would like to lay the groundwork for now. Do you have a few minutes to talk? It's on me."

I was beginning to warm up to this guy. He was candid and warm, even on the phone, which I have always thought to be so impersonal.

"Of course, Roger. Let me organize my pad and pencil and I'll take some notes. OK, there we are, shoot."

"OK, Harold, here's what we have on the burner right now. Have you heard of the 'Truth or Consequences' program on TV?"

"Sure, we don't have television up here, yet, but I have certainly read about it. I think I even saw one program when I was 'outside.' "

"Outside?" he asked, curiously.

"Sorry 'bout that, Roger. That's just an expression used up here. It means, down in civilization."

"Got to remember that one, Harold," he laughed, then said, "Well, if you know the program, you know that there are contestants on each show who are asked certain questions. If they give the wrong answer, they must perform a penalty, the consequence ... get it?"

"Of course, sounds like an interesting format."

47

"Yeah, it works well. Anyway, one of the contestants has a consequence which requires him to travel to the Klondike and pan for gold. Is there still any gold 'in them thar hills?' " he said, coupled with a boisterous laugh.

I just knew I was going to like this guy.

"Only if you salt the river bed," I replied, joshing him.

"Geez, Harold, you sure are the right guy for what we have in mind. It may come to that. I sure hope not, but if he doesn't find gold naturally, that is, well, let's deal with that when we come to it. This contestant will be 'on stage' all the time he is up there. We're sending up a television crew, a director, script girls, makeup people, and the whole damn lot. From the moment that his plane arrives in Whitehorse, until he gets back on it again in four days time, he will be pampered, powdered, wined, combed, dressed, undressed, watered, fed, dined, wiped, photographed, and televised, all in living color. At the end of all this, he has to return to the studio, go back on the program and report his findings. That will be followed by the edited version of the pictures we take up there. He is a lawyer from Los Angeles. Name of Rollie Goldberg (not his real name), I think that's it. Anyway what we need is to have him met at the airport, then taken up to Dawson City, near which he will pan for the gold. It has to be in the Klondike River. We will need hotel accommodation for about twelve people, including me, a chartered aircraft, leased vehicles ... you know ... trucks for the equipment and cars for the gang. We would like you to round up people who will dress in the attire of the 'gay' nineties. We want to have that entourage, of those costumed people, follow him wherever he goes. Let's get say, oh ... eight or ten of them. Of course, we will pay for everything. What we want you to do is to set up the whole thing and be in charge of the entire show. What about it?"

Was this guy kidding me? This was a "feature" dream come true. I might not be able to handle the whole scenario, but I sure as hell would give it my best shot.

In a voice which I hoped would not disclose my anxiety and over enthusiasm, I allowed that I would be interested. I would require a comprehensive brief on the matter, together with a firm budget, names of cast and crew, and all specific timetables.

"Ya got it, Harold. I'll also enclose a cheque. Great to talk with you. Call you soon. If you need anything or have any questions just call me at the number I left with your secretary.

See ya."

With that he hung up and left me gasping. Now what had I let myself in for?

Over the next few weeks, I heard from Roger often. I was gradually getting a feel for the objectives and he and I were developing a good rapport. I went to some friends of mine in the drama club, from which I extracted volunteers. I spoke to the mayor. He assured me that there was no way in which he would miss such a deal. Wild horses couldn't pull him away. Ken Bowman, the tall, handsome, muscular, former hockey player turned druggist, eagerly accepted the challenge. Thelma Olsen, a rare beauty, and a double for the movie actress Ruth Roman, agreed to participate. Others involved were George and his fiancee Diana Whittal; Noreen Morin, another beauty and Thelma's best girlfriend; Doctor Nori Nishio and his lovely wife June; Joan "Rusty" Veinott, my other secretary; Rusty Erlim, a leading light in the drama club and future newspaper editor/publisher. There were many others, whose faces and/or names will not come back to me at this time, which I regret.

Mr. Justice Jack Gibben jovially concluded that no event of such a nature could be complete without an authentic judge involved. I remember him, fondly, as being a mischievous sprite at times and this was one of them.

I leased one of the paddlewheelers, which was tied up on the shores of the Yukon River. Her name was the *Klondike*. Boats like this one had all the historical background that any site director for a movie could ask for. They were the real thing! These boats used to ply the river from Whitehorse to Dawson. Soon after leaving Whitehorse, the boat could glide leisurely and without incident across Lake Leberge, (immortalized by Robert Service poetry). Once having traversed the lake from south to north, it was back onto the tortuous Yukon River again. At about the half way point, (between Whitehorse and Dawson) the boat would reach the treacherous Five Finger Rapids. To get by these rapids the captains would have to send out a boat and crew to carry an anchor hundreds of feet ahead of the boat. The anchor would be cast into the river. The cable, which joined the anchor to the capstan on the boat, would then be wound up at the boat, thus pulling the boat through the narrow, rock strewn, gorge which created the rapids. Within a matter of but a few miles, the whole procedure had to be repeated at Rink Rapids. The boat then resumed its challenge of the tortuous bends in the river where sand bars shifted with such rapidity and regularity that the pilot, (usually the captain) could never rely upon them being in the same place twice. The *Klondike* was known to have carried a load of one hundred and fifty tons of freight. She drew about thirty-eight inches of water. When we leased her, she still had her commodious barroom, ship wide counter, full back bar mirror, and murals of reclining, voluptuous nudes. I believe that these were all aboard during the Great Gold Rush. She was within easy access of the downtown core and to say the very least about her, she was one of the most picturesque elements of the gold rush days.

Laura, June, Noreen, Thelma, Diana, and many other women who fast became interested in the proposed "costume party," formed an informal committee dedicated to locating genuine, museum quality clothing for both men and women. How they did it, I'm sure that I will never know, but secure them they did. There were period pieces galore. The girls either found or made dancehall costumes with the low cut, snug fitting bodice, with the tight waist and the multi-crinolined, cancan skirt. Each "dancer" wore black net stockings and a large brimmed, tilted, plumed, hat. Others wore the long gowns with the puffed sleeves, apron front, and ruffled hem. Wearing a boa stole and carrying a parasol was, apparently, a popular caparison.

Happily the menfolk were also able to locate and acquire appropriate attire. We obtained a few bowler hats which had seen much better days; some striped shirts with white, starched collars and cuffs; and some colorful, wide lapelled vests, which were short and tight fitting. We got many of these items from a costume house in Vancouver. I already had the striped trousers and black vest, which I sometimes wore in court. Someone, I cannot remember who, produced morning dress consisting of a cutaway frock coat and gray trousers. There were two buffalo coats and some beaver hats which we borrowed from the Mounties.

Costume wise we were ready.

We decided to have a dress rehearsal on the boat. The "cast" showed up with a mass of well-wishers in tow. One of the bars sent in a case of mixed bottles of liquor. Another case contained ice; yet another, glasses. What happened then did not constitute rehearsal. Most of those in attendance were well beyond the stage of novice at the art of boozing. It became just another of the many spontaneous, impromptu, animated parties for which the Yukon has a well-earned reputation. It could not properly be categorized as a rehearsal but it certainly was a harbinger of future events in Dawson.

Eventually, I received the telegram which instructed me to initiate all activities. The guest would arrive aboard a CP Air flight, at a specified date and time. Out went the word around the town. Notwithstanding the weeks of preparation, there were some anxieties, frustrations, petulances, depressions, excitement, and last minute hitches.

But we made it!

The air crew had been put on notice to let all the sane passengers off the flight first, followed closely by the television crew. They were to "entertain" the guest, i.e. detain him with free libations or whatever, until the TV cameras were set up, then usher him down the stairway.

What a sight greeted him. Bearded prospectors wearing plaid shirts and/or red longjohns, cork boots, black pork pie hats turned up at the front, and some carrying picks and packs. Clean-shaven faces sported morning attire and top hats. Others wore the Mountie's furs. Lovely ladies sashayed about the apron, swishing long skirts and twirling parasols. There were six gorgeous females doing the cancan with enthusiastic flair. The mayor struggled, uncomfortably, under the weight of his personal buffalo coat which was not intended to be worn in the heat of a day like this particular day. Even the weather man had blessed us with unusually fine weather for this occasion. The official greeting party was backed up by dozens of other people, who were either aware of the event and wanted to be a part of it, or who were passers-by waiting for the next plane. Regardless, it was an appropriately large crowd for such an auspicious event.

Down the stairs came Mr. Goldberg. Heads of the crew poked out of the doorway to watch the proceedings. Another impish face kept bobbing up at various windows or alternatively at the open door just momentarily, then back to a window.

There was no band, but a loud cheer went up. The contestant, our guest, looked apprehensive. The mayor stepped forward and greeted Goldberg warmly. Then Gordie gave the shortest speech any of those present had ever heard him give. That coat did have some redeeming qualities. Goldberg appeared to relax somewhat, as the dancers surrounded him and escorted him to a car. He was a rotund, short man, of about forty years. His round face broke easily into an engaging smile. He posed frequently for the cameras. At one point, for example, he turned himself and the mayor into a better stance for the benefit of the TV crew. He then leaned in, towards Gordie, so as to insure that they were both within the scope of the picture. It occurred to me that he might have been coached before leaving for the gold laden north.

That evening, the "locals" had a party. The contestant was, quite naturally, tired from his long trip so he retired early. For him, that was both a wise move and a blessing. Remember that impish face? That belonged to Roger. What a bearcat! This guy should have been named Omar, he certainly believed in "Ah, make the most of what we yet may spend, before we, too, into the dust descend." But all at once? WOW! What a guy, a great guy. Bright, witty, and intelligent. He was slight of build and not tall. He had dark hair and a five o'clock shadow; a long, narrow, pointed, nose; an elongated face and small jaw. Rather large, round, deep set eyes looked out of place on such a face. When I left the blowout at 3 a.m., Roger had just got his second wind and was dancing with the dancehall girls in rotation. That is, he was dancing with those whom he had not already worn out or crippled. What a guy!

The next day about noon, (thank God) we took off as scheduled on the charter flight. The plane belonged to CP Air and was crewed thereby. The pilot was a friend of mine by the name of Ernie. He was the right guy to have along on a jaunt like this because he enjoyed a good time and could, therefore, overlook some of the shenanigans which would surely happen on this trip. Inasmuch as he wouldn't have to fly for several days, while we machinated in Dawson, he might even deign to join us ... to a limited extent. The stewardesses (now "flight attendants") fell into step immediately after we were off the ground. There was a lot of healing to be done, for all the self-inflicted damage from the night before. They ministered to Roger and to all the others whom he had kept up ALL NIGHT.

During the initial stages of the flight, someone reported that one of his or her forebearers had either lived in, or had been born in Mayo, a small community not on our flight path but not far off it. Shortly following this announcement, the plane banked to the east and soon was making a smooth landing on the gravel airstrip which serviced Mayo. We were using a DC3 for this trip which, as any person knows who has ever traveled in one, is a noisy but highly stable and reliable plane. When the dust raised by the plane's presence had settled, many of us got out and wandered around the deserted field. A car came out from the town, picked up a small group, took them for a tour of the town, and brought them back again. It seems that Roger had something to do with all of this. I couldn't help but think how accommodating he was. In fact, this very thought was on my mind as the vehicle returned. The group unraveled itself from the confined quarters in the Jeep and I noticed a case of a particular type of booze was off-loaded. It seems that an order had been placed for a specific drink and the air crew did not have that particular brew on board. Hence the landing.

Well, no one said that this was going to be a conservative, orderly affair, did they?

Dawson had received advance notice of our arrival and our purpose. When Ernie taxied the DC3 up to the tie down spot on Callison's Field, the high jinx were already well under way. There was a sea of people all wearing period costumes. They were certainly not going to be outdone by that young upstart city, Whitehorse. Dawson had at one time been the capital of the Yukon, with a population of some 50,000 people. Whitehorse had been named the capital, in or about 1953. There was still an air of friendly resentment and rivalry abroad in the land.

These people had really outdone us. They not only had authentic period costumes, they had authentic period automobiles, and carriages. I couldn't identify all of the vehicles, but I did recognize a 1908 Ford Model "T" town car, a 1905 Buick Model "C," and a Daimler 1904 Landaulette. At least, I think that's what they were.

There were several curry combed, clean, shiny horses, with plumes stuck into their harnesses at the forehead. The carriages shone brightly as though recently waxed and polished. Each horse had a shining, light chain traveling from his halter to a small, round weight, which rested upon the ground. The weight was called a "nag anchor."

A makeshift bar was set up in the open field. It was well patronized.

When the dust settled and we disembarked, a band started up. Another item which we did not have available in Whitehorse. The band members were all dressed in similar attire, which I took to be that of firemen's off duty, nonemergency clothing. A man in morning coat and top hat lead the parade toward the plane. On his arm was a beautiful lady, wearing a long dress with a lace ruffle at its hem and on the edge of the short, puffed sleeves. She wore a bonnet with identical lace trim. It framed her lovely face and was secured by a ribbon which tied under her chin, with an exaggerated bow. They were the official greeters. I feel certain that this couple were Mayor Howard Firth and spouse. The others formed up behind them to fashion a parade, of sorts. Some found difficulty in keeping the line straight. My guess was that they had been here for hours. They would not have known about the "pit stop" in Mayo.

Roger was frantic. He wanted these people to "hold it." He wanted the TV crew to get off the aircraft "immediately." This scenario was too good to miss. He demonstrated his superb organizational skills that day. Somehow he was able to have them repeat the performance almost precisely, and to make the same speeches again, verbatim. Taking into consideration the near proximity of the bar; the fact that everything was on the house; coupled with the fact that all our people, including the TV crew, script girls, writers, directors and everyone else, were frequenting that bar, hastily, and repeatedly, the results were nothing short of a miracle.

Horse and chaise or horse and carriage went through their paces, aided and abetted by tippled drivers and worse off passengers. The cars startled the horses, the horses intimidated the city folk. The conflicting orders, directions and demands, were universally loud and occasionally hostile. Too many chiefs and not enough Indians. Ladies vied for "center stage" and men played the fool. It was bedlam of the nicest kind. Most of us had never been exposed to this big city movie and/or TV production stuff. It was interesting and infectious. Everyone, including me, has a streak of "ham." That day we all had a chance to posture, pose, and have our pictures taken. Sorrily, most of those pictures would end up on the cutting room floor, never to see the light of day.

When the high jinx at the airport wound down, we all headed for Dawson City. It was several miles away over a dusty, gravel base road. Many of the people from the "outside" were having their first experience on such a road. Their lives centered around blacktop and concrete. I found this to be an interesting commentary on the diversity of ways of living. Some had never actually seen a horse or a cow, up close, in the

54

flesh. Incredible, isn't it?

The hotel which I had leased for the occasion was a lulu. It had been constructed during the gold rush era of the 1890s. It was totally wooden. A lot of the heavier timbers had been cut right there at Dawson. Much of the siding, and certainly the fascia boards, had come from the surrounding hills. The interior decoration of the barroom had been shipped in from "outside." Maybe even on board the *Klondike*. There were dark stained, hardwood pillars, which may or may not have been load bearing. They most likely were totally decorative. Mirrors were everywhere. Bottles of various shapes, sizes, and content, lined the back bar mirror. The bar proper was over fifty feet long. It was made completely of mahogany. Shaped mahogany rolled over the top front edge of the bar. The front exhibited blended patterns and divers colors in the wood, terminating on bare floor boards, which had been oiled for generations. Around the base of the bar stood a brass rail, which shone as though recently polished. A flight of stairs went up the east wall. They led nowhere. The landing at the top had long ago been covered over for some reason or another. All of the lighting, save and except some fluted glass shading lamps on the walls were vintage chandeliers. There was a player piano which performed without the necessary encouragement of a coin. Aged tables and chairs filled the place, completing the suggestion that this was a museum, rather than a going concern. Two men stood behind the bar, each wearing arm bands on striped shirts. Aprons covered most of their fronts. They greeted this crowd like they were all long lost friends. I'm sure, that at least some, were friends of long standing.

I excused myself and went to the registration desk. I knew the proprietor and his wife. I had stayed in this hotel on other occasions, and loved the quaint atmosphere. Displaying the list of proposed patrons, their room requirements, other idiosyncrasies and food preferences, I left it to them to become hosts. They would get the tagged luggage to the proper rooms without confusion. At least so I thought.

I must not leave off here, without telling you of two unique features of the hotel and the city, respectively. Firstly, the doors to the rooms. Due to the constant movement under the hotel, of the permafrost, the building had tilted and shifted aimlessly, on an annual basis, for generations. The result was that the doors would get caught up on the floor and on the top of the jambs. A partial solution, adopted by the management, was to cut off the top and bottom four inches of each door. It might have been drafty, but it was at least semi-private. Secondly, I refer to the sidewalks of Dawson. They had been constructed in the early 1900s by the town fathers. Where there were any, they were made of wood, like so many other structures in that matured city. Some of the walks, in order to be level with their terminal points at the end of each street, were as high as five feet off the ground at some points. I had been told stories about the town constables who would, on their early morning rounds, find bruised and more seriously injured people, lying near these sidewalks. Not all of those unfortunates could properly be accused of making the misstep to their downfall as a result of over indulgence in a saloon.

That evening most of us enjoyed a meal of moose steak. It was a novelty to many present. There were no complaints, and lots of compliments, so I assumed that all who tried it enjoyed the inventiveness.

The partying went on to all hours. Some of us departed for our rooms earlier than others. It was now after midnight. It was not really dark. At this particular time of the year, Yukoners enjoyed the midnight sun.

As I went into the foyer and started up the stairs, I heard strained voices. The female was angry. The male was persuasive, or trying to be. When I reached the top of the stairs, I saw the reason. One of the members of our party had thought it a cute ploy to change the name tag on the luggage belonging to this lovely, young lady. Her luggage had been deposited in his room, along with his. She said, heatedly, that she was not interested. He was trying to "sweet-talk" her into changing her mind. Doors started to open to investigate the commotion. Some were grumpy, others merely interested in watching the action. She had her own room, she asserted, and was tired. She wanted to retire. Anyway, she didn't know him that well. Could she please have her things. He said she was beautiful ... that he had admired her, secretly, for a long time. She said that was nice, but wasn't he married? No way he exclaimed. Did he have objections to marriage she asked. Not really, he allowed, if the parties got to know one another. How about breakfast together in the morning she inquired. How about a nightcap now he wondered. Only a nightcap she wanted to know. Sure thing, just a nightcap and talk. Just talk she asked. Honest, he insisted, as he opened the door wider. She walked in. The door closed, and so far as I know, they were not seen by anyone until the late serving of breakfast next morning.

Faint heart never won fair lady, did it?

During the course of the early morning hours, there was one hell of a disturbance out below my window. I woke up, looked at the time, and discovered that it was close to 3 a.m. I stuck my head out the window and saw two male figures below. They were squared off for battle. The abusive language, amply flavored with powerful profanity, was increasing in volume with each retort.

"I saw her first ... I bought her the first drink ... so you butt out you # @*%#!+%#&" screamed the smaller of the two.

"Don't be ridiculous, you Yankee bastard, I've known her for years ... she wants me, not a little #$*&@$%*+$@!, like you," bragged the bigger one.

Smack! The smaller guy belted the big one directly on the jaw. Down he went. He didn't get up. He was out cold.

The stunningly lovely girl, over whom the fight had occurred, stood on the sidewalk proud as a pea hen. They had fought over her. How exciting, how medieval. However, the wrong one had won the fight. She turned around and went to her room, alone.

(In the event that readers think that the scene which I have just described sounds a bit far-fetched, I can assure you that there will be three people who read this book, who can verify that it happened, virtually as described.)

About 6:30 a.m. that morning the TV crew, in whole or in part, either got up, or were still up. In any event, they went around gathering their equipment and the people who were to figure in the picture taking. I got myself organized and tried to locate the various members of the Whitehorse gang, who were to figure in the day's "shoot." This was not an easy task. Many were off visiting friends of theirs who lived in Dawson. Others were definitely not where they told me they were to be located. I borrowed a car and drove out to Bear Creek, one of the minor tributaries to the Klondike River. We had visited a bar there last evening. Maybe some had stayed over. All was quiet when I stopped the car outside of the saloon. The doors to the saloon were not locked. It was not the custom, in the Yukon, to lock doors. Entering the bar was an insult to my nostrils. The foul, tainted air reeked of old tobacco smoke and stale beer. With no difficulty whatsoever, I found three of my party in the fireplace (now cold) on the bare floor, huddled up under a grizzly bear skin. There were no blankets ... no sheets ... no pillows ... just three, fully clothed bodies. No need to name them here ... they remember who they were. If only I had brought a camera. Possibly just as well that I didn't.

They got up, in good humor, still enjoying the nectar of the grape from the night before. Why not? An event such as this may never happen in their lives again. "Make the best of what we yet may spend?" Put yourself in their shoes, for a moment. On how many occasions might you be able to get to this historic, gold rush community, appear on television, get all you want to eat and drink for free, including housing and transportation, and meet a contingent of mostly happy people, all bent on the same objectives. Not many, eh?

We went out to Klondike Creek. It is only a short drive from the downtown core of Dawson. From there, one can look northeasterly and see "Moosehide Hill." Allegedly, it got its name from the fact that when a portion of the hill slumped away, the residual bare surface thereby exposed resembled the hide of a moose. I don't know the actual facts, but I do know that there is a small river at the foot of that hill, which bears the name, Moosehide. To our left was Bonanza Creek where, on August 14, 1896, G. W. Carmack staked the Discovery Claim which caused a world to stampede to the Yukon. On September 24, 1896, he, Skookum Jim, and Tagish Charlie filed their claims with the mining recorder in Dawson. All around us, the visual remains of the gold strike were manifested. Tailing ponds and mounds were everywhere. A huge, Guggenheim Mining Company dredge rested where it had been left. A thick, rusted, wire hawser, somewhat frayed, secured this huge craft to a massive concrete anchor. It was this type of "mining" which replaced the shaft; the windlass; the hand shovel; the tram cars, laden with gold bearing gravel; the sluice box; the gold pan; and the smaller mounds of tailings. This floating building housed all of the features of gold mining under one roof, including assaying the results. A huge arm extended from its front. This arm was mobile in about 180 degrees. It dug, or dredged up the gravel, then fed it to the grinder, the separator, the shaker, and finally the sluicer, all of which were contained within this barge. Once the gravel had been totally divested of its gold, the residual crushed, cleaned and sifted sand, was cast out the rear of the barge. The barge would have been brought to this part of the Yukon in sections, assembled on the river, then surrounded by sufficient water to make it float.

The water served a second purpose also. It sluiced the gravel for the precious metal. The barge moved about the riverbed and through the river valleys, on its own pond. Ingenious, eh wot? These gold dredges were perhaps fifty feet long and thirty feet wide. They towered up to possibly thirty-five feet. They were highly visible and provided the camera crew with an authentic backdrop to the shenanigans.

Once we had collected all pertinent bodies, and in particular Mr. Goldberg, we set about getting the film footage which had prompted this escapade. Rollie was dressed in dungarees, high leather boots, a plaid, flannel shirt, which exposed red flannel underwear at the neck, and a black Stetson. Others were dressed in similar miner's clothes, including a few ladies. I may have been one of those miners. Rollie dug into the gravel at the water's edge and tossed the results into his pan. He bent down, scooped some water into the pan and swirled the gravel. He was panning for gold and the cameras hummed. The director called for this and that. The "grips" (the people who lift, carry and/or move things) wrestled with boulders, which should or should not be, in their particular location at any given moment. The makeup artists had a field day. Beards, heavy eyebrows, sweat or no sweat. Rollie either stood and did nothing, or was ordered into ridiculous stances or positions. The lighting was either good, or "atrocious," depending upon the point of view of the director or cameraman, or both. Many diverse scenes were contrived. Many were performed over and over again, for reasons best known to the director. At the close of the day of filming, everyone had had enough, particularly my group. They had thought it would be all glamour and exhibitionism. It was far from that. It was hard work and professionalism. When the director finally called something like, "that's a wrap," we all headed again for the comfort of our rooms, showers, and the bar. Getting the makeup off was a bore. Probably, because some of us were not used to it. Maybe we tried to hurry that which was not to be hurried. Anyway it was a tired, exhausted, unenthusiastic group which wound up in the bar some hours later. There weren't even any pugilists to be found, nor patent amorists. Docility was the norm.

The next day we all flew back to Whitehorse. Gordie made one more short speech. The group disbanded, never again to reunite for anything remotely similar to this wonderous event. Rollie found a gold nugget. He probably has it, even to this day.

Chapter Seven

Giving birth—an exciting time,
And usually a great big deal
And if there is a doctor there
You'd better make sure he's real.

The Spurious Doctor

On or about Friday, August 3, 1956, my secretary Joan "Rusty" Veinott, was languishing in the General Hospital in Whitehorse. She had just given birth to her first child, Rick. Her husband "Dutch" was out celebrating this magnificent event. He was being helped in this objective by two of his friends and cohorts. One was Stewart Enderton, then a law student with van Roggen, Nielsen and Hine (Now Judge Enderton of Nelson, B.C.). The other chap is well-known to us all.

Rusty is the charming girl about whom I have written earlier. She had a dazzling smile. Her temperament was high in sociability. All the clients commented on how fortunate I was to have someone so competent and universally, constantly pleasant. She used her training in a law office to great advantage. She is today the Public Administrator for the Yukon Territory as well as its Chief Coroner.

Dutch was the town's refrigeration specialist. Great guy, always eager to help. Constantly involved himself in community endeavors. He won the annual beard growing contest for the most luxuriant growth. Typical of him—to enter such a contest.

In any event, on this particular date and time, Dutch felt disposed to go up to the hospital to visit his wife. The fact that it was not visiting hours, coupled with the fact that all three parties had been drinking most of the day, appeared not to deter him one bit. Possibly the chaps with whom he was traveling that night, had a hand in such an attitude.

Up to the hospital they went. Checking the entrance and corridors carefully, they made their way to the doctors' lounge. One of Dutch's companions had a personal friend who was a doctor. The companion had been at the lounge many times. The trio snuck into the lounge and "cased the place" for what it was they sought. They were in luck. They each donned a white smock. One of Dutch's companions "borrowed" a stethoscope and dangled it from his neck, just like doctors do.

Peeking out of the door of the lounge, they made sure that the coast was clear in the direction they wished to go. Dutch had, of course, been up to the hospital when he brought "Rusty" in earlier that day. Therefore, he knew in which room she was to be found.

Finding their pathway free of nurses and other potential threats they walked brazenly into the maternity ward.

There were only two ladies present. Rusty, and Mrs. Des Duncan.

When Dutch and his confreres entered the room, Rusty saw and recognized them immediately. She was further to the right than Mrs. Duncan. She sat up and was about to admonish this trio, when the one with the stethoscope went to the bedside of Mrs. Duncan. He said nothing. He placed the stethoscope against the swollen tummy and uttered medical terms such as "Hhhummmnn," "oh yes," and "uh huh," while shaking his head up and down in a knowing manner. Then this fake obstetrician, in a most positive way, assured the good lady that the birth was to be expected within but a few hours. As if she didn't already have a pretty good idea that such was the case.

Then this intruder approached the bed where Rusty lay shaking her head and holding back a burst of laughter. Dutch, who was known to Mrs. Duncan, held his wife's hand and silently conveyed to her his affection and pride at her accomplishment. Enderton stood near Rusty's bed, arms folded across his chest, as though awaiting the arrival there of the specialist. I, of course, being the one with the stethoscope. As this interloper sauntered, confidently, over to Rusty's bedside, she barked, "Get away from me with that thing, Harold. We're not about to start playing doctor. You guys better get out of here ... right now!"

Just as Rusty uttered those words, the nurse for that ward stepped into the room. For a moment, she took us to be the genuine article. Upon closer scrutiny she recognized Dutch and said, "What on earth are you doing in here. You'll have to leave, and you, Mr. Hine, you shouldn't be here at all. Mr. Enderton, you just wait until I tell Jean about this. Out you get. All of you ... out! Come tomorrow during the proper visiting hours."

For the record, Mrs. Duncan did have her son the very next day, on August 4, 1956.

Not bad for a spurious obstetrician, eh?

If Mrs. Duncan reads this book, it may be the first time that she learns who that "doctor" was.

Chapter Eight

A pleasure flight to Anchorage
A break from courtroom chores,
Stirred up emotions, hot and strong,
The kind that started wars.

Innocence was set aside,
It had no role to play,
Power has to flex its might
No matter what you say.

This power, in the hands of some,
Could havoc wreak in time,
But pleasant endings do occur,
When luck is yours sublime.

Bungled Flight

During the course of the next year, I spent a good deal of my time both in the courtroom and flying. In fact, I would often make an early morning flight out to a designated lake where I would either drop off one or more prospectors, eager to make the "big strike," or pick up one or more prospectors, whom I had taken out months earlier. Later that same day I would make my appearance in court. Flying during the early part of the day was advisable for one particular reason; the sun had not had time to set in motion the factors which cause air turbulence, thus the flights were usually more comfortable for all concerned.

During April, 1954, I had been involved in a continuous series of heavy trials. While I enjoyed that experience, it was nevertheless tiring, and on occasion, exhausting. Getting up very early on some mornings in order to fly, then conducting a trial for some five hours (with a lunch break during which the lawyers researched law or rearranged their respective tactics) became too demanding. I decided that I wanted a short holiday.

One of the lawyers with whom I was involved in the trials was James King. He and I were approximately the same age and were forming a strong bond of friendship. I respected his talents and integrity as a lawyer and felt comfortable with him as a crony. His wife, Jean, and Laura had become good companions as well. Moreover, Jim had been a pilot during the recent war.

After the conclusion of the final trial on the court list, I asked Jim if he would like to join me on a weekend jaunt to Anchorage, Alaska. It was the Easter break in both the U.S.A. and Canada. Maybe the girls would like to go, we could make a foursome of it.

"Sounds like a great idea to me, Harold," said Jim. "I'll ask Jean and give you a call tonight, OK?"

"Great, Jim. I'll talk to Laura as well. I haven't said anything to her as yet. She hasn't been feeling too well, as you know. By the way, do you still have those RCAF air maps and radio frequencies? We could use them on this flight, if they cover Alaska."

"Yeah ... I think I could locate them ... I'm sure that they cover the route to Anchorage ... I'll let you know when I phone tonight, OK?"

"Sounds tremendous to me ... see you later, Jim," I said as I picked up my bag which contained my court gown and accessories, and left him to finish changing into his street clothing.

That evening Jim phoned as planned. It turned out that neither Jean nor Laura were going to make the trip, but both of them encouraged Jim and me to take the time off while we could. Jim confirmed that he had the flight maps. We mutually agreed to meet the next day over coffee to plan the flight and the timetables.

Flying any time usually contains the promise of excitement. Flying in a small plane, over foreign air space, sometimes provides excitement which can be both unexpected and unwelcomed.

Getting air maps of Alaska would not have been an easy task. Not only would I have had to order them from the Federal Aeronautics Administration, probably in Fairbanks, and endure the delay created by mail delivery both ways plus the usual administrative delays in the government offices but at this particular time the "Cold War" was at its peak. The tension created by that phenomenon permeated Canada as well. The isolationist policy of the Americans was formidable, albeit unofficial.

On the appointed day, at the established hour, Jim and his family arrived at the airport. Jim strode over to the plane and in a feigned uncertain attitude said, "Is this plane of yours airworthy, Hine?"

Jim was then about thirty years of age. He was not tall. He was about the same height as me and about the same weight. He had dark hair worn in the brushed back, off the forehead, style of the day. He had a quick, dazzling smile. He affected a James Cagney type of cockiness, stance, and walk. He had a buoyant spirit, and endless energy.

"She has just had her 100 hr. inspection and has been certified by Gordie (Gordon Cameron, an aircraft engineer based at Whitehorse, who was well known to both Jim and me. Gordon eventually became the commissioner of the Yukon Territory and was well-respected by all who knew him) as totally airworthy," I replied with pride. My plane, at this time, was a S.17 D. Staggerwing Beechcraft. She was the type of plane which was flown by Amelia Earhart when she competed in the International Air Races in the U.S.A. and won many of them. She was designed to accommodate four passengers and a pilot. She had a well-appointed cabin of soft leather seats and wall paneling. The instrument panel was specifically designed to be totally visible without impediments from the control column or any other interfering parts. She had a 450 horse power Pratt and Whitney Junior Wasp engine which supplied a tremendous amount of power for that size of aircraft. The "Beaver," which is an international air workhorse, carries the same engine.

This plane is distinctive from all other types of aircraft in that of the two wings which she had, the lower one protruded AHEAD of the upper wing by some eighteen inches. Most two-winged planes have the wings parallel and equidistant in set back from the engine. This unique arrangement gave the plane quick lift, immediate response to controls, and great stability. She was noisy but this was compensated for by the high speeds which she could develop. She was "clean," in flying parlance, meaning that her aerodynamics had been well-conceived; air could flow over her various foils and do all of the flight things that they were supposed to do quickly and properly without drag, inefficiency, yaw (to deviate on her own from the straight course) or inconsistent behavior. On this day she had retractable landing gear which added to her clean look in the air. At other times she had floats attached.

"I've checked the weather and we should have nothing but the best of it both going and returning," I said with enthusiasm.

"Yeah, so did I," said Jim with a smug look. "I may have been born at night, but not last night. I do my own checking."

Then he feigned a punch at my middle and danced around like a boxer.

"What a couple of kids," said Jean, "just look at those two, Laura, they're worse than the children."

The ladies had elected not to fly with us for several reasons, two of which were that the children were still very young and would be particularly miserable if left with a stranger, coupled with the fact that we were going to fly over the most rugged terrain in Canada and the United States. Our planned flight path would take us near Mount Logan (19,500 feet), the highest peak in Canada and Mount McKinley (20,500 feet), the highest peak in the U.S.A. Both ladies felt that they could do more constructive things at home and "after all, both you and Jim have earned the right to blow off some steam together." At least that is what they told us.

The flight plan (which we filed with the tower in Whitehorse) was to fly from Whitehorse directly to Burwash Landing in the Yukon, where there was located an abandoned airstrip which paralleled the Alaska Highway. Over it we would "blow" (let run into empty) our starboard tank, switch to the port tank, then head for Northway, Alaska, where we could refuel. From there with both port and starboard tanks full, together with the belly tank reserved for take off and landings, we would be fuel "organized" to finalize our flight to Anchorage.

Northway was described, on the air maps, as being a gravel airstrip on the perimeter of which were located three low buildings; being a coffee shop, a hangar, and a flight service workshop where fuel was available.

After leaving Northway our plan was to fly almost southwest toward Anchorage, keeping mainly to the high valleys.

Just as we were climbing into the plane at about 6:30 a.m. on that Good Friday morning, I asked Jim if he had brought along his Air Force flight maps. He showed them to me, then stashed them into the pouch on the passenger door of the plane.

After all the kisses good-bye, and being warned for the umpteenth time to be careful, Jim and I climbed aboard the plane. I waved everybody back from the aircraft so that they would not be blasted by the propeller wash, and then started her up.

We cleared with the tower, where they, too, added their admonitions for us to be careful.

The flight up the Alaska Highway towards Burwash Landing was flightwise uneventful. The panorama of the mountains was breathtaking. A mere 100 miles west of Whitehorse we were flying parallel to the Kluane Mountain Range in which is located the Kluane National Park (Canadian). The closest settlement of consequence is Haines Junction, Y.T. On our starboard side (right) there were miles and miles of pasture land which erupted, 'way off in the distant northwest, into the coastal mountains. Directly to port (left) there was a massive wall of granite, thrusting craggy peaks high into the cloudless sky. This was the "Snowcapped Grandeur," about which one reads in the travel folders.

While Jim and I chattered excitedly about "that peak," or "that river," or cried "look over here," or "what's the name of that" ... the engine stopped. Suddenly, it was deathly quiet in the cabin. The noisy but comforting roar was not there. The propeller windmilled lazily without the power plant providing it with revolutions.

"It's Burwash Landing ... we've blown the bloody tank!" cried Jim.

"Right," I yelled, "Let me get to that tank valve ... move your legs ... I can't see it ... I'll switch tanks."

Frustratingly, the tank valve was on Jim's side of the plane. It was bolted to the side wall near his right calf. Consequently, it was out of my line of sight. As I reached over, being careful not to put downward pressure on the control column, all I could find was Jim's hand.

"Get out of the way, Jim ... let me do it!" I insisted, with urgency in my voice. The plane was losing altitude fast and I wasn't the slightest bit interested in making an emergency landing on that abandoned, unattended, potholed airstrip.

"Jim, will you get your bloody hand out of the way ... I'll do it ... move your legs ... get your hand out of the way!"

"I've got it, Harold ... I've got it, I tell you ... it's switched to the port tank ... start it up ... hurry up," he urged.

Just as suddenly as she had stopped, she started up again. What a lovely deep roar that was. What a wonderful noise.

The entire episode had taken only about thirty seconds but it had taken on the tone of distress about which we both now laughed uncontrollably.

"Jeez, Harold, you almost tore the bloody fingers off my bloody hand," bellowed Jim. "I've heard stories about the fastest two-handed game in the world but I thought it was something else," he howled.

"Yeah man, with all that careful planning about blowing the tank, and there we were like a couple of tourists gawking at the scenery instead of concentrating upon the fuel indicator. What a couple of goofs," I responded and joined in Jim's laughter.

Aside from absorbing some of the most beautiful scenery in the entire world, the rest of the trip to Northway was uneventful.

"We should be over the Northway strip in two and a half minutes," said Jim, who was acting as navigator while I flew.

"We should intersect their runway anytime now, if our calculations have been correct. Flying mainly by magnetic compass, this far north, demands many adjustments but I think I've made them OK. We should be over it any second," Jim insisted.

"There it is!" Jim cried, as we flew over what had to be considered a very well-camouflaged setting.

"Did you see it?" he asked, as he rotated his head far to the right and to the rear.

I banked the plane to port and assumed the reverse of my previous compass heading. This of course would take us back over the exact same path which we had traveled while flying in the opposite direction

"Yes I did ... boy that is difficult to see ... there it is ... man that is a narrow runway ... I had better make a pass over it first just to get my bearings and check the surface."

When we touched down on the hard, clay surface, a huge cloud of dust billowed up under and behind us. I deliberately waited at the end of the strip for a few minutes to allow the dust to settle before taxiing to the fuel center.

"How are you guys today?" said the gas jockey. "How was the flight? I understand that it is CAVU all around us." (Ceiling and visibility unlimited)

"It sure is," I responded. "I can't imagine seeing those mountains under any better conditions than we just did."

"Shall I fill 'er up?" he asked.

"Yes, please, and I'll check the oil," I replied.

"Are you guys going on further into Alaska?" a voice to my left interrupted.

Jim and I turned to see a young, slender, pleasant-faced man dressed in clean coveralls and jack boots. He had his hand extended in greeting.

"Yes, we're on our way to Anchorage," I said as I accepted his hand and shook it.

"Well, come on over to the general store when you're through here. You'll be my first customers. I've just been appointed the customs and immigration officer for this region, haven't even got my uniform or badge yet ... just the official letter. I'll fix you up with the necessary documents covering you and the plane." So saying, he wheeled on his heel and strode off in the direction of what we took to be the store he referred to.

Once airborne again and on course for Anchorage, I stashed the entry documents into a secret compartment in my briefcase. Just habit, I guess.

We flew along, chatting, admiring the vastness and the beauty, when my flight watch on my wrist sounded its alarm.

"Time to contact that US airbase at Elmendorff, Jim. We should radio and let them know of our presence. I'm sure that they must have us on radar by now but it's still a good idea," I said.

"OK with me. Let me check the right map and I'll give them a call," responded Jim.

In just a moment or two, Jim had a flight map on his lap and was reaching for the radio dials. I couldn't really hear what he was actually saying because of the noise in the cabin, but I realized that he would know what he was doing. I saw his mouth move as he spoke into the mike, then saw his arm come down from his mouth as he waited for a response. He was wearing the earphones. He did this several times then turned to me and said, "I can't seem to reach anybody on these frequencies. I'm getting no response."

I was about to respond to Jim with a suggestion or two when I saw Jim's eyes bulge. He was looking past me, to the outside of the plane. He made some sound which was, to me, unintelligible and pointed out the window on my side.

Turning automatically, as one does when someone points like that, I was astonished to see a USAF jet fighter passing our left wing. It had on full flap and had its landing gear in the down and locked position. Only this way could he fly slowly enough to temporarily match our airspeed.

The pilot of that jet was signaling that he wanted us to land. His right hand was raised with his gloved thumb turned down. With his repeated jerking motions of that thumb we had no doubts as to what he meant. He was doing it with authority.

All of this took but a few seconds, then the jet fell off to its left. He had probably stalled trying to fly at our much slower speed. He circled, then came alongside again. He signaled that he wanted us to communicate with him by radio. I nodded affirmatively and pointed at Jim, who held up the mike so that the jet jockey could see that we had one and understood.

"For God's sake Jim, get this guy on the radio. He isn't acting too friendly. What the hell would he be doing here anyway?"

Jim struggled with the dials as the jet fell away again.

"I'm going to try the tower at Anchorage. Maybe they can intercede for us," barked Jim.

The seconds drew into agonizing minutes and they into about half an hour before Jim finally found a frequency that drew a response from Anchorage. By now, we had two jet fighters on our tail, side, top, underneath, or wherever they wanted to be at their discretion. They would fly directly at us in what could only be described as a menacing manner. As they "swooshed" by, our much lighter plane would bounce around like a balloon in a wind tunnel.

By now we had reached Anchorage. We had been given clearance to land at the Anchorage International Airport.

I had just nicely touched down and was braking to slow down when a US Army truck pulled onto the runway directly in front of us. It had a huge, crudely scrawled sign on the back of it which said, "Follow Me."

"How nice," I thought, "this is the type of courtesy which has given the many airports, at which I have landed in the US, such a good image."

Upon closer examination there was something different about this particular vehicle. It was the dirty green of the military and had a flashing red light on the roof. I could see people in the back, through the small windows, but I could not quite make them out. They seemed to be very intent on what we were doing.

The truck pulled up to a building. It almost touched it. Suddenly, the two back doors of the truck burst open and out jumped eight military policemen. Each wore a white helmet, white gaiters, white belt with white holster, and a white lanyard. Each was carrying a rifle with a white sling. They seemed to be very familiar with their armament. They looked ominous.

On the taxi strip, immediately in front of that building, there had been painted a large white circle. We were directed into that circle by the police who stood outside of its perimeter.

One of them, who appeared to be dressed slightly differently and who did not carry a rifle, drew his right forearm across his throat. I took this to mean that he wanted me to shut off the engine, which I did.

As soon as the propeller stopped whirling, but before the gyro compass stopped whining, my door flew open and there stood a major in the US Air Force. It was he who ordered me to shut off the engine.

He, too, wore all white trappings but was different in the one respect that he carried a pistol in his hand. It was pointed at me.

He was tall, good looking, blond, and immaculate in his uniform. I would guess that he was not yet 35. His chest was beribboned with campaign colors. He was the epitome of a military officer and he knew it.

"Alright you two, get down out of there. You are both under arrest and your aircraft is under seizure. Come on ... get out!" he ordered in a most demanding, authoritative voice. His manner was arrogant in a way in which only those people who hold authority can be.

"I am Major Bradner, T. J. Bradner, (not the real name). I now formally place both of you under arrest for unlawfully invading the airspace of the United States of America, without permission so to do," he pontificated.

It was all I could do to keep myself from bursting out laughing. Here was a crown prosecutor for the Yukon being arrested for some alleged international offense. I didn't laugh on the outside. This guy was serious.

"Alright then, Major, if you feel that way about it. Can we take our belongings out of the aircraft?" I asked.

"You just leave everything the way it is. You won't need any of that stuff where you guys are going," he snapped.

"Where are we going?" asked Jim, who had been silent up until now.

"Into the lockup there," said the major, pointing at windows in the building beside us. I had not really looked at them prior to now, they were barred.

"Major, we are both lawyers and I am carrying a client's confidential documents in my briefcase. My oath requires me to protect that confidentiality ... at all costs," I asserted, hopefully.

The major was obviously stumped for a moment, but not for long.

"OK, you may carry your briefcase with you, but only after I have checked it for firearms and other contraband ... AND you have proved to my satisfaction that you are lawyers. I can hardly believe that two lawyers could let themselves get into such a fix."

"Firearms and contraband?" who the hell do they think we are, I thought.

The major holstered his pistol, wheeled upon a sergeant and ordered him to search the plane for a briefcase. When the sergeant returned with mine he handed it to the major.

"Check it!" snapped the major.

"Fall in," the major yelled, curtly.

With that order, the eight policemen formed two parallel lines. One on each side of Jim and me. They were about four feet apart with their rifles on their shoulders. I felt a bit intimidated.

The major strode, no, paraded to the head of the two lines then stood in front of Jim and me, did a snappy about face, and marked time waiting for the two of us to join in. Unconsciously we started to get into step with this haughty, imperious, overbearing toy soldier. Jim and I were still in good humor but the edge was being stripped off by the awesome scenario being painted by the major.

"Quick march!" he bellowed, and away we went to jail.

The cell was much like those that one sees on TV. It had four walls, three of which were cold concrete blocks. The other wall had a door cut into it. There were bars in a hinged door fixed into the concrete. Another door, on the outside of the barred door, was solid metal except for a small peep hole of wire-filled glass.

Jim and I had just nicely examined our new quarters and were choosing bunks when the metal door opened and the sergeant pushed my briefcase through the bars.

"Good, now at least we can play cribbage while we wait," said Jim, who knew that I carried a miniaturized cribbage set at all times.

"We can do more than just play cribbage, Jim, if my hunch is right," I said smugly.

Quickly I opened the case, searched in the back compartment, and cried out, "Hah ... Hah! ... look what they missed."

"What is that?" asked Jim as he saw me waving a document over my head.

"It's the immigration and custom clearance we picked up in Northway, remember?" I whispered softly, conspiratorially, "You heard what that pompous peacock said, 'we are arrested for having invaded without lawful authority.' It's obvious that he is not yet aware that we have this document. Let's have some fun with that egotistical bastard!"

Whether it was the absurdity of the situation in which we found ourselves, or the fact that we now felt that we had the upper hand, I don't know, but both of us burst into laughter and tears.

"This is no laughing matter, you clowns!" said a voice. We had not heard the metal door open. There was Major "Puffed Up" who had heard us and stepped over from his office across the hallway. "You Canadians are all alike. You think that because we are neighbors, you can behave any way you please. Well, you can't! Yours will be the third aircraft that I have seized this quarter ... and like yours, they are never going back. Do you understand me? This is our country and our airspace and you are going to learn to recognize that fact the hard way!"

Having said his piece he slammed the door, hard, and we heard him parade away.

"How long are you going to keep us here, jailer?" Jim cried.

The door opened again and the major reappeared. "Still think it's funny, eh? ... you wait ... just sit and wait, ... until we get damned good and ready to deal with your case. I'm doing some checking on you two ... until I'm satisfied ... you just sit and wait, got it?"

"Please, sir, do we get to choose our last meal?" I sniveled, dramatically, hands clasped at my chin.

"Just because you're a couple of bloody lawyers doesn't mean that you're going to get away with this ... this," he stammered in frustration.

"This RAP," I offered, solicitously.

"Sure, you can be the smart aleck now, but just wait. Just you wait," spat the major as he stormed off, slamming the door again. Harder this time.

"Shouldn't we tell the poor guy?" asked Jim, smiling at the idiocy of the situation. "He's liable to have apoplexy if we keep this up."

"Well let's have a couple of games of cribbage first. We came over here to get a change of pace, and we certainly have had that, eh, wot, old chap?" I said, doing my best mimicry of Colonel Blimp. "Let's let him have another real good outburst before we tell the pompous ass, OK?"

"Yeah, I suppose we should capitulate to good sense sometime in this crazy charade," replied Jim, just as he burst out laughing again.

Jim and I played crib for about two hours without any interruption. We were just at the point where we started talking about calling Major Puff Puff, when the metal door opened, the barred door swung wide, and in walked a civilian. He was wearing a Harris tweed sports jacket, complimenting slacks, a plain, pastel colored shirt, and a blending tie. He wore a fedora with a pastel band.

It was the major!

"What's with you, Major? Are you off duty already?" I cried, with mock astonishment.

The major looked as though he was in pain. He twitched nervously, wrung his hands which he kept looking down to, cleared his throat several times, and shifted his stance repeatedly.

"You guys bloody well know why I'm here in mufti."

"In mufti! God I thought it was only in the British Army that they used that expression."

"Yes, in mufti," he started to growl, then changed his voice to contain more warmth. There might have even been a hint of a smile. A sort of "invitation to treat," as we lawyers call it.

"Well, we made a mistake," admitted the major, "more accurately, I made a mistake. It is my responsibility to check the data on all incoming aircraft but when the jet fighters weren't able to communicate with you and you hadn't checked

74

in at Elmendorff Air Base ... I ... I ... well I ... "

"Jumped to conclusions," I offered.

"Yes, jumped to conclusions, erroneous conclusions, as it turned out," the major agreed, dejectedly.

"You found out that we had recorded our entry into Alaska at Northway, right?" I asked.

"Right," he replied. "I hadn't read the notice about the appointment there. The notice was on my desk but for some reason I hadn't read it."

He no longer fitted the term "Major," as he had, out on the tarmac. He was now exhibiting some of the qualities of a 'nice guy' even a likable guy.

"I tried to contact the air base and the jets but got no response from either," said Jim, quizzically.

"What frequencies were you using?" asked the major.

"Those on the flight maps out in the plane," explained Jim.

"I'll go out and get them," volunteered the major, "and by the way my first name is Tom, if you care."

When he left he carefully shut both the barred door and the metal door behind him.

"Tom" did not have to announce his return. We could hear him laughing all the way down the corridor to the cell.

"No wonder you guys weren't able to contact anyone. These maps are obsolete. They're at least eight to ten years out of date. No wonder everyone thought you were invading aircraft."

I looked over at Jim. He looked at the floor and said, "Oh, boy, I never thought about that."

" 'Oh, Boy,' is that all you have to say about our being arrested, threatened with death, having our aircraft confiscated, being accused of being in possession of guns and other contraband, attacked by armed jets, just ... 'Oh, Boy'?" I roared, in mock hysteria.

I must have overplayed my hand with that outburst. I had no sooner completed the last syllable when all three of us crumpled with laughter.

When we settled down again, Tom said, "Look you guys, if my commander ever finds out about what has happened I will get 'busted' to corporal. What can I do to make amends?"

"Well Tom," said Jim, with an impish expression on his face, "the first damn thing is to let us out of this bloody cell."

75

"Christ, you're right. I'm so discombobulated that I forgot about saying ... you are not under arrest ... and your plane is not under seizure ... and ... and you are free to leave ... any time ... but first, is there anything I can do to make amends?"

"Certain ideas spring to mind, Tom ... don't rush me ... let's give this some thought," I said as I held my right hand to my forehead and tilted my eyes upward in a stance of muse. I winked at Jim while stroking my chin and walking in a small circle. "Jim and I don't know this city at all. Do you have a passing acquaintance with it?" I asked, with a glint in my eye.

"How about showing us the sights?" erupted Jim.

"I'll do anything to make up for this bungled mess ... first I'll take you to your hotel ... then to a great steak house for dinner ... then the 13 Club for after dinner drinks and ... uh ... entertainment. It will all be on me," offered Tom, then "Oh, by the way ... just for the record ... can I see those immigration entry forms?"

"Sure you can, Tom" I said, "and also, just for the record ... we too were at fault ... using those outdated maps ... so let's split those costs ... everything after dinner is on us, OK?"

"Can't think of a better deal than that ... except to add that I do hope that no word of this ever gets to the ears of the general ... deal?" Tom asked.

"Deal, there will be no complaint filed by us. I don't know what explanation you'll give to the jet jockeys and the others but you'll have no problems from us," I responded. Jim nodded in compliance.

That was more than thirty years ago and unless the general reads this book and is still Tom's commanding officer, I doubt that anyone in authority will now give a damn about our bungled flight.

Chapter Nine

To Haines, Alaska, we were bound,
A festival was there,
We saw the boundless works of God,
His art was everywhere.

Huge mountains piercing to the sky,
All blues and grays and whites,
And mantles shrouding spires of rock
White clouds, at rest, in height.

More mundane the arid waste,
Which covered most the way,
The contrast was a shocking thing
As we went down to play.

Down from desolate valleys high
To reach the coast below,
Then a dance and revelry
And a toast, which lost its glow.

The Inexcusable Request

In June of 1955, Laura and I thought that it would be a good idea to take advantage of the fact that the upcoming long weekend consisted of both the Canadian national holiday of July 1 and the American national holiday of July 4. This meant that we could have Friday, Saturday, Sunday, and Monday, away from our usual activities. Talking to some of our friends produced results. Why not go over to Haines, Alaska, where they have their annual "Strawberry Festival" on their holiday, July 4.

So well was this suggestion received amongst our friends, that we arranged four carloads of enthusiastic holidayers within the week.

One of the people whom I attempted to contact was a young Irishman by the name of Mickey. I know his last name but as I have not been able to contact him, prior to this book being published, I will use only that first given name. He, and the others who were present on the occasion about which I now write, know to whom I refer. There is nothing sinister involved. Just an unusual weekend.

Mickey had come directly to Whitehorse from the "old sod," as he called it. He had been born and raised in Belfast. An unhappy love affair had driven him away from Ireland and brought him directly to Whitehorse, Yukon Territory, Canada. Now there is a peregrination if I ever heard of one.

Mickey had been a bartender in Ireland. He had learned the business through the apprenticing system. He was about thirty-five years of age at the time I refer to. He was small of stature, slight of build and weight. He always looked emaciated. His eyes were always rheumy, and he smoked ceaselessly. He was addicted to the demon alcohol. Oh, he would go for weeks without taking a drink but then he would go for weeks without eating, just drinking. He told me that he always knew when he had been drinking long enough. He would become severely nauseous, throw up, then sleep for a few days. He would then return to working near his true love, in a bar. He would, as he would say, "join what's left of the human race."

Mickey was a pleasant man. He liked people and they responded in kind. He could "chat you up" for hours and when you parted from him, you would invariably leave thinking what a fine chap he was, notwithstanding that the subject matter of the conversation was completely inconsequential.

I got to know Mickey quite well. Whenever I went into a bar for a quiet and private drink, alone or with an intimate friend, I always went to whatever bar Mickey was working in at that particular time. As he was transient minded he worked for a lot of different bar owners.

On the day that I went to see if Mickey would like to come to Haines with us, he was apparently away on a binge. I left a message with his alternate bartender, which in essence informed Mickey that a group of us were going over to Haines for the long weekend.

Early on the Friday morning, a caravan of revellers left Whitehorse for the 240-250 mile drive over to Haines. We consisted of four cars, all of recent vintage and each having had a thorough check before departure.

Haines is an anachronism in many ways. Its existence at that time was principally as a result of events which had long ceased to be of importance. It had become a military outpost for the Americans when they purchased Alaska from the Russians for $7,200,000 in 1867. Located there was a huge barracks with four or five large buildings. They had been designed and built to house the military complement, which had been established there after the said purchase. Those buildings, or some of them, had been renovated and made into tourist accommodations. It was in one or more of them that our party was housed on this trip. A main feature of this confine was a large bar which contained a sizable dance floor. It was at this precise spot that the focal point of this story is located.

Haines had a large dock installation. I was told by some of the people we met in Haines, including the lady mayor, that Haines had been almost as popular a disembarkation port because of the Yukon gold rush, as was Skagway, in the late eighteen hundreds. The town itself was quite small. My recollection now is that it then consisted of maybe four or five main streets which ran downhill to the bay. Haines, by the way, is on a small peninsula which juts out into the Chilkoot Inlet at the northern portion of the Lynn Canal, which terminates at Juneau, the capital city of Alaska.

The drive from Whitehorse to Haines Junction is a distance of about 100 miles. Obviously this community got its name from the fact that it was here that a traveler either turned south to go over the desolate, sometimes barren Haines Road down to the ocean at Haines, or remained on the Alaska Highway which continued on to Fairbanks. This "Alcan" highway is 1,671 miles in length. It is a gravel road which traverses endless miles of wilderness, muskeg, clay, and sometimes shallow rivers without the benefit of the implacement of a bridge or culvert. The highway begins at Dawson Creek, British Columbia, and terminates in Fairbanks, Alaska. I have driven the entire length in counter part trips. The road was completed in 1942. It was built by Canadian and US engineers and civilian contractors. It was completed end to end in just seven months. The invasion of Alaska by the Japanese, in June and July of 1942, and their establishment of an invasion force

79

upon the small islands of Kiska, Attu, and Agattu, in the Aleutian Island chain, confirmed the urgent military need for such a land link between Alaska and the mainland U.S.A..

Anyway, back to the story. The drive along the said highway was, in itself, uneventful. Those of us in the caravan were familiar with the dusty surface of the road, so we stayed well spaced. There was no thought of passing one another. A driver could not see even the car ahead, at say, an eighth of a mile. He also could not see to pass. Frustration on the part of many drivers on the Alaska Highway has caused many white crosses to be stabbed into the road edge. They commemorate the passing of impatient drivers and their hapless victims. While the road bed was constructed through an arid valley, mountains rose on both sides. To the right was the Ruby Range, and to the left, the Coastal Range. Directly in front of us and slightly to the left, rose the huge St. Elias Mountains. It is in this range that we find the Kluane National Park (Canadian). We also find Mount Logan, which is Canada's highest peak at 19,850 feet. The grandeur of that sight is truly awe-inspiring. Haines Junction, for example, is at approximately 2,150 feet. Less than ten miles to the west the mountains reach 8,190 feet and some 50 to 60 miles in the same direction they tower to 12,750 feet (Mount Queen Mary); 14,250 feet (McArthur Peak); 16,971 feet (Klog Peak); then Mount Logan, still further to the west.

When we reached Haines Junction we all stopped in to say hello to mutual friends, John and Sally Backie. They operated a tourist lounge and motel. On this particular day they were having some festivities of their own. Their small, young daughter, also named Sally, was practicing riding a new pony which her parents had given her. Having a young daughter of my own and about the same age, I somehow became intimately involved in that situation.

The reason that I have focused upon the pony episode is that many years later I flew to the Junction with my son, Larry, who is also a pilot. We were accompanied by a business associate on this trip. His name is Rod Hardie, who still lives in the Yukon and is a big game guide. I landed upon the airstrip and we walked over to the lounge. Many things had changed in the thirty years since I had last been there. Upon entering the bar I recognized the lovely young woman bartender. She did not recognize me. The three members of our entourage sat on the stools at the bar. I engaged this young lady in light

80

conversation. She reported that John and Sally had passed on to their respective rewards. She studied me with uncommon interest but said nothing, then her curiosity got the better of her. She returned from chatting with some of the locals who were at the far side of the bar. She sized me up again and eventually said, "Do I know you from somewhere? You've been in here before, but I can't place you. How would I know you?"

"Maybe if you can remember what I do for a living. I'll bet you can't guess what I do for a living," I said. "As a matter of fact, I'll bet you two bucks against that sign there, that you can't guess what I do."

The sign had words scrolled across it saying, "We make the best Bloody Mary in the world." I thought that it would look good on my bar after she autographed it, when I eventually won it.

"OK, you're on. Two bucks against my sign," she said. "You're a salesman, now I remember!"

"Darn it, you're right," I replied. "But, I'll bet you another two bucks, against the sign, that you can't tell me what it is that I sell, wanna bet?"

"Sure, I'll take that bet. You're on, again," she said with confidence.

Placing the four dollars upon the bar I waited for her response. She asked me to stand, which I did, then sat down again. She wandered over to her cocktail waitress and they whispered together. The waitress came over and sized me up. Then the young woman returned and said, "You're a post card hawker."

"Wrong!" I cried in a loud voice, "I'm a condom salesman!"

Just for a moment, it was as though time stood still. There was a hush throughout the bar. The two women stared at me in surprise. My son turned away from me as though he didn't know me. Our business associate looked shocked. There was that pregnant pause, then both he and Larry crumpled with laughter. The bartenderess and the waitress acted as though they hadn't heard correctly, but knew that they had. I couldn't contain myself. Even if one isn't supposed to laugh at one's own jokes, I did. The ladies realized that it was all a joke, then they too, joined into the levity.

"You're Mr. Hine," cried young Sally. "I'd know that laugh anywhere. You are Mr. Hine, aren't you? I'm sure you are. How are you? Where have you been? I haven't seen you since ... since ... ."

"The day that we played outside there with your new pony?" I offered.

"Right! That's right. Come here and give me a hug! How are you? You look fine. I don't know why I didn't recognize you. You've changed, but not that much ... too bad Mom and Dad aren't here."

Incidentally, I did end up with the sign. That was in 1980, I think.

Now back to the story of the Haines trip.

After leaving the Junction, we traversed the same type of barren, dusty terrain that we had previously. At Dezadeash Lake, some thirty to forty miles south on the Haines Road, we encountered a family of bears. The proprietors of the cabins there discarded their garbage into an old square wagon box and the bears appeared daily to scavenge for food. They were black bears. It appeared to our party that these were a mother and two cubs. The cubs were mature, but not as large as the mother. No one ventured out of the cars, but many pictures were taken. I looked at ours just recently.

Continuing on the southward trek, we remained contained within a valley. The land was parched and the vegetation, what there was of it, was withered, adust, and desiccated. For mile after mile, and as far as the eye could see on each side of the road, there was utter desolation. The spindly trees and bushes looked forlorn and wretched. The sunbaked earth, which but months ago laid covered with snow, was a blanket of powder. The entire area looked as though it had been the victim of an atomic explosion. The sky was clear and the sun shone but it did no good here, it only inflicted punishment. Soon we neared Dalton post, one of the historic points of interest. It was here that the cattle wranglers, bringing a herd of beef up to the meat starved gold diggers in the Klondike, set up a camp. It had long since been abandoned. Then near 136 degrees 30 minutes west and 60 degrees 30 minutes south, we crossed over the boundary between the State of Alaska and the Province of British Columbia. I do not remember there being any Custom or Immigration building. My current research indicates that there was none.

Then, without forewarning of any kind, after all those many miles of desert and arid landscape, we rounded a sharp turn in the road and came into a very narrow valley. I can remember this event as though it occurred yesterday, so startled was I by the change. It was as though someone had opened a door to a new existence. There was a definite demarcation between the barren past and the lush present. The distinction between the two was so well circumscribed that it could be photographed. Ahead were the visual results of the coastal precipitation, behind were the visual results of the lack of the same. Tall firs rose up from the side of the road, where previously there had been no trees, or if there were, they were stultified, spindled, arboreal freaks. Bushes pressed out toward the edge of the road. They were full of energy and promise. Everywhere there was verdant beauty. What a contrast!

Once that turn in the road occurred, we were in a different world. This was the change which makes the rest. We had only approximately 35 miles to drive before reaching our destination. It was going to be the pleasant diversion we sought.

Having arrived at about mid afternoon we all agreed that we should seek out our respective rooms, get settled, have a shower to remove the last vestige of the dust, and meet in the bar at 5 o'clock.

The festival lived up to its reputation. There was plenty to do and to see. There didn't appear to be too many strawberries in sight but that was a matter of minor concern. Some of the more bizarre events which were witnessed are as follows.

A certain lawyer from Whitehorse had armed himself with a water pistol. He filled it with Southern Comfort (a liqueur which has a bourbon base). He wandered the streets, restaurants, and bars squirting people in the mouth. At one point, he was seen to encounter the local town sheriff. The sheriff wore a huge revolver hanging in a leather holster strapped to his waist. Upon meeting on the street, each traveling in a different direction, the lawyer assumed the crouch of the gun fighter. The water pistol was stuck in his belt. He stalked the sheriff, face to face. The sheriff good naturedly crouched also. They came together slowly, step by step. It was like a scene from "High Noon." Just at the crucial moment, when they were about six feet apart, the lawyer whipped out the gun and shot the sheriff in the mouth. Thank God he only laughed and slurped it up, otherwise, I would have been in potential trouble.

Another situation occurred near the same point. Someone claimed that he could run at a telephone pole, run up it to about six feet, no hands involved, then whirl around and run down the pole without falling. A bet ensued. The chap made the run and succeeded. It looked so easy that another in the group decided that he, too, could perform the feat. He charged at the pole, thrust one foot against it, then another, then fell back down into the circle of trash and broken glass which had accumulated at the foot of the pole. He had smooth leather soles on his shoes—I wore runners.

One of the most interesting side shows at the festival occurred in the large dance hall to which I have earlier referred. During the course of the dance, which was to last all night, a huge local resident had become very intoxicated and was making an extreme nuisance of himself.

No one will ever know if he was a quiet docile person by nature when sober, or whether he was habitually the bully. When I say that he was huge, I mean a man standing six feet four and weighing about 240 pounds. He had large shoulders, like those of a dock worker, and he had paws for hands. He wore a plaid flannel shirt which had not seen a laundry in months—he was filthy both in clothes and mouth.

He would sit at the bar and annoy anyone who came within his range of vision. His modus operandi was to slap, jab, poke, guffaw and in general, create havoc wherever he went. He frequently went onto the dance floor, grabbed a girl and shoved her partner away. This caused no end of fracases. He was quarrelsome and wanted to brawl. Each time he got out of hand, the bartender, who appeared to know the bully well, came after him with a sawed off baseball bat enwrapped in black, electrician's tape. One tap across the shoulders got the attention of the belligerent ass and he would return to his seat.

On one of his reluctant returns to his stool he found a small, young, slightly but muscularly built youth seated upon the next stool. It appeared that the youth may have just gotten off work. He was clean-shaven and looked freshly showered. He wore blue jeans, a "T" shirt, and hush puppies. The young man ordered a drink. It had not arrived before the bully started to verbally berate the man and then shove or push at him. All eyes were on this event. Dancers swayed in one spot, watching to see what transpired.

The youth, who stood maybe five feet four, no more, and who weighed maybe 135 pounds, looked as though he was about to be massacred by the massively muscled antagonist. I heard the young man say, "If you touch me once more, you will probably regret it, for the rest of your life. Now leave me alone!" The bully had been waiting all evening for someone to pay attention to him. He stood up and lunged at the youth. The blow never landed. The young man, obviously skilled in the art of fisticuffs, ducked, jumped to his feet and punched the bully squarely on the nose. So efficient was the punch that blood splattered everywhere. Then the youth bobbed, twisted, and pranced all around the plodding giant. Blows rained all over the head of the bully. His eyes were glazed, he was out on his feet. Then down he went like a felled tree.

Not content to let the matter rest at mayhem, the youth grabbed the bully by his shirt and dragged him outside into the rain. The cold rain revived the bully slightly, enough that he could again stand. The youth beat the bully unmercifully. The bully eventually fell down again. The youth sprang upon him, grabbed him by the ears and pounded the bully's head into the blacktop. The time had arrived to pull the youth away, before he was faced with a murder charge.

An ambulance was called, and the bully removed. The bartender had called the police. I thought it strange how they emerged from the shadows of the building after we tore the youth away from the bully. We heard no car drive up. They said not one word to the youth. He just stuck his hands into his jean pockets and wandered away, where to, no one knows.

Upon returning to the dance, where a lot of us would now feel more relaxed, I saw a familiar face. It was Mickey! He was sitting at the bar chatting with some of the group from Whitehorse.

"Mickey, how the hell are you?" I yelled. "Where on earth have you been? I tried to find you in Whitehorse for several days before coming over here."

"What do you mean where have I been? I've been here for the last week. Where have you been?" he slurred.

Boy, was he smashed! He certainly looked like he could have been here all week, and I mean right in this bar the whole time. I sat down beside him and chatted as best I could under the circumstances.

He had heard about the festival, got the urge, and came over. He was staying at the same hotel. It was great to see so many people from Whitehorse all in one place at one time. Why didn't he reciprocate for all the times that they had bought him a drink, he thought. It would be a great idea, he concluded.

At a break in the music, he jumped up on his stool and hollered until he got everyone quietened down. He made a short, almost incomprehensible speech, but we all knew where his heart was. He wanted to make a toast. Would everyone come up to the bar and order a drink of their choice. Drinks were on him! Come up and get the drinks, then he'd make his toast. There had to be 30 to 40 Whitehorse people in the bar. That mattered not a whit to Mickey. When Mickey drank, everybody drank. Or so he said.

While the orders were being placed and filled, I drew Mickey aside and said, "Mickey, when did you last have something to eat? You look terrible."

"Ach, you know, Harold, I have no idea, man. Why, they tell me that there's lots of the calories in the booze, sure'n I don't need the food, man," he replied.

I saw some tins of shrimp behind the bar. I got one from the bartender's helper, who opened it for me. He poured off the liquid and put the shrimp on a plate. He supplied a fork and put the plate in front of Mickey. I persuaded Mickey to eat what he could while waiting for all those drinks to be made so that he could then make the toast.

He was impatient with me because his mind was focused upon the toasting. To please me, he gobbled down the plate load. At the last swallow, he looked at me with the eyes of a truant child, who had just accomplished a good deed. Now, he was at liberty to pursue his quest.

There was another break in the musical set. Notwithstanding that the others had not yet gathered up their respective drinks, he decided that this would be a good time to "do his thing," while the music had stopped. He leapt up on his stool again. He loved the attention and sensed that he was in command of the entire situation.

He said, in that beautiful Irish brogue, "I tank ya'all for having me as your gist. I want to repay all my many friends, here from Whitehorse, for their kind patronage over these past years. Please, gather 'round and pick up your drinks, for what it is, that I have to say is: May the wind always be at your backs, and may you be in hiven an hour before the divil knows you're daid. Come on now git up here and git your drinks."

The entire Whitehorse group pressed in around their host and started to pick out their respective drinks.

Mickey, having made his toast, downed his drink in one gulp. He had thrown back his head and, as a result, had lost his equilibrium for a moment. He sat down upon the stool with a plop; then he shook his head and tried to focus upon me. He squinted, opened his eyes wide, then turned away from me and puked. He had turned toward the bar. Sputum and chunks of shrimp encompassed all of the drinks which had just been poured for his friends. Vomit and fragments of shrimp floated in every glass. Mickey surveyed the scene as though it couldn't possibly be real. He leaned over the mess, then lifted his head back, turned and looked at me, failed to focus ... then bent over the corruption, again. Those who had been pressing and gathering at his feet during the toast shuffled back out of the epicenter of this tragedy.

"Ooops! Excuse me!" Mickey said in a loud voice. He reached out, picked up a glass, stuck his fingers into it, chased a chunk of shrimp until he caught it, pulled it out, then offered the glass to a girl standing near to him. The girl recoiled in horror, as did the rest of those who moments before had been responding with respect and affection for this fallen celebrity.

Chapter Ten

Scorn a woman and expect the worst,
All hell knows no such fury,
With heart of steel and cold as ice,
She'll get even, in a hurry.

Not sleet nor snow, nor fridged veil
Will keep her from her task,
Rejection is the fatal move,
She'll don Lucrezia's mask.

Cold Revenge

It has been said many times, and with much evidence to support it, that "Hell hath no fury like a woman scorned." The word "hell" conjures up images of fires, heat, steam, agony, and immense discomfort caused by pyrogenics. I know of a case, which I am assured by "unimpeachable sources," actually occurred in our little community. In this case "hell" meant, and in fact was, the opposite of many of the features normally associated with that word.

Nancy, whom some might refer to as the heroine of this story, was, at the time in question, employed as a stewardess. She had bid on the Vancouver-Whitehorse run, instead of the more glamorous runs to Europe or Hawaii, because there lived in Whitehorse a certain young man whom she had decided was going to be her husband. As it turned out, she should have gone to those other romantic places because his ideas differed, in one critical aspect, from hers. He was not interested in matrimony. Like most ladies bent on that status, she had confidence that she could change his thinking.

This story is the culmination of that conflict.

Nancy was a most attractive female. Her short blond hair made a frame for her perfectly sculpted face, with its high cheek bones, small uptilted nose, and a well-defined, short, tapered jaw. She had large, blue eyes. As a stewardess her training in personal makeup taught her how to emphasize her best features including how to outline her generously full, heart shaped lips. Nancy was always well-dressed whether in uniform or street clothes.

In the eyes of most men she would fulfill their fantasies of the perfect woman. Not so with Nick. At least not completely.

Nick was a local businessman. He had the best business in town in the particular field of business which he pursued. He was a classic example of the saying, "Sell yourself first and the public will seek you out to buy whatever it is you have to sell." Nick was tall, very huskily built, (this feature had helped him win a football scholarship in college football) and still very athletic. He had dark, wavy hair which he wore in a pompadour style. His teeth were a perfect line and white as snow, as became obvious each time he smiled, (or leered as some claimed) which was often. He was gregarious, sociable, and a leader in many of the community projects. He was often referred to as a "smooth character" by the ladies in town. Nick was an officer in some of the local service clubs. He was often seen at dinner dance functions, squiring some local lady, (other than Nancy) who acted as though she were the belle of the ball.

Nick had flash and panache. He drove only the latest model of car. The one he had, at the time of this story, was one with the electric windows and the automatic, push button, signal seeking radio. It had a push button gear shift as well. In those days such items were the wonders of the new age of electronics.

Nick's large modern house was furnished with all of the newest gadgets. Its decor featured expensive brass and leatherettes. Nick was a parvenu of the first degree.

Nancy had first met Nick at a party in Vancouver. It was a huge social event thrown by one of the companies with whom Nick did business. It was really a client prospecting occasion. They met and both went prospecting, for one another. That chance meeting is the basis for this story.

At the time in reference they had been going together for over two years. Nancy was flying up to Whitehorse twice a week and during her "layover" time, stayed with Nick in his wonderous surroundings. In fact, Nancy was almost as well-known in Whitehorse as was Nick. The reason being that, inasmuch as Nick attended every public function in town, he took Nancy with him whenever she was available.

Nancy could have stayed in the Crew's Quarters which were supplied by her employer. They were reasonably comfortable and close to the downtown core. However, she had learned a long time ago, possibly from her mother, that "The way to a man's heart was through his stomach." Nancy had trained herself to be a fabulous cook. She also shared his bed.

Due to her seniority with the airline, Nancy was able to take her holidays at the most sought after times. On this particular occasion she elected to take her leave over the Christmas vacation period. There was a specific event being staged at the Air Force Officer's Mess, which she wanted to attend with Nick. The function was to honor two ladies whose husbands were civilian members of the Mess. The ladies had both recently given birth to new babies. Christmas time was a universal celebration of the birth of a child, thus the theme. Nancy knew both of the women and naturally enough wanted to be there to help them celebrate.

It was, as usual, a fabulous party. The Mess cook had made figures out of ice, butter, and marshmallows. The foodstuffs were epicurean delights. The Air Force Band played popular songs of the day, with beautiful competence.

Everyone enjoyed the party. Nick had been his usual ebullient self. He had been the life of the party. He also had too much to drink.

"Darling, please let me drive home," Nancy insisted, as they reached the parking lot and found the car.

Nick fumbled with the car keys and said, "Don't bug me Nancy ... I'm OK ... you just butt out ... I'll drive." He slurred his words badly.

"Nick, you told me to tell you if you got too drunk to drive ... that's what I am doing ... now give me those keys ... please?"

"Oh for God's sake, OK! ... Jeez what a nag ... here take them," Nick roared, as he threw the keys at her.

Nancy searched in the snow for the keys. It was a cold winter's night with the wind blowing snowdrifts here and there. A solid crust of ice lay under the skiff of snow. There had been a type of Chinook recently. The warming wind had come up the coast from the Pacific and had caused a partial melting of the snow cover. When the wind left and the freezing temperatures returned, the whole of the Yukon had become an unwelcomed skating rink.

"What the hell are you doing now?" demanded Nick as he saw Nancy squatting and rummaging through the snow near to where the keys should be.

"I'm trying to find the car keys ... you big oaf ... where the hell did you throw them," she said through her tears.

"Chriz' ... broads!" Nick exclaimed. "Get out of the way ... I'll find the bloody things."

Just as Nick was rounding the rear of the car Nancy found the keys.

"It's OK, dear ... I've found them ... see?" Nancy held the keys up, in numb fingers, but she had achieved her goal. She, not drunken Nick, would drive.

"Well it's about time, for Chriz' sake. Here let me drive!"

Nancy didn't respond, she just opened the car door, flicked the switch which opened all the other doors, jumped in, and started the car. She had become fully familiar with Nick's toys. This was one time when that familiarity paid off. There was to be another.

"There, Nick, the door on your side is open, get in," Nancy said sweetly.

With obvious reluctance and some petulance Nick got in and slammed the door shut. He sat sullenly as he searched himself for a cigarette.

Nancy was letting the engine warm up a bit before moving the car because of the extremely cold temperature that evening. There was hoarfrost on the windows, together with a patina of snow. Heating the interior should melt those vision barriers so that she could see to drive home.

"Where the hell are the cigarettes, Nancy?" Nick growled. "You had them last. What the hell did you do with them?"

"They're in your shirt pocket, dear," she replied as calmly as she could through the tears.

"No, they're not!" he exploded, flaying at her hand as she reached over to help him get his smokes.

Astonished at his aggressiveness this evening, Nancy withdrew her reddening hand and her intention to be of help.

"OK, never mind, I found them," Nick yelled as he withdrew the pack from his shirt pocket. "For Chris' sake, what's holding us up now? Let's get this bloody show on the road, NOW!"

Nancy was just about to get out of the car and return to the Mess Hall and get a ride home with someone else. Others would be happy to assist her under the circumstances. As she started to move, she realized that if she left Nick alone now he would most certainly drive, or attempt to drive, home; an act of which he was not capable. In addition, if he did make it home, he might not let her in. He had done this once before. The lesser of the evils was to stay, even though she knew from past experience, that things would likely become very unpleasant; Nick being in the boorish mood which now controlled him.

"Alright, dear," she said placatingly, "I was just letting your car warm up, as you have told me to do many times. It should be OK now, now that I can see out the windshield."

"OK then, broad, let's move it!" Nick said harshly.

By the time they got to Nick's house he was fast asleep. Nancy backed the car into the garage. Nick had installed an automatic garage door opener, so she did not have to get out into that cold, blustery weather, with the snow swirling like little twisters. Nancy merely pushed a button in the glove compartment and ... presto! ... the door lifted up. She pushed it again and the cold winter night, which was getting worse, was shut out. They were then surrounded by the warm, heated garage. Nick insisted on having his garage heated. He liked to get into a warm car on those cold winter days. Sometimes he never even wore an overcoat because the garage at his office was likewise heated.

Such were the amenities of the wealthy, young bachelors in the modern world.

Once inside the house, Nick, who had enjoyed a nap, became alive and animated. There was no trace of the objectionable person who had reviled Nancy earlier. Nick flung his fashionable fur coat on the chesterfield, then helped Nancy out of the lovely fur which he had given her for Christmas.

"Here honey, let me help you. What do you say to a nightcap?" he said, as he gave her a big hug from behind.

"OK, Nick, just a short one for me. How about a hot rye," she responded, trying not to show how hurt she had been by his previous behavior. She seethed below the friendly veneer. Nancy was agitated, but this was certainly not the night for a confrontation. Not of this kind anyway. She had promised herself that this was to be the night for the pursuit of matrimony. Some grave doubts were creeping into her thoughts but she had seen the good side of Nick as well. Harmony had to be the key mood for the balance of this night.

"OK, honey ... good idea ... I'll plug in the electric kettle ... why don't you have a shower and get comfortable," he said as he turned into the kitchen. "Sure was a good party tonight, wasn't it, honey?"

"Yes, dear ... it was a particularly good party. Wasn't it nice that the Officer's Club gave those wonderful gifts to those new mothers. I didn't realize that they did that for civilian members' wives, did you?"

"Uh ... no ... I don't think I ever thought about it, Nancy. Do you want sugar or honey in your drink?"

"I'll take honey, Honey," Nancy said as she wrapped her arms around him from the rear and hugged him carnally, "and I think I'll take you too, Honey."

"Wow! What a tiger. Just wait until I get you into bed tonight, Baby," he said, salaciously, "you're in for the ride of your young life."

"So are you, big boy," said Nancy nasally while moving away erotically.

"Hurry up with that drink," she hollered, as she moved across the living room carpet, undoing her clothes.

By the time Nick showed up with the two drinks, Nancy had undressed, showered, and was semi-reclining, in the nude, under the bed sheet. She had tossed the blankets back to the end of the bed. The bed sheet was pulled over her in such a way as to delineate her entire body, except her ample breasts, which were exposed.

"Gads, you look gorgeous like that, Honey. You look good enough to eat," crooned Nick, as he deposited the drinks on the night table and dove across the bed to land on top of her.

"Hold it, Buster! Hold the fort!" she joshed. "Try getting your clothes off first, all of them."

"Right you are, Baby. I'll take a quick shower, too."

When Nick came out of the washroom he too was in the nude. He picked up the drinks and slid in alongside Nancy. He handed her one and they both sipped the libation.

Nancy smiled invitingly at Nick, between sips, then cooed, "Do you know, sir, that you make a great hot rye?"

"That isn't all that I make well, Honey," he said lascivi- ously "Wanna find out?"

"I could be talked into it ... m-a-y-b-e," Nancy purred, in her most coquettish manner.

Nick rolled slightly to his right in order to put his drink back on the night table. As he rolled back, filled with sensuous intent, Nancy skittered out from under the sheet. As startled as Nick was, he couldn't help but appraise the beauty before him. She had, in his opinion, the perfect female form. Small waist, well-rounded hips, and particularly full breasts. The nipples were pink on a large, light brown background of the areola. Was she teasing him? Was she trying to heighten the erotic stimuli of the moment?

"Get back into this bed, you little minx!" he cajoled, as he reached out to grab her.

"No ... not yet, Nick ... I want to talk to you ... just for a minute. Just sit back there and have your drink ... just for a moment ... let's talk," she pleaded.

"Let's talk ... talk ... woman, are you crazy? You pick the craziest times to want to talk ... can't we talk afterwards? Oh God, Nancy ... are you going into your marriage routine again? Christ Nancy, not now ... not right now ... come on ... be a good girl and get back into bed ... daddy wants to make love ... OK? ... come on, Honey," he pleaded.

"I want to, Nick ... you know I enjoy making love with you, and there are no other men in my life ... just you ... but I have to know where I stand ... are we going to get married? ... and if so, when? ... I want a definite commitment ... tonight! We have been carrying on like this for over two years. I think that is long enough for you to be able to make up your mind. I want to marry you ... why do you hesitate marrying me? I want a family while I'm still young ... do you really love me? When we are alone and making love, you tell me that you love me ... but do you really? Show me that you do. Marry me. You know that I will be a good wife for you. What do you say, Nick, when can we get married?"

Nick sat in the bed leaning against the headboard; he shook his head from side to side and raised his eyes to the ceiling. He extended his arms plaintively, palms turned up into a begging position. He repeated this several times as he searched for words.

"Jeez, Nancy, you pick the goofiest times to pull this routine. It's always the same. You get me all steamed up then pounce upon me about getting hitched. You know that I love you. Haven't I demonstrated that to you? ... I buy you expensive gifts ... look at that fur coat I just got you. It set me back a grand. What about all the other clothes, the shoes, the trips? I could take any other broad ... lots of them want to be with me ... but I take you ... what else do you want?" He knew instinctively and immediately that he had asked the wrong question.

"I want to get married, that's what I want," she spat. "How many times do I have to ask you ... you big clot!"

"Christ I don't know, Nancy, you must have asked me a hundred times by now ...."

" ... and I always get the same run around. You sweet talk me into waiting 'just a little longer,' until you get a house ... until you get a new car ... until your business is built up a bit better ... well, you now have all those things and I'm not waiting any longer. Either I get a positive commitment tonight or I'm leaving right now. I'll go to the crew's quarters. You'll never see me again. So what is it to be?" Nancy demanded.

She put her drink down on the bureau, folded her arms over her breasts and glared at Nick. This was typical of Nancy's personality; she took a long time to make up her mind firmly, but when it culminated, as it had tonight, she was a determined woman. She had a great deal of patience and had used up a lot of it on Nick. Tonight she was angry, hurt, and felt used and scorned.

"Oh, to hell with it, Nancy. You pull this routine every time some broad you know has a kid. I should have realized that tonight's recognition of the birth of those kids would have this effect on you. Frankly, I'm just getting plain tired of this nonsense. Isn't what we have good enough for you? I'm damn sure that there are many other broads out there who would love to be in your place."

"Well go and see them, then, you bastard, if that's all that our relationship means to you," she snapped. She gathered up her clothes and headed into the bathroom. She locked the door.

"Ah, cumon, Nancy, ... what the hell is wrong with you anyway? ... you're ruining a perfectly good evening ... we had lots of fun earlier ... come on out and we'll have more fun. Why do you always have to bring up the subject of marriage? Let's not fight ... let's make love."

There was no response from the bathroom, whatsoever. Suddenly the door flew open and there stood Nancy, fully dressed. She was livid. This time, unlike all of the many previous episodes, she was enraged beyond control.

Nick was startled to see Nancy clothed. She had gone into the washroom on many previous occasions when they had fought, but she had always, meekly, returned to bed.

"For Chriz' sake, Nancy ... cool off ... let's talk a bit," Nick pleaded.

"Talk? You don't want to talk ... you bastard ... all you want is to get me back into bed ... to use me ... my body ... for your selfish pleasure ... that's all I'm good for as far as you are concerned ... to hell with you!" she snarled.

As she passed his prone, nude figure she snapped up the keys to his car and ran for the garage doorway.

"Come back here with those keys, you bitch ... you're not taking my car ... you can bloody well call a cab!" Nick yelled after her. He leapt out of the bed and chased after her disappearing figure. "Put back those goddamn keys you minx ... you've seen the last of me ... but you ain't taking my bloody car."

Nancy had made it down the stairs and had the car doors opened as Nick swung around the stairway, still in the nude.

She slammed and locked the doors just as he got to her driver's window. Nick pounded on the window and screamed, "Give me those keys ... you slut ... open this window!"

Nancy dangled the keys on her fingers. She pressed the automatic switch which rolled the window down, just a bit. She then started up the car and turned to Nick and gave him a glare which would curl a rasp.

"You can pick up your beloved car in the morning. It will be at the crew's quarters."

"Like hell it will. Give me those goddamn keys you seamy slut!"

Nancy rolled down the window just a little bit more. Nick saw his opportunity so he thrust his arm through the window to try and grab the keys. There was barely enough room to get his thick arm in, but he got it in as far as above the elbow, and grasped and shoved in an effort to get it in further.

Then Nancy wound up the window on his arm.

Nick looked at Nancy incredulously. He couldn't extract his arm. It was through the window at a right angle. He was standing on his toes. He was in the nude.

Nancy pushed the button in the glove compartment. The garage door opened.

Section of the Alaska Highway like that traveled by the author on his way to Whitehorse to practice law.

Harold Hine taken on the occasion of being appointed a Queen's Counsel.

Harold on graduation day at law school, University of British Columbia, May, 1950.

Harold as a youth of 15 in the uniform of the Canadian Navy.

Four generations of ladies in Harold Hine's life. From left: wife Laura, daughter Cathy with granddaughter Lori, mother-in-law Isobel Davis, 1971.

Courtroom similar to that in which the author was called to the Bar of the Yukon Territory.

The three law partners, left to right, Harold Hine, Erik Nielsen, and George van Roggen at office Christmas party, 1955.

Gordon Armstrong, Whitehorse mayor, with Harold Hine's secretary Joan "Rusty" Veinott, at the same Christmas party.

Mr. Justice Jack Gibben, court stenographer Wynn Clarke, Judge A. H. Gibson, and registry clerk "Musty" Thompson, at the same party.

Harold stands alongside the aircraft in which he just made his solo flight.

Fleet Canuck CF-DPM, in which Harold (right) took Laura flying. With him here is Gordon Dickson, a successful prospector.

Deed of Land for one square inch of Yukon Territory, issued to Lowell Jay Lunden, when he was a child. He is now manager, marketing service, Quaker Oats of Canada, Ltd.

Whitehorse residents, dressed in period costumes, and Mayor Gordon Armstrong, in buffalo coat, greet Truth or Consequences contestant.

Left to right are Doctor Nori Nishio, his wife June, and Laura and Harold Hine, all dressed up for the costume party.

Harold, left, Dianne Whittal (the future Mrs. George van Roggen), and druggist Ken Bowman were also at the airport to greet the contestant.

Local residents aboard MS *Klondike*. The author, lower right, alongside Ken Bowman. Top right, the contestant, with his arm around Thelma Olsen.

Gold diggings on Bonanza Creek at the point where gold was originally discovered in the Yukon.

Gold seekers work hard at their digging and panning on Bonanza Creek. (Yukon Archives)

This gold dredge is like the one described by the author. (Provincial Archives, Victoria)

MS *Klondike's* **sister ship, the** *White Horse*, **navigates the Five Finger Rapids.** (Yukon Archives)

Recent picture of Dawson City from atop Moosehide Mountain.

Dawson City, 1903. Note appearance of bull moose with rack on side of Moosehide Mountain (top center right). Yukon River is at left, the Klondike River to the right, with Bonanza Creek up the Klondike to the right. (Yukon Archives)

Elevated sidewalk fronts this house in Dawson City.

Gold may still be panned from many Yukon creeks. (Yukon Government Photo)

Staggerwing aircraft flies over terrain that awed the author on his trip to Alaska.

The Staggerwing cockpit. Note the two fuel switches at lower right, just below the panel. (Photos by Ken Holmberg. Courtesy of Doctor J. V. W. Johnston, Surrey, B.C.)

This is the grand scale of scenery encountered on the driving trip to Haines, Alaska.

Harold flew prospectors over Dall sheep in a similar setting en route to the "frigid lake."

It was a glacier like this that fed the lake into which the author waded with prospectors and their gear. (Yukon Government Photo)

This Staggerwing is beached much like Harold's in "Cold Side of Hell" and "A Guiding Light." (Photo by John Mrazek. Courtesy of Walt Lannon)

Harold does a handstand on a chair set on pop bottles, left, while on leave from the Navy. With him as Santa Claus (right) are grandchildren Lori (right) and Chris (left).

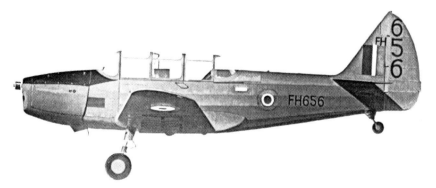

A Fairchild Cornell: The type of plane flown by the author on his trip to get a court order from the judge.

The log tower building at Aishihiak, Y.T., (left), now abandoned, was built during WW II as part of the staging route for aircraft constructed by allies and flown to Russia. It was at this airstrip that Harold Hine encountered wild horses on the runway.   (Rod Hardie)

It was in a serene setting such as this, that Harold and Nikko encountered a bear.

As we flew overhead, we observed a young grizzly taking a river fish.

Harold and Nikko thrilled to see a moose charging through lake shallows.

This is the actual Staggerwing, CF-HSK, in which the fishing party traveled and returned late to find the car lights guiding them down to the Yukon River. (Robert Cameron)

This regal Dall buck is quite at home on mountain rocks. It was near Pilot Mountain that Nikko and Harold saw sheep like this one. (Yukon Government Photo)

The Palace Grand Theatre was one of the buildings that Harold and Nikko visited. This renovated hall houses the Gaslight Follies.
(Yukon Government Photo)

It was on a becalmed lake like this one that the fishing party became temporarily stranded. (Yukon Government Photo)

Whitehorse Rapids "dance like horses with shaggy white manes" through Miles Canyon (top). Center photo is Whitehorse in 1902, with Yukon River

in foreground and paddlewheelers along stretch where headlights helped Harold to land. Below is Whitehorse today.   (Top and center Yukon Archives)

In addition to his busy legal career and airborne duties, Harold Hine is also an accomplished painter of water colors.

"You crazy bitch, leggo of my arm!" he cried. "You're going to break it off ... it hurts ... let it go ... you stunned slut!"

A blast of frigid air was all that Nick got as a response. The snow swirled into the garage and twirled around his bare legs.

"Nancy ... for Chriz' sake don't. Let's talk. I'll freeze to death. Nancy ... be reasonable ... put the door down ... stop the car ... I'm freezing ... let's talk it over. Nancy, for God's sake don't do it!"

Nancy pushed another button and the car eased forward. Nick kept pace. She accelerated slightly. The car began to move out into the street. Nick kept pace. Snow enveloped the car together with the nude figure running alongside it. That figure was pleading, yelling, screaming, but to no avail. His plaintive cries were now falling upon deaf ears. She was about to even the score for all the months of insults, frustrations and what she now clearly believed as being the abuse of her rights. She wanted marriage, a home, and a family. He knew that and had taken advantage of it. He conned her. She would have her revenge.

She drove at a snail's pace down the block and a half to the Main Street intersection. There she turned towards the bright lights of the Whitehorse Inn. Down there she would find all the bars and grills, many of which would still be open.

Nick pranced alongside the car like a ballerina. He was hoarse from screaming and cold as hell. The combination of the ice, snow, and cinders spread out by the city works trucks, had placed Nick in absolute, inscrutable agony.

Whatever remonstrations Nick made, and there were many, they served not one whit to thaw this woman's frigid determination. It only served to fuel the fires of this dedicated chastizer.

Nancy had reached the intersection where the hotel and bars where located. She started to blow the car's horn. It was a one car parade. It might have resembled a wedding procession except that there was but one car and the would have been groom was nude and freezing his bunns off. The would-be bride was Lucrezia Borgia, reincarnate.

The honking horn had the desired effect. The late night, early morning revellers, who were patrons in the restaurant of the Inn, came tumbling out to see what was causing the commotion. What they found was ludicrous in the extreme,

97

even for their condition. The nude had long stopped calling out. He just dangled there, his arm still caught in the tightened window.

Nancy stopped the car and wound down the window. Nick's arm popped out and he fell in a heap, in the ice and snow. Nancy drove away, without once looking back.

The next morning, in Whitehorse, the story was on everyone's lips. Everyone, that is, except Nancy's, who had caught the early morning flight back to Vancouver.

Chapter Eleven

A bet in a bar is a sacred thing
For men who live in the north
And rather than welsh on a valid bet
They'd give up all their worth.

To define the bet—an important part
To avoid things getting bitter
Like to bet a suit and win the bet
Then find it has no zipper.

A Bet in a Bar

You may recall that in a previous chapter I told you that I had been a physical instructor during my tour in the Canadian Navy. Prior to joining the navy, I had attended at the YMCA regularly. My father had been a highly athletic person and encouraged me in sports and gymnastics. Keeping in mind that one is to be modest when talking about such matters, I am required to say that I was only fantastically good at all forms of gymnastic endeavors. I now watch the competitors in the various Olympic games and hear myself saying, "I could do that," or "now let's see if he (she) can do a cut-away from that position," or other statements which are designed to indicate that I used to be able to do such things. It is a circuitous, esoteric way of bragging, particularly when no one is likely to challenge me to prove it.

One of my claims to fame was that I was particularly adept at balancing myself on my hands. On the mats, on the parallel bars, even on chairs set upon coke bottles (see picture herein). I had no difficulty in walking up and/or down a flight of stairs on my hands.

Walking on one's hands is much like riding a bicycle, once you learn, you never forget. Two factors, over which none of us have too much control, interfere with the continuation of that ability. One is age, the other is the additional weight which one acquires with age.

Anyway, while in the Yukon I did not have those two problems.

On the occasion of the birth of our son Laurence (Larry), I was kidnapped by a group of our friends and taken to a cocktail lounge in Whitehorse. I can't honestly claim that the abduction was entirely against my will. The object of the party was to celebrate the birth of Larry. Not that there ever was any need to have a specific cause for a party in Whitehorse.

During the course of the carousal, the subject of flowers arose. I had already performed my part by sending a large bouquet to Laura, but nonetheless, my captors insisted that a telephone call be placed to the only florist in town. Someone made the call, and every flower of every nature, type and description which Miss MacDonald had on her premises was purchased and sent to Laura who, of course, didn't attend the party. She was in the Whitehorse General Hospital looking after Larry. When I went up to visit her I received several comments about the fact that Laura's room was completely full of cut flowers, pots of flowers, and baskets of flowers. So was the hallway on both sides of the doorway to her room. Some of the comments were polite and complimentary.

As was customary in the cocktail lounges in Whitehorse, games of chance soon became part of the festivities. Rounds of drinks were paid for by various forms of gambling. "Birds in the bush" was popular. In this game each person involved at the table, and often people from other tables, would hold between zero and three coins in one hand, which had to be up on the table during the game. The object was to guess the exact total being held, collectively, when all those hands opened and exposed the coins. It was a process of elimination. As a person guessed correctly, he or she was eliminated from the obligation of paying for the upcoming round of drinks. This continued until there were only two persons left, one of whom obviously had to buy the drinks.

At our table one of the prime instigators of this party, was one Jack Arens. He was one of the local haberdashers. He had become one of my good and close friends and was a member of my regular poker group. His wife, Joan, looked forward to the evenings when the poker night was at her home. She would try out some of her new recipes on the five men. She was a great cook. The men also looked forward to those guinea pig nights.

I am not sure how the subject matter of the bets changed from buying the next round to performing some physical deed. It is probably immaterial, anyway. The fact is that it did. Some of the bets are well-known and well-worn. For example, Jack was bet that he couldn't hold a broom handle in both hands in front of him then step over the broom without letting go of it, and then step back through his arms under the same conditions. Jack performed the deed with aplomb and won the bet.

Another member of the group allowed as to how he was considered by many to be a softball pitcher of note. It was too bad, he said, that there was no ball available or he would show us his skills. By sheer coincidence, the proprietor of the lounge sponsored girls' softball and there was a ball available. A pathway through the crowd of patrons was cleared. A stool from the bar was placed at one end of the premises. A wastepaper basket was layed lengthwise upon the stool so that the mouth of the container faced the pitcher who stood some thirty feet away. The ball was produced, bets were made and our Dizzy Dean went through his warm up antics. With a flourish he circled his right arm. Then, after some high jinx to entertain us all while he had the spot light, in one simultaneous motion he took one step forward with his left foot and as his arm came down from its final circle and reached its lowest point in the arc, he let the ball go. Our hero demonstrated lots of style and terrific speed, but no aim. The ball went right through the huge plate glass window at the roadside wall of the lounge. The wastebasket remained totally unmolested by the ball.

There were other bets, none of which produced the dramatic impact of the pitcher. Then, somehow, it was my turn. Jack bet me a brand new custom-made blue, pin strip "banker's suit," that I could not walk the length of the bar on my hands. I was to get up onto the actual bar top and perform this feat. The ceiling in the lounge was not high, it was probably the normal ten feet. The bar, per se, was about four feet in height. Above the bar and for its entire length, there ran a box containing fluorescent lighting. This consumed more of the space between the ceiling and the surface of the bar. Glasses hung from slats suspended at one end, from the box containing the lighting, and supported at the other end by brackets on the wall behind the bar. I figured that there might be, at the very most, five feet of clearance. Being short, but being more than five feet in height, the bet posed a genuine challenge. That made it interesting.

Firstly, I would have to get the bar surface wiped dry to obviate slipping and consequent falling. Falling off the bar into the lounge area was threat enough, but to fall behind the bar where all the bottles and glasses were kept was a serious, much greater threat. Especially for a new father. I would have to keep my legs bent at the knees so as to clear the suspended glasses. I didn't want to be responsible for breaking them. Most certainly, I didn't want any kicked off so that they would fall and break on the bar under my hands.

Well this was an interesting challenge.

I paced off the length of the bar. It was just over twenty feet. I stood on the bar to judge the separation; it was a tight squeeze. I called for quiet. This was going to require a great deal of concentration. I asked for assistants to help me off with my jacket, vest, and tie. Several lovely ladies in the lounge volunteered for that distinction. I removed my shoes. Yet another volunteer took care of those. I flexed my muscles and fingers, I shook my arms to insure that there was ample circulation, I bent over to touch my toes several times, and I again called for quiet. I closed my eyes and held my fingertips pressed to my forehead for a moment. Then without notice I leapt up onto the bar, levered myself up onto my hands, bent my knees, walked to the far end, did a pirouette, still on my hands, then walked back the length of the bar again. To conclude the act, I did a flip dismount from the bar onto the carpet.

The lounge was bedlam. Cheers and congratulatory shouts filled the air. Prancing and jumping about seemed to be commonplace. Only one discordant cry could be heard, it was a cry of "foul." It appeared to eminate from Jack Arens who was laughing with his buddies but crying foul. His was the only negative note amongst the applause and general conviviality. Pandemonium infected the lounge. Where had I learned to do such things? Would I do it again? How about a back flip? A front flip? A cartwheel, perhaps?

Through all of this I sat and basked in the glory of the moment. My clothes and shoes were returned. Drinks flowed like water. The fervor of the party accelerated, it became another night of intemperance in Whitehorse.

Through all of this Laura remained incarcerated in the hospital. A bored non-participant, yet the causa causans of the event.

About six weeks after the bar scene I received a call from Jack Arens. Would I come to his shop and pick up my suit? True to his bet, he had measured me the day after the party and sent the details "outside" for the suit to be made in Toronto.

I attended his place of business and tried on the jacket. It was a perfect fit. Next I tried on the vest, same result. Then Jack ushered me into the changing room to try on the trousers. Only then did I discover how strongly he felt about his cry of "foul." There were buttons in the fly instead of a zipper.

Whenever I wore that particular suit thereafter I grew not to be surprised when I was asked by men and women alike, "How are the buttons holding out, Harold?"

Chapter Twelve

In dark of night, there are things done
By people who should know
That acting like a wretched teen
Is not the line to toe.

A backhouse wends its silent way
Down Main Street one fine night
'til rowdies see it as a toy,
Albeit, they were tight.

Poor backhouse surging down the ice,
With auto as its thrust,
Sliding, gliding, like a sleigh
Until there is a "bust."

A policeman comes to do his job,
But things get out of hand,
Then wiser counsel, in the guise of judge
Gives lesson which is grand.

The Whitehorse Backhouse Caper

When that rambunctious little boy, housed in the body of most mature males, gets loose the results can be most unpredictable.

The Lions Club were having a convention in Whitehorse. I wasn't a member of the Lions but I had been invited to attend, along with the mayor and some civic dignitaries. I was there as the solicitor for the city. The mayor, who had become my good and dear friend, was Gordon (Gordie) Armstrong.

I believe that the convention was in either March or April. In any event, the streets were still heavy with ice, although the weather was not that cold for Whitehorse.

I write this chapter with considerable trepidation. There will be many readers who will conclude that as the crown prosecutor and city solicitor, I should have known better. They will be right. However, most of the other chapters show my better side, this one shows my foolish side.

On the afternoon of this fateful day, the mayor contacted me and said, "Harold, how about coming with me to the festivities tonight. I have to make a short speech of introduction and greeting. We could visit with the visitors from the other cities for a few drinks, OK?"

There was a difference in our respective ages but that had never appeared to present any challenge to our becoming friends. He was several years older than I, possibly fifteen. I guess that we respected one another for what we were and that was all that was required.

"OK, Gordie, I'll see you there."

We arranged a mutually suitable time and concluded the call. We were going to a place which was still referred to, by the locals, as "Silent Smith's." This hall had, at this date, become the best semblance of a convention center that the town had to offer; yet it was really only a small building of, maybe, 3,800 square feet. Its chronology included being a bank, a gold commissioner's office, and more recently, a gambling saloon. The saloon was once operated by a man euphemistically referred to as "Silent Smith." When wide open gambling in the Yukon was to be closed down, it became one of my responsibilities to see to it that Smith ceased his operations.

There may be irony in the fact that the events of this night originated from this place.

I went to the Lions "do" at about eight in the evening. When I entered the hall, I looked over the crowd to see if I could locate the mayor. While I was getting my eyes accustomed to the smoke filled room and my ears attuned to the horrific din, I heard someone call my name.

"Harold, come on over here and have a drink."

I looked in the direction of the voice and saw a friend of mine, Doug Bennett. I wandered through the maze of tables and exuberant people. When I reached his table he jumped up and greeted me effusively.

"Hi, Harold I haven't seen you since I got back from outside. I've been meaning to phone but I have been just too busy getting caught up. You know Noreen, don't you? We just got engaged today!" Doug said in high spirits.

"Yeah, Harold, come over and sit next to me. Maybe I should have sought the advice of a lawyer before accepting his proposal. Come sit here. Doug, get Harold a drink while he and I talk," said Noreen, joshing Doug and giving me a facetious, exaggerated, big hug.

Doug was a successful businessman who was well-liked in town. He was about my age, height, and build, but he was rounding out with the good life. His dark brown hair was wavy and more often than not, looked like it needed a barber's touch. He was loud but not offensively so. His business was sales and he believed in the old saw that a salesman must sell himself before he can make a successful sales presentation. As a result, he made a point of memorizing hundreds of jokes which he would intersperse amongst his sales pitch. He knew every joke that anyone ever started to tell him and it became frustrating at times. He and I curled in the same league so I got to see him at least twice a week. He and I had become good, close friends. Noreen, his new fiancee, was the close friend of Thelma Olsen, about whom you will have read, in a previous chapter. Noreen was a school teacher who had come to Whitehorse as a result of encouragement from Thelma. She was unusually attractive. Her smile was full and friendly, she had a habit of speaking through her smile, so often was there one upon her face. She had long blond hair combed back from a pale white face. Her sky blue eyes sparkled as though there was a massive secret behind them. Her smile was truly like that of the Mona Lisa, which also bespoke of some secret.

After a few drinks with Doug and Noreen, I heard the mayor and his usual entourage arrive. Apparently he had been enticed to a "before party" party. He was a very popular person. Wherever he went there were people who wanted to pass a few words with him. He always had time for his constituents. As a result, he was almost invariably late, except for council meetings for which he was meticulously punctual.

I knew that Gordie would be glad handing his way to the table which had been reserved for our group. This would take a few minutes and as Doug was away getting our drinks from the bar, I turned to Noreen and said, "How about a dance?"

"Love to," she replied, "I just love to dance but Doug

doesn't care if he ever gets up. By the looks of him, I'm going to have to sit a lot tonight."

While we were dancing, Noreen talked about the engagement and why she had finally decided affirmatively, after Doug had asked her many previous times. She told me that Doug wanted me to be his best man.

"Only if I get to spend the first night with the bride!" I joked.

"It's OK with me if you can talk Doug into it," she teased.

"Let's go ask him," I challenged.

"Go on your own," she said, as she disengaged herself and headed for the ladies' room. At the entrance to the lounge she turned around and stuck her tongue out at me.

Just at that exact moment a huge, heavy, bear-like paw, landed on my shoulder.

"OK, Hine, where the hell have you been?" boomed Gordie.

"I've been here for an hour, you big clot," I said, with a smile. "You just haven't had your nose out of your glass long enough to find me!"

Gordon laughed in his huge, inimitable way. He was a handsome man. Huge. Everything about him was oversized. His teeth, which were uneven but not unattractive. His face, his nose, his large powerful hands. He stood about six feet two in stockinged feet. I think that he took a size fifty suit jacket. Extra large of anything was a tight fit for Gordie. His thinning dark hair was combed straight back from his forehead and pressed close to his skull.

"I'll see ya at our table over there, when I get back from the john, OK?" he ordered.

"Yes, Your Honor," I said mockishly.

"Don't 'Your Honor' me, you little twirp. I got both of us a supply of drinks, they're on the table, go stand guard. I'll be back in a minute."

As the festivities progressed, everyone's enthusiasm for partying expanded. The atmosphere was charged with levity. The band played well. The drinks were many, and the hall was overheated by the many dancers.

Just as I was settling into a nice slow dance with Noreen, I heard Doug calling to me over the tumult.

"Harold, drop that broad and get out here!" he screamed. "You've never seen anything like this before."

Noreen wasn't about to be "dropped." She tagged along to the doorway. Doug was right. I had not ever seen anything like that which was taking place out on the main street of Whitehorse.

One of the well-known truckers in the area was pushing a backhouse down the center of Main Street. He was using a pickup for the job. It was no great feat for the truck. The streets were quite icy and the backhouse was on skids. It was much like a case of a children's sleigh but with a more unusual object on the runners. The "john" was not affixed to the truck's bumper. He was using the element of inertia to hold it in place.

"Let's go get that bloody thing," a loud, booming voice behind me yelled.

You guessed right—it was the mayor.

Quick as a wink, several bodies charged out of the hall. Each headed for a car parked on the street. One car took aboard two people, one a driver and the other one carrying drinks. Doug was driving and Noreen was not only refusing to be dropped, she was proving that she could be useful, in what turned out to be a most unfortunate way.

In no time at all, there were three or four cars careening out onto the main street. It was early in the morning, there was little or no traffic; the streets had been virtually deserted for hours. Hence the idea of moving the "john" from one location to the other while it would create no traffic problem.

That's what he thought!

Gordie pulled up alongside the trucker and yelled, "Hey, Red, where the hell are you going with that 'john' at this time of the morning?"

"I'm moving it over to the new house that I bought, Gordie. I'm renovating the inside. The people I bought it from moved outside and forgot to turn the water off before they left. Everything is frozen solid. I need the 'john' over there, so I thought I'd make the move now while there's no traffic," replied Red.

Red and Gordie had slowed to a crawl, they were almost stopped at the intersection of Second and Main. I saw Doug's car gliding out from behind the building on the northwest corner, the old Bank of Commerce building. He had only his parking lights on. Gordie must have seen it too. He continued to engage Red in conversation. Red had to lean across the seat in order to talk out of the passenger's window of the pickup truck.

Then it all began. Doug revved his motor and yelled, "Ya-hooooo," out of his open window. He picked that "john" off the bumper of Red's truck without even so much as a nick. Down Second Avenue he charged, with the backhouse leading the parade. Cars appeared from all angles. The streets, which had been devoid of traffic, were now seething with roaring engines and loud, unintelligible yells. Somehow the mayor got down a back alley without notice. In a few minutes, he showed up at the intersection of First and Main with the backhouse preceding him. Doug shot out of the shadows with obvious intent to relieve the mayor of the "john." The mayor careened down Main Street to the west. Doug surged out of the south on Second Avenue. Just as the two of them reached the crucial moment, Doug veered off to the east. There was no way that he was going to test the nerves of the mayor. He had no nerves. If he did, they were made of steel.

For a few minutes there were cars, people, and a backhouse skidding around the various streets near Main, or those which intersected it. The "john" transferred from car to truck to car. At one point, it was left in the precise center of an intersection and some of the revellers tried to kidnap it. The arrival of a Jeep, sounding its horn and gently shoving its way into the pack, preserved the "john" from the intended abduction. I drove around the block so as to come down Fourth Avenue going south. I waited in the cover of the new Court House (Federal Building) until I saw enough of the backhouse to start my run. Out I charged in my new Oldsmobile. The driver of the Jeep saw me coming. He also saw something else which I did not see. He jammed on his brakes just prior to the intersection. The backhouse had lots of momentum and kept traveling west. Just as I got the backhouse nicely onto my bumper, a flashing red light started up behind me. So interested was I in the plan of attack upon that "john," that I did not notice that the long arm of the law had arrived.

By this time, both sides of the street were lined with people in parkas or other heavy clothing. Our antics must have emptied the hall. Most, if not all, were holding drinks. They were wildly and boisterously cheering the contestants.

Just as suddenly as it had all begun, it appeared to cease. Not a participating car, save and except mine, was in sight. Were they lurking in the dimly lit side streets or had they seen the policeman and taken off? Only time would tell.

"Take that thing back to where it belongs and quit fooling around on the streets," ordered the RCMP officer. He was being diplomatic, yet getting the job done.

I drove around the block, still pushing the backhouse and with the intent that I would deliver it to the bumper of Red's truck. He had parked, after the initial foray, at Second and Main and had been waiting for this moment. The policeman followed me without his lights flashing.

Just as I reached the intersection, the mayor's car zoomed in front of me and picked the backhouse off my bumper. I stopped dead in my tracks. The backhouse careened west on Main Street. The policeman took off after him, lights flashing.

The moment the mayor saw the red lights he applied his brakes. He had made it just about as far as the intersection of Third and Main. When he stopped, the backhouse kept sliding, as before. It was in this manner that he lost the backhouse to Doug, who picked up the self propelled "john," right under the nose of the cruiser. The patrol car veered away to pursue him. Obviously Doug had not seen the cruiser in time, either. In a few minutes, the backhouse, Doug, and his car and the cruiser with the police officer returned. Everyone parked near the intersection. I didn't recognize the constable nor him me. I had heard that two new officers had arrived in town but I had not yet met them, this was one of them.

"They told me in depot, in Regina, that I would find this posting to be novel and different in many ways, but no one said anything about pushing 'johns' around the streets in the middle of the night," he said, laughing.

The police officer walked over to Doug's car.

"It's all over,sir, no more backhousing, OK?" he barked, loudly enough for all of us to hear.

Doug got out of the car, showing a big smile, and carrying a glass of booze. The policeman grabbed the glass and took a sniff.

"Sir, have you been drinking and driving? Come here a moment, I have some tests which I would like you to perform."

"Tests? What kind of tests? Why take my glass? Look at all the others here, look at them, everybody almost has one. Why just me?" asked Doug.

"Because it appears that you might have been driving AND drinking. Just step this way a moment. Can I see your driver's license, please?"

Just at that moment a woman's hand flashed out of the crowd and grabbed the glass from the officer's hand. It was sent crashing to the icy road. It was Noreen.

The constable was speechless. So was I.

The crowd started to disperse. The aura of fun had disappeared. Things were getting serious. Many headed home. Others went back into the hall. The mayor and I stood there watching the action unfold, unsure as to what should be done, if anything.

"Just a minute, Officer ... " said the mayor.

"Let me handle it, Gordie. I'll talk to him. You should leave, or go into the hall. I'll see you in a few minutes," I urged.

"Constable, could I talk with you for a minute," I asked, in what I hoped sounded like a plaintiff, pleasant tone.

"Just back off there, sir! I'm about to make an arrest here. This man has been drinking in a public place and may have been driving while under the influence of alcohol. You just butt out," he ordered.

"Well, I would like to make a statement, Constable. Doug isn't the only one involved. Would you mind letting me take him home, we can get a taxi. I'm sure that he will not cause any disturbance, and as I have said, there were many others here who were drinking publicly, when you selected him," I said.

By this time Noreen had disappeared. About the only people left on the street were a few stragglers, Doug, the police officer, and me.

"Look, Officer, couldn't we handle this in a different way. I don't want to interfere with your duties but what about giving him a reprimand and letting him come with me?" I urged again.

"You ARE interfering, sir. Why don't you just leave. I may have to arrest this man and take him in," replied the officer.

"Look, Officer, uh what is your name, please," I asked.

"Never mind that, you just get along unless you want to join your friend in the lock up," he snapped.

"But, Officer, I'm just trying to point out to you that you may not have a valid set of circumstances upon which to base a case, maybe not even enough to justify a charge."

"Look you, just butt out. Get moving or you're coming along too."

"Officer, I am a crown prosecutor for the Yukon .... "

"Yeah and I'm Santa Claus," came his retort.

"He really is, you know," boomed a big voice behind me.

It was the mayor, he had come out from the hall. He became impatient waiting for me and wanted to see what was happening.

"Is your name Hine?" asked the constable.

"Yes, it is, Officer. Why don't you let me take Mr. Bennett home. I'll produce him in court in the morning, if you and/or your superiors think that I should. Will that be OK?" I asked solicitously.

"Well, I suppose that should be alright, if you give me your undertaking to do that. Court is at what time ... 10 a.m.?" he asked.

"That's correct, I will be there and so will Mr. Bennett if it becomes necessary."

Little did I know how prophetic that statement was.

"OK, if the mayor says that you are the prosecutor, then I will act upon that authority. I'll let you take Mr. Bennett. I'll check with the sergeant when I get back to the office," he said, as he put his unneeded handcuffs back into their pouch.

In the middle of the night, or so it seemed, the telephone rang. I was jolted into reality on the first ring. When I lifted the receiver I was greeted, (if that is the correct word) vociferously, by a voice that I recognized. He was yelling so loudly that I'm sure that I could have heard him directly, without the aid of a phone from the police office, which was only three blocks away.

"Hine, where is our prisoner?" demanded the owner of the voice. It was Inspector Steinhauer, the officer-in-charge of the RCMP detachment in Whitehorse. "You get that guy Bennett here and I mean NOW! Immediately! I mean before this phone stops rocking in its cradle. Have I made myself clear?"

"You sure have, Dick," I mumbled.

"Don't you 'Dick' me Hine, you've seconded our prisoner. I want him here, now!" he snapped. "Do you understand?"

"But, Inspector, he was not arrested. He's not your prisoner in the proper sense," I pleaded.

There was a long drawn out pregnant pause at the other end. I thought that he might have put his hand over the receiver and called to someone. The pause became prolonged. I waited remorsefully.

"I don't care if he wasn't our prisoner, I want both of you, both of you, understand, at my office at 8 a.m." he snapped as he slammed down the receiver.

It was already six o'clock. I might just as well get up and find Doug. I was most certainly wide awake.

Boy! He must really have been angry. We had become fairly good friends, I thought. I ruminated about the fact that I may have fractured a good relationship by trying to help another.

As I drank my first sip of coffee, I started to analyze the ugly scenario. Youth and enthusiasm, inspired by drinks and people who should know better, including me, had put me in a most invidious situation. I couldn't see a clear way out of it short of admitting my wrong doing, which I was prepared to do, notwithstanding that no one had accused me of anything short of relieving the police of a "prisoner."

Now, I had to find Doug. I wouldn't be able to locate him by searching for his car. That had been parked and locked at the scene of the event. I dialed Doug's home number and let it ring many, many times. There was no response. Maybe if I telephoned Noreen, she would know where he went? I dialed her number, a small, drowsy, depressed, but sweet voice answered. Did she know where Doug was? No. The last she had seen of him was when he left with a bunch of the drama club crowd. Others had brought her home. Then suddenly she was awake.

"What has happened to Doug? Harold, tell me, is he injured or, or, what?" she insisted. She was near to tears.

"Calm down, Noreen, nothing has happened to Doug. At least, not that I know of. I just have to find him, to make sure that he appears in ... in ... uh ... court on time. We have an earlier stop to make, so I must find him sooner. I'll telephone again when I find him. Go back to sleep, if you can," I suggested.

"Thanks a lot, Harold. Anyway, you phone me now, you hear!"

When I entered the one large room which comprised the drama clubhouse, a place in which I had spent many happier hours, I witnessed a scene of uncommon pollution. Glasses were spread, indiscriminately, from one end of the hall to the other, some were not broken. Spillage must have been the order of the day. Pools of liquid discolored the usually highly polished floor. Paper towels lay in lumps around the edge

113

of the room. The furniture was strewn about the perimeter. There was an irregular opening, free of furniture, roughly in the center of the floor, which might have been the place to dance.

Walking with great caution, I entered the hall to check the chesterfields for bodies. Eureka! There was the body I sought. It was Doug, or what was left of him, strange fellow. He was celebrating his engagement without his fiancee. Oh well, to each his own.

"Come on, Doug," I yelled, "wakey-wakey time."

His response cannot be set out verbatim in a family book, but it dealt with my ancestry and a popularly used directive, meaning that I should leave.

"Doug, wake up! We're in trouble!" I shouted, as I shook him diffidently. I had heard about his unpleasant reaction to being disturbed out of sleep.

Slowly he opened his bloodshot eyes. He looked at me as though I was a stranger. He surveyed the surroundings as though they were foreign to him.

"Where the hell are we, Harold? What are you doing here? Where's Noreen? Is she here? What time is it? What's going on, Harold?" he stammered and shivered a few times.

"Sit up, Doug, get your mind organized. I need you alive."

"Need me? For what? What do you mean alive, alive? I'm alive. What happened? Has something happened to Noreen? Where is she? How come she's not here? Tell me, Harold, what is going on?" he pleaded.

"There is no serious problem, well not in the way that you are thinking, Doug. Relax, get yourself together. Noreen is fine, I just talked to her on the telephone, trying to find you. There's nothing wrong with her but there sure as hell is something wrong for you and me. We have to be at the police office in the courthouse at 8 a.m. That gives us one hour or less. Let's get over to your house. We can talk more on the way."

"Jeez, Harold, what did you do?" asked Doug quizzically.

"It's not so much what I did, as it is what I didn't do. I may have allowed my heart to overrule my head," I suggested. "I didn't mind my own business last night when that police officer was dealing with you. Do you remember that?"

"Oh God! Harold I hope that you are not in trouble over me," he said, shaking and holding his head in his hands.

"Well, I'm not sure as to the extent of the trouble, Doug, but let's get you organized to go to court. Come on, let's go. I'll drive you home and wait for you."

At exactly eight fifteen we walked into the police detachment headquarters. I told the sergeant on duty that I was there to see the inspector.

"Jeez, Harold, he's going to roast your ass," retorted the sergeant. "How could you do such a stupid thing?"

"I didn't think that it was stupid at the time but give me a break, will you, I'm going to get hell from the inspector, please don't you get on my back too," I begged.

He gave me what I took to be a friendly smile of encouragement, then left to beard the lion in his den.

"We're here as directed," I volunteered in a friendly manner, as Dick rounded the corner of his office.

"And it's bloody well about time, Hine. Where is our prisoner?"

"If you mean Doug Bennett, he's right here," I said, gesturing to the figure in the seat beside me.

The inspector strode up to Doug and snapped, "Is your name Douglas Bennett?"

Looking up, haplessly, Doug said, "Yes sir."

"OK ... both of you remain here until I return ... and I mean right here!" he ordered. He whirled around and strode off in the direction of the judge's chambers.

"Why is he wearing his street clothes?" I mumbled almost inaudibly.

"What did you say, Harold?" asked Doug.

"Nothing ... nothing important," I replied.

The time dragged with a terrible slowness. Doug and I must have had five cups of the terrible brew that the label on the dispensing machine indicated was supposed to be coffee. Alternatively Doug and I paced, puffed cigarettes, paced, shuffled, stood, looked out the window, then repeated the routine.

"What time do you make it, Sarge?" I asked.

"Just about nine, Harold," he answered smartly.

Had I noticed a smirk on his face? What the hell is going on? We had been sitting here for about half an hour without any sign of the inspector or anybody else involved in this fiasco. Dick's secretary had gone down to the judge's chambers just a few minutes after he had. She had taken her stenographer's note book with her. She had returned in about fifteen minutes.

I didn't know her too well, but didn't she give me a strange look, with pursed lips and shaking head?

Where was Dick? I should be getting prepared for my daily chore as crown prosecutor. Where was the court list? I was becoming agitated and unnerved. What a bloody dolt I was. What a rectal cavity. Stupid, stupid, stupid!

My thoughts must have showed. Doug looked over at me and asked, "Harold, are you likely to get into trouble too?"

"I'm certainly beginning to wonder about that possibility, Doug ... I ...."

I was just about to make further comment when I was interrupted by the court clerk. I hadn't seen him come up behind me. He had come from the direction of the judge's chambers.

"Mr. Hine, the judge would like to see both of you in the courtroom now," said the clerk.

"Mr. Hine?" I thought. "What the hell is going on here? He and I have been on a first name basis for years. Jeez, I could be in real trouble."

"Jeez, Doug, I'm afraid that we are in for it," I said with patent concern. "I don't like the way things are shaping up. It's all so strange."

"Why do you say that, Harold?"

"Well, several things, including the fact that it is only nine o'clock and I'm told that the judge wants to see both of us in the courtroom. Court doesn't convene until ten. The inspector is wearing his street clothes and he doesn't usually go in to deal with the judge personally. The clerk called me Mr. Hine instead of the usual Harold. It doesn't add up," I replied.

"This way, Sir!" said the clerk.

"Reg, will you knock it off with the Sir bit. What the hell is going on?" I demanded.

Reg didn't even turn to acknowledge my question. He led us directly to the courtroom doors, pulled one of them open, and stood back.

We were greeted by a startling sight. At least it was for me. The judge was already sitting "on the bench." Dick was standing in the witness box. He held a file in his left hand. It was a genuine official RCMP folder. When I reached the prosecutor's table, I saw the daily court list. There was but one case on the docket. Strange? I glanced down and saw that it said Regina vs Douglas Bennett. "Oh God!" I thought. "How can I carry out my duties as prosecutor and at the same time be a principal witness. For which side? The crown or the defense, or for myself?"

At that moment I wanted a hole to open up and swallow me. I had heard of many reasons for giving up that devil alcohol. Now I had reasons of my own.

My reflection on the use of alcohol was shaken by the sound of Reg's voice saying, "Mr. Bennett, would you please step into the prisoner's dock?"

My thoughts were racing wildly. There had been no call to order in court. What the hell is going on?

Usually the accused person is allowed to stand when called, listen to the charges, then make a plea. He says either "guilty" or "not guilty." If the accused contests the crown's case, then he asks for a date upon which the the trial will be heard. The onus upon the crown is to prove that the accused is guilty. If the crown fails in this endeavor, the accused goes free. Today the accused was being sent to the dock without a plea? What the hell was going on here?

Poor Doug, he looked stunned, hungover, pathetic, and unsure of himself in these strange surroundings and very, very sorry. His eyes pleaded for some succor, some indication of help. Anything that would lighten the aura of fear and uncertainty. If eyes alone can speak, he was telling me how absolutely ludicrous and helpless was his state.

Once again, my wool gathering was shattered by the judge instructing the clerk to "read today's list."

Reg rose from his seat, majestically, a bit ostentatiously, I thought, then pointedly, while looking directly at me, he held up the list and read aloud, "Regina versus Douglas Bennett, Your Honor."

The judge looked sternly at my demoralized friend, and said in a loud voice, uncommon to me, "Are you Douglas Bennett?"

"Yes, yes I am, Your Honor," stammered Doug. His voice sounded as though he was pleading for the intervention of the Divinity.

"Then let us proceed with the case," said the judge tersely.

No one had asked Doug to plead guilty or not guilty. What the hell was ... ? I picked up the docket file. It should contain the answers to my questions. I would read the resume of the evidence which I would normally present to the court. The docket file was empty! The bloody file was empty! What the hell ... ?

I couldn't follow these proceedings at all. No one had read a charge to Doug, no one had asked him to plead to the charge, which was as yet unread. I had an empty file which was supposed to contain the evidence, upon which I (or another prosecutor) could prosecute the case. My friend was standing in shock, watching this farce. What was I to do?

"Your Honor, I have a motion to make. May I make it at this time?" I asked submissively.

"No, you may not!" he pronounced.

"Witness, are you prepared to testify in the case at bar?" the judge asked the inspector.

"You bet I am," snarled Dick. He snapped out the words as though he was on a parade ground.

"This must be a dream," I said to myself. "They haven't read the charge, haven't asked Doug to plead to the charge and yet they are going to start accepting testimony from the OC/RCMP and he hasn't yet been sworn as a witness." What the hell ... ?

I was a mite disoriented. I was also devastated by what was happening. It had to be a dream! I wasn't sure of what I should do, if anything, but ....

"Your Honor ... " I started to submit.

"Please be quiet and do not interrupt these proceedings again, Mr. Hine!" said the judge sternly.

"Proceed, Inspector," said the judge. Did the judge glower at me as he said that? Was it just my imagination?

"Oh God," I pleaded fervently, "let this be a dream."

"Your Honor," Dick began, as he opened his file with a flair and scowled at me. "Last night, or more accurately, early this morning, Constable Werner (not the real name) of this detachment, while making his customary rounds of the community in the RCMP cruiser, was confronted by an automobile pushing a backhouse on Main Street, in this city."

"A backhouse!" exclaimed the judge.

"Yes, Your Honor, a backhouse," confirmed the witness.

"Who was pushing this ... this ... backhouse?" queried the judge. He had a look of incredulity upon his face.

"The automobile in question, Your Honor, was being driven, at that moment, by one Harold Hine!" said Dick. I thought that he had said that with a touch of relish and too much dramatic flourish. I could have been mistaken.

"Our Harold Hine?" asked the judge.

"One and the same, Your Honor," said the witness.

"Proceed, Inspector. Our Mr. Hine, you say ... well, well."

"The backhouse has as yet to be identified, Your Honor, but it is believed to be in the possession of one "Red" Carter, a local businessman/contractor."

"Yes, yes, Inspector, but what happened to it?" asked the judge, displaying what I thought to be an uncommon interest in the scenario of last night's improprieties.

"Well, Your Honor, the constable pursued the car, and the backhouse, his 'quarry' if you wish, to the intersection of Second and Main. The quarry took a circuitous route by going around the block, actually several blocks, to get to that destination on our city's main thoroughfare. Then suddenly, without notice, a car registered to our mayor, Gordon Armstrong, and driven by an unidentified person, shot out of the cover of darkness and peeled the backhouse off of the front bumper of Mr. Hine's car without hesitation or contact. The new quarry tore off down the street traveling west on Main Street, in this city, with the constable in hot pursuit."

"Hot pursuit, my God! That phrase is usually reserved for a car chase involving bank robbers, or other serious matters," I thought.

"In hot pursuit, eh? My ... my," said the judge. He looked over at me, shaking his head admonishingly.

"When the mayor's car reached the intersection of Third and Main Street in our city's downtown core, there appeared a car registered and driven by one Douglas Bennett, the accused, Your Honor," continued the inspector.

I felt, more than I saw, Douglas wince as his name came up in the evidence for the first time.

"Go on, go on, Inspector, what happened then?" urged the judge, with demonstrated curiosity. Or was it spectator interest?

"The accused's Pontiac picked that backhouse out of its forward momentum, given to it by the mayor's car, with startling grace and aptitude, then raced away with it down Third Avenue to Black Street."

"Grace and aptitude?" I mused. What the hell is this all about?

"Yes, yes, how very unusual. Please continue Inspector, please do," encouraged the judge.

"Well, Your Honor, at that point my constable, a new recruit mind you, was placed in a genuine dilemma. Should he pursue the mayor's car, Mr. Hine, or go after the backhouse in transit, so to speak?" said Dick with dramatic flair.

"Backhouse in transit?" I repeated to myself. I closed my eyes, rolled them backwards and shook my head. This is just too strange to be real.

"So just what did he do? The constable I mean. With all the players in this event, one might have trouble understanding to whom I referred," said the judge in a pontifical manner. Once again he glowered at me.

"The constable, although a new recruit mind you, quite properly elected to pursue the car driven by the accused there."

"And the backhouse, what happened to the backhouse? Was it apprehended? I mean did the constable locate it as well as the accused?" asked the judge, encouraging the inspector not to leave out any of the interesting details.

"Yes, Your Honor. I am proud to say that the constable, although a raw recruit, did catch his man with the exhibit ... which is yet to be identified. All of the cars involved finally came together at the intersection of Second and Main. Indecision on the part of the drivers as to who was to get the use of the backhouse next, allowed the constable to interject his presence without damage or injuries to citizens, cars, or to the backhouse, and put a stop to this backhouse caper," said the inspector with patent pride.

"Good for him!" exclaimed the judge. "Oh, excuse me," he apologized as he clapped his left hand over his mouth. His eyes roved, from me to Doug, then back to me again.

Did my eyes deceive me, or did I catch a glint of satire in the judge's actions?

"Please go on, Inspector. Did the constable catch the culprits and arrest them?" asked the judge.

"Culprits? Hot pursuit? Backhouse in transit? Quarry? Startling grace and aptitude?" my mind boggled at this summary. This has got to be ridiculous.

"No, Your Honor, being a young, raw recruit, the constable failed to arrest any of the culprits. Nor have any summons been issued in regard to this caper, but two of the participants have agreed to appear this morning voluntarily," said Dick, with a broad grin.

Voluntarily my eye! I had responded to what I took to be a verbal summons. My mind then started to go over the events of the last fifteen minutes. There had been no reading of any charge. The court had not been called to order. The judge was on the bench and the "witness" was in the stand when I arrived. Nobody had required the inspector to be placed under oath. The constable, the true witness, was not present. All of Dick's testimony was pure hearsay evidence, he was in mufti and my court file was empty.

"Wait a minute!" I said, half to myself, but loud enough for the judge to hear. I started to rise when the judge bellowed, "Just remain seated, Mr. Hine. The inspector may not have finished telling me about this most interesting event. Have you, Inspector?"

"Not quite, Your Honor. Once my constable had rounded up the various participants, and the backhouse, he was about to disperse this unruly crowd when an event of drastic implication occurred. The constable seized some evidence which was suddenly removed from his control."

"No-o-o-o-o-!" exclaimed the judge, with an expression of horror on his face.

The judge removed his glasses, placed them upon his desk, rubbed his eyes and forehead, then stared at Doug and me. Dramatically, he lifted the glasses and slowly placed them back on his head. He brushed the hair over each ear, with his fingertips, while he glowered at Doug, then me.

"What happened next?" he said, spurring the witness on.

"The constable was just about to arrest the accused person, was about to place his hand upon him, when Mr. Hine interceded and made off with the accused," said Dick, with obvious relish.

"Our Mr. Hine did that?" exploded the judge, throwing his arms into the air and with disbelief written, expansively, on his face.

"Yes, Your Honor. I'm sorry to say it, but it is one and the same person," said Dick, with what might have been mock sorrow.

I wanted to get up and interject but I was now almost sure that what was happening was going to be for my benefit, in a constructive way. Better quiet than sorry.

"Is that the sum total of your testimony, Inspector?" asked the judge, patently hoping to hear more.

"Almost, Your Honor. To be fair, I should tell you that Mr. Hine did return our 'almost prisoner' early this morning. He has thereby redeemed his otherwise incomprehensible, and for him, highly unusual behavior."

"Thank you so much, Inspector, you're excused," said the judge.

"Excused? Not before I get a chance to ask some questions, but did I have any questions which could be of any help in what sounded like a bloody ridiculous situation?" I thought.

I was about to leap to my feet when I was cut off by the judge. He had not spent all those prior years in the courtroom without learning something about timing.

"It might behoove you not to say anything Mr. Hine, and if you did on whose behalf would you speak? The crown, the accused, or possibly yourself?" he said through a large grin. I turned to look at Dick. He, too, was grinning from ear to ear. Reg could hardly contain himself as he stifled an inner explosion of laughter.

"Mr. Bennett, do you think that the inspector's resume of last night's events, involving you, and others," continued the judge, as he looked pointedly at me, "is a fair, accurate, and unbiased recounting of what occurred?"

"Yes, Your Honor. There is no doubt that something, much like that, did occur last night," responded Doug dejectedly.

"Alright, Mr. Bennett, you can sit back down. It looks to me as if you need the rest," asserted the judge, with a twinkle in his eye.

"Now, Mr. Hine, what do you suggest that we should do in this most unusual situation?" mused the judge aloud. "You are obviously aware that this is not a properly constituted court of law. It is a behavior lesson for both of you. Mr. Bennett admits his wrongdoing. You must be involved or you wouldn't have returned the 'culprit,' as referred to by the witness ... and what about the mayor ... and the others. Hmmmm! ... difficult to say ... but I have a suggestion ... actually two suggestions, One ... don't do it again ... and, if I was going to adjudicate such an event I might impose a fine of say ... twenty-five dollars. Possibly, if you two feel it to be appropriate, you could make a donation, in that amount, to a suitable charity. You might even let the mayor know that I think he might do the same," said the judge.

"Thank God for all mercies!" I exclaimed.

"And well you should give Him thanks," said the judge with a smile, "and you might thank the inspector. He realized that what happened was really a combination of youthful enthusiasm, group idiocy, a convention which spawns this sort of thing, but a convention of people dedicated to doing good for the community, and a young recruit. I don't know what I should say about the mayor. I understand that the police had been told to relax their presence and vigilance during the term of the convention. Maybe the recruit didn't have the experience to understand fully. Yet he did his job admirably, to a point. The inspector persuaded me that a lesson was in order, under the circumstances. After all, no measurable offense of consequence occurred, and it would not be right to single out but two of the many who were involved. Some were not even identified, and probably just as well at that. I am sure that we have succeeded in that objective, haven't we?"

"You certainly have, Your Honor, and thank you for handling the matter as you did," I said.

"I have one last burning question, Mr. Hine. Where on earth did you get the idea for a caper involving a backhouse?"

Chapter Thirteen

A businessman came into town
to market what he sold
And so successful was the trip
He drank more than he could hold.

Arrested then and put in jail,
All sympathized his plight
So set the bail and let him out
So he could catch his flight.

While acting as chief magistrate
The mayor said, "let him free!"
Police released him from the cells
But said "it might not be."

When man was gone—the question posed,
Was mayor chief magistrate?
He wasn't, but the plane had left,
Oh, God!—did cops berate.

The Illusive Magistrate

In 1954, in the early summer, a businessman from Vancouver came to Whitehorse. He was a good friend of my partner George. The particular business pursued by this man, whom I will call Fred, required that he could spend only the one full business day in Whitehorse. He absolutely had to be back in Vancouver to close some bids on Wednesday. He had arrived on Saturday or late Friday. He had return reservations on the Tuesday morning early flight. Taking into consideration his propensity to party and the fact that he was in the party capital of the world, I have to assume that he had never been in Whitehorse before. Otherwise, he would never have made travel plans of that nature and simultaneously joined the marathon drinkers of the local relay team. So dedicated was that team to insuring that "outsiders" enjoy the hospitality of the city that, as one faded, another materialized to fill the potential gap. So it was on this escapade.

All day Saturday this hapless individual was shown the bars of Whitehorse. On Sunday, when he felt sure that he was safe, he was taken to a bar which seemed to have the habit of being "cleaned and aired" on that particular day every week. That meant that the proprietor was in the bar purging the premises of the dust and other corruption which fell upon the place during the regular business week. What it also meant was that "friends" might drop in to visit with that proprietor, who, abiding by the code of the Yukon, felt obliged to offer his visitor(s) a drink, or two, or .... The fact that it was contrary to local ordinances to be open for business on Sunday, at any hour, didn't seem to deter this practice. After all, no money actually changed hands, the drinks were not sold in the true sense. The bartender kept a secret tab.

On Monday, that all-essential one business day, Fred was almost too exhausted to do any business. He was encouraged to have a "bit of the hair of the dog." He did. Once he received signatures on certain stereotyped documents, he was again inveigled into joining a group of potential customers at the same bar while he awaited the availability of one final signature. He had about two hours to kill. George and that omnipresent mayor, Gordie Armstrong, were there as well. I'm not sure if they were the instigators or the followers but they were most certainly there.

After several hours of constant rounds and meetings and greetings, Fred asked if he could borrow a car to go and get that last signature. "Sure! Take mine," someone yelled, "it's parked right outside. You know ... where I parked it when we drove up."

Fred did.

Hours passed before Fred was missed. The party was exceptionally good. There was even a slight justification for this particular party. There was a visitor from "outside." Any excuse will do, but if it sounds genuine, there is less guilt attached the following day.

The regular dinner hour came and went. No Fred. Soon a

phone committee was detailed. Calls went to every conceivable place. Except one. That was not conceivable.

After a few more rounds and numerous more phone calls, the unthinkable suggestion was advanced. Should the police be called? Maybe there had been an accident?

"Good idea, George," said the mayor, "give them a call. You're known to them, your office is that of the crown prosecutor."

The call was made. Yes, they knew a person by that name. In fact, Fred was in the cells. He had been arrested for several offences involving intoxication. Maybe there was a fracas involved as well. Something about resisting an order from a uniformed police officer? My God, we had better get down there right away.

"It won't do any good to come down. The judge is trying a case down the Alaska Highway and won't be back until Wednesday morning," said the officer in charge at the RCMP detachment.

"Wednesday morning ... hell that's preposterous! Fred has an extremely important meeting 'outside' on that day. His plane leaves tomorrow at 10 a.m.," cried George.

"Nothing that I can do, George, sorry," said the sergeant.

The party fell flat upon receipt of this disheartening news. The best that could be done under the circumstances, was to go to the cells and commiserate with Fred. It was almost closing time at the bar anyway.

During the night, when the body is at rest, the mind sometimes does some of its best thinking. In this particular instance, I think it is fair to say that the minds of several interested parties were working hard on solving poor Fred's dilemma. There were three prosecutors in Whitehorse at that particular time. I believe that all three were enlisted in arriving at a solution. After all, if the judge had been in town, the problem would not exist.

In the cool, gray hours just about dawn, one of those prosecutors awoke with a start. All that was needed was a magistrate. The Criminal Code provides that under the exact circumstances of the charges against Fred, a magistrate, having jurisdiction in the community where the offences were alleged to have occurred, could set bail and release the prisoner. Eureka! The problem was solved. Fred could still catch the plane if a court could be convened in time.

> "get home early." She wanted to get the children
d three) to bed at a reasonable hour. They would
or 6 a.m., possessed by curiosity and full of anxiety.
d their sleep.

ng a bachelor, had been invited by Laura to spend
Eve and Christmas dinner with us. Without know-
was that he might be in for, he had accepted.

you think that we should slide out of here, while
e the ability to navigate," I suggested. "The kids
ed early so we can, if you want, go out and do some
er that, or you can stay now and I'll pick you up

Hal ... Oh, boy! Am I in trouble ... God! How
so damn thoughtless, so stupid?"

, Al, hold on. What are you talking about? Don't
ed up. Did you forget to call some gal?" I asked,
friendly punch on the shoulder. "Did you overlook
us little school teacher?" (I had seen him out with
some weeks before, but never teased him about it.
t shy where girls were concerned, that's probably
still a bachelor).

al, it's much worse than that, this is serious. Oh,
could I? I forgot to get presents for your kids.

h as I knew that the children would be truly dis-
their favorite Uncle Al failed to bring them a gift,
that the same Uncle Al would suffer about it far
they would.

ll the stores are closed now. There's not much that
about it," I said.

about Rolfe Hougen, he's single, maybe he would
and open up his department store for me. What
k?" Al offered.

he just might. Let's call the store, he may still be
, we can call his home," I suggested.

t Rolfe at the store. He had been taking a
as he called it. I called it an after work drink.
exceptionally busy in his store. It was a popular
p for the entire community. Rolfe and his mother
h his younger brother "Blondie" were responsible
agement of the store. Rolfe was the moving force

In most communities the mayor is the chief magistrate. The statutes (ordinances in the Yukon) which create the communities, almost invariably makes such provision. Ergo, Gordon H. Armstrong was a magistrate. He was the mayor of the city of Whitehorse.

Urgent phone calls were placed. The mayor was still abed. Get him up! It's essential that he be at the RCMP detachment office within the hour!

Fred's belongings were collected from the hotel and his bill paid. At 9 a.m. a sad lot were seen to gather at the detachment. The senior NCO paraded the prisoner before His Honor, Magistrate Armstrong. There was reluctance on the part of that NCO. He sensed that there was something irregular about these proceedings but he, too, had become familiar with the fact that the mayor, in the numerous areas in which he had been posted, was the chief magistrate.

Fred stood and faced his compatriot of yesterday. The prosecutor read the charges. The magistrate, who was not in any way familiar with such proceedings, asked what it was that he should do. The prosecutor counselled the magistrate, while Fred sagged and constantly checked his watch.

"Released on your own recognizance," pronounced the mayor. "Now let's get out to the car and get you up to that bloody plane."

The three perpetrators of this peculiar event rushed off in the prosecutor's car. Fred boarded the plane. It was taxiing to the runway in preparation for takeoff when a police car, with lights flashing, drove up to the terminal building. The roar of the plane's engines almost drowned out the NCO's yelling at the mayor and the prosecutor. He had checked into the ordinance which established Whitehorse as a city. The goddamn mayor was not the goddamn chief magistrate. The two of them had just shanghaied one of his prisoners, illegally! Goddamnit!

Chapter Fourteen

At Christmas time across the land,
The hearts of many change,
From work a day, exhausted, bored
To a more emotive range.

That little man, in beard and suit
Bright red and trimmed with fur,
Brings out the better side of man
Good will to all assured.

And yet a wistful soul still cries,
To do this once per year
Has hollow mockery at its base,
No constant views adhere.

The Great Santa Claus Saga

What happened on the eve of Christmas, 1953, started out as a private, family prank. It has repeated itself, in one form or another, for thirty-two consecutive years thereafter. The nature of the event has always been of the same intent. Only the number of persons involved and the varying locations comprise the changes in the format.

During Christmas Eve day, I had been conducting the conclusion to a long, demanding, civil trial before Mr. Justice Jack Gibben. My opponent counsel, "my learned friend," was Allan Bate. He was then, and is now, a well-respected lawyer, with a wealth of experience. He and I had gone to law school together and had formed a strong bond of friendship. Al was single and there were no special women in his life at that time. He was tall, maybe six feet two inches in height. He was well-built, not

powerfully but staunchly. He was
size and lack of weight. His dark
it would not stay in place. It forev
of his forehead. He was handsom
reluctantly, even passively. Only
on a party, did he seem to beco
Other times he was somewhat dis

The judge, the court staff,
court reporter, Wynn Clarke, ar
court system, were eager to hear
being made by me and Al. The
lowing the hearing. We were cut
frame. Everyone, including the r
terminate the serious and get o
positive, but when the last word
heard a faint cheer go up from out
walls. Mr. Justice Gibben, in hi
thanked both counsel for the ass
would receive from our submissic
the holidays. Then I was certain
chorus of cheers.

Within moments, long before
gowns to street attire, the law lib
place had been chosen for the f
It contained a large, elongated
regated from the rest of the fede
door to the washrooms.

A polyglot crew was in atte
(Bob) Friend; his deputy Cece N
omnipresent mayor; the registrar
lawyers; representatives of the m

As the group swelled, the pa
nuances, colors, and flavors. The
tion of the distinctive divisions
the usual reserve arising from th
"forces" and the rank involved
the font of camaraderie, fellowsh

As much as I was enjoying
must break away and assume a
responsibility was to Laura and
home. They were waiting impat
Saint Nick." Laura or, "the Bi
affectionately by many, had give

morning,
(ages six a
be up at 5
They need

Al, be
Christmas
ing what i

"Al, d
we still ha
will go to
visiting af
later."

"Jeez,
could I be

"Who
get so wor
giving him
that delici
a real cuti
He was a
why he wa

"No, I
God! Hov
Damn!"

As mu
appointed
I also knev
more than

"Well,
we can do

"What
come dow
do you thi

"Yeah
there. If n

I caug
"breather,
He had be
place to sh
together w
for the ma
therein.

"Sure thing, come on over, bring that big oaf with you. I still have some toys and Christmasy items left. There aren't as many here now as there were recently. That'll cut down the period of agony and indecision," Rolfe said, laughing about one of Al's noticeable quirks.

Rolfe responded to the bell, which we rang as we arrived at the front door of the store. The main lights were out. He soon had the interior ablaze with neon lights and occulting tree bulbs. Tinsel and other decorations hung everywhere.

"Do you guys want a bit of good cheer?" asked Rolfe as we went into his private office.

"Great idea, Rolfe, you and I could have one while Al does his shopping," I said with a wink.

"To hell with that," said Al, "that invitation was for all of us, eh, Rolfe?" cried Al.

"Yeah, what both of you guys need right now is another drink, like another hole in the head. What a couple of jokers. Where have you been, at the judicial blast?" asked Rolfe.

"I didn't realize that the party had taken on the status of having a formal title," said Al. "Must remember that."

"OK, Al," said Rolfe as he handed each of us our respective drinks. "You come with me. I'll show you what we have left and give you prices. I suppose you want the discounts, too, even if it is after the sale has terminated," joshed Rolfe.

"Bloody right, man! I'm probably buying stuff that nobody wanted and that's why it's still here ... eh, Hal?" asked Al. He followed by putting an arm around Rolfe and laughing, "OK, Rolfe, let's go and get'um."

I headed to the doorway slightly behind them. I had no clear intent. I was merely wandering while sipping my drink. My attention was attracted to a large cardboard box which was tucked to the side, just outside Rolfe's office door. What had caught my eye was a flash of red, trimmed by white fur. It might be a Santa Claus suit. When I lifted the top, my suspicions were confirmed.

Maybe it was the drinks. Maybe it was because Rolfe was a friend and I, therefore, felt at liberty to try on the suit. Maybe it was fate. I'll never know the true answer, if there is one. In any event, I removed my top coat and suit jacket then put on the jacket of the Santa Claus costume. It wasn't a good, nor proper fit, but it felt good. Before I knew it, I had donned the entire outfit and was making with the "HO ... HO ... HO's."

131

The costume was replete with fur trimmed black leather boots, a black leather belt, from which dangled little silver bells, and a luxuriant white beard. The beard had an elastic attached at each side which went up over my ears then around my head. The substance of which the beard was made tickled my face and ears. A droopy mustache attached to the beard sent little hairs up my nostrils, giving me a tendency to want to sneeze. The precarious angle at which the elastic encompassed my head, was made more secure by the white wig, which was just a tad tight for my skull. This particular wig came down over my forehead, then applied itself, like a beanie, from there to the nape of my neck. The white tresses were shoulder length. There was no mirror, but if I looked as good as I felt, I had to be a reasonable facsimile of good old Saint Nick himself.

Succumbing to the ham in me, I picked up my drink and wandered off to find Rolfe and Al. When they saw me they burst out laughing and made rude comments about "the shortest Santa in captivity" and "you certainly don't need any padding there, Hine."

"OK, you guys, enough of the insults. With Rolfe's permission I may play one of me better roles tonight. What say, Rolfe, may I borrow this until tomorrow?"

"Going home to surprise the kids, eh?" asked Rolfe. "Sure, Harold, keep it until after the holidays are over. No need for it until next year, anyway. Hope you get good use out of it. Have fun, and a Merry Christmas to both of you guys and to your families."

"Thanks, Rolfe, I'll just do that. I'll take good care of it. I'll bring it back day after Boxing Day," I said.

"Don't worry about it—I won't. Have fun," Rolfe responded.

"OK Al, let's get out of here. What have you bought?" I asked.

"You are going to love this little item," Al said, as he pulled a small drum off of the counter and started to beat it with sticks which looked like toothpicks in his large hands.

"Yikes! Laura is going to kill you for sure, Al. She's going to have to listen to that being pounded all day long. I don't envy you her reaction Al, but get it if you must," I cajoled.

"I must!" Al insisted, as he thrust it into a large paper bag which Rolfe had supplied. "I'm not going to show you the rest of the things, Hal—you're a party pooper," he said feigning annoyance.

132

One could always tell when Al was starting to feel his drinks. He lost the facade of the big city attorney and became the big, loveable, teddy bear that he really was.

Al and I tried to sneak into my house through the back door. We were being "as quiet as little mice." Suddenly, the door flew open and there stood Laura, wrists on hips and with a mimicked hostility.

"It's about time you two jokers got here. Where on earth did you get that outfit, Harold? It looks great! Come on in, I want to see the reaction of the children," she said.

"Who are you calling Harold, madam," I insisted. "My name is Santa Claus."

"Yeah, and mine is going to be Lizzie Borden, if you don't get in here before the children get too tired waiting and go to sleep on me," Laura retorted.

Al had been standing directly behind me, holding that ominous huge, paper bag. He stepped (maybe staggered) forward and proferred the bag to Laura. "It's for the kids, nothing's wrapped. Could you do that for me, please?" he said shyly, even though we three had been well-acquainted for at least eight years.

"Al, you dear man, of course I'll wrap them for you ... whatever 'they' are."

"It's just a few things for you, this guy, and the kids. You'll be able to figure out which is which," he said.

"I'm sure that I will be able to figure them out, but where are you going that you won't be able to tell me yourself. Are you going out again?" Laura asked suspiciously.

"Well, I thought ... that is, Hal thought ... that we should go and visit some of the families we know which have children. I'm sure that they would love the idea of having Santa drop in on them, like a private Santa. Hal can jolly up the children, tell them about the reindeer, the sleigh, the gifts, the elves, and things like that. I think it is a great idea," Al said most seriously.

"Sure, and getting the children all excited, so that they won't go to bed or to sleep. It's truly a lovely idea and a charitable thought Al, but you two guys are already half smashed. What will you be like after visiting a few of your pals?" Laura mused aloud.

"Well, let's try it on our kids, and see what happens," I said.

"Let's try it on our kids, then talk about it further," said Laura, as she led the way into the bedroom where our daughter and her younger brother were already in bed, where they had been waiting for Daddy and Uncle Al.

Cathy had just turned six years of age on her recent birthday, which was December 3. She had long, reddish hued hair and the lovely complexion which usually goes with red hair. She was bright, healthy, and athletic. She was above average intelligence for her age and loved going to school with Wade Jorde, another six year old, who lived across the street. We had got to the point where we said that Cathy was "six going on sixteen."

Art, on the other hand, who was just three years of age, was more interested in music and being cuddled, either by his mummy or by Cathy. One might doubt that Cathy had a true mother complex for Art when one hears that she had put Art into the Bendix combination washer/dryer machine, then turned it on. Art would have been wrinkled and dizzy if Laura hadn't investigated the cause of the sound, just as the machine got started.

I suppose I should list "curiosity" as one of Cathy's characteristics, as well.

Laura opened the bedroom door and peeked in. She found that the children were, or appeared to be asleep, so she waved Santa into the room. As I entered, I flicked on a wall switch which controlled a small table lamp. The lamp went on, but the little darlings did not move a muscle. Art, as he so often did when he was tense, had crawled into Cathy's bed. Somewhat abashed by their lack of attention, I let go with a loud "HO HO HO."

In a most matter of fact way, Cathy sat up and surveyed this ersatz Santa. Art, as usual, copied her every move. Both sat there in bed, supported by their arms behind them, and blinked.

"Daddy what are you doing in that funny outfit?" inquired Cathy.

"Daddy look silly," said Art.

"What do you mean 'Daddy'? Don't you two know the real Santa, when you see him?" I inquired, using a put-on voice.

"Daddy, you are funny," said Cathy, as she and Art started to giggle. Each encouraged the other. Before we realized what had happened, the three adults were caught up in the humor of the moment. We, too, were laughing with the children. It was a delightful moment.

"OK, you guys, just see if Santa brings you any toys tonight. You've hurt Santa's feelings now, so he's going to leave and take his toys back to the North Pole," Santa pouted.

At this sobering suggestion, Cathy flew out of bed, closely followed by her shadow, Art. She wrapped her arms around Santa's legs in a big hug. Art fought to find space enough for his hug too. I picked both of them up and carried them out into the living room, where we all fell into a heap on the chesterfield. Hugs and kisses abounded. Cathy investigated the beard, the wig, and the suit. Art checked out that which was nearer to his level, the boots. Then we snuggled for a few precious moments.

"OK, you chillun's, time for bed. Maybe the real Santa will show up tonight. Give Daddy another hug, then one for Uncle Al, then off to bed, quickly now," said the Big Chief.

"Goodnight, Daddy Santa," called Cathy as she pulled the covers over her head and started to giggle loudly. Of course, Art had to emulate Cathy's every move, so they were at it again.

"Thanks a lot you two," said Laura as she joined Al and me after trying, unsuccessfully, to get the children settled down. "I knew what would happen if you went in there wearing that outfit. I don't think Cathy was a believer and possibly she had told Art that there was no real Santa. Now there will be no doubt in either mind, and now you want to go around town doing the same thing to other families?"

"Well, it won't be the same thing, the other children won't know me intimately enough to see through this disguise. Anyway, they really did get a lot of pleasure out of Santa's visit didn't they? Did you ever hear such artless, carefree laughter?" I asked.

"I had to go into the living room," said Al. "I knew, that if I once got started laughing with them, I would be a basket case. A child's laughter is so guileless, spontaneous, and innocent, it becomes completely contagious to me. I'm never certain, at the time, whether I'm going to laugh with them or cry with the beauty of it all."

"You're such a big softy, Al," said Laura. She went over and gave his arm a hug.

"Well, I've decided, I'm going out to visit the children of our friends. Are you with me, Al?" I solicited.

"Well, I've gone this far with you Hal, might as well keep going. Somebody has to look after you," replied Al.

"Now there is a real case of the blind leading the blind," offered Laura.

"Should we have one more for the road, Al?" I asked.

"No you don't, you guys have had enough. If you're going, get, otherwise you won't be home 'til midnight. Scoot, get going. You'll probably be 'forced' to have a few while you're out. Try to get back early, and I mean tonight, not early tomorrow, OK?" Laura insisted.

"Jeez, Hal, what a witch you married. Now you know why I stayed single," teased Al as he and I headed for the door.

Laura held the door open for us and kissed us both good-bye. We didn't know it then, but we were off on an adventure that many of the "oldtimers" from the Yukon still talk about whenever they get together at Christmas time.

Stopping at the first home which we had selected for Santa's visit, I knocked on the door with some trepidation. Christmas Eve is, after all, an evening which is set aside for a quiet gathering of family members. Particularly, this is so if there are youngsters involved.

I was not at all prepared for the reaction which I received when Audrey opened the door.

She stood there for a moment or two, just staring. Then she cried, "It's Santa Claus! Look it really is Santa, and his helper. Come on in. Pretty big to be an elf, isn't he? Come on in, Al ... is that the name of your helper Santa? Look Phil, it's Santa!"

Phil Iverson who was a pilot for CP Air, was also a law student in our office. Audrey was his beautiful wife. She was a very practical lady. She was exactly the right woman for Phil, and was truly his helpmate. Audrey was a good and loving mother to their two young boys. Phil was industrious and ambitious. Not long after he was admitted to the Bar he was killed in a flying accident near Anchorage, Alaska.

Audrey led us into the living room, then placed her head against the window and asked, "Where are your reindeer, Santa?" Without waiting for an answer she turned and joined us. I assumed, correctly, that their sons were still awake and what might have appeared to be a rhetorical question was, in reality, being overheard by the children.

"I left them up on the airstrip," I responded. "Al, here met me and said that he knew of some children who had been good and he wanted me to meet them. Are there two children in this house who have been good, and who might like to meet me?" I asked in a stage voice.

"They're down this way, Santa," said Phil, "they're probably asleep, but you can look in on them." He shook his head in the negative and smiled, all the while he was saying this.

I poked my head into the room. Phil turned the lights on and two young heads bobbed up from the pillows. The light bothered their eyes but they were otherwise wide awake.

"Come out and say hello to Santa, dears," said Audrey.

The children didn't move. In fact, they were a bit retiring. This apparition in the red suit appeared to overwhelm them. I waited, patiently, for them to make up their minds about me.

"What is it that you want for Christmas?" I asked the youngest one.

"A bike," he responded immediately.

"And what about you?" I asked the older of the two.

"I want a bike too," he declared.

I looked outside the room and saw Audrey nod to me in the affirmative.

"Well, I've heard that you have both been very good this year, so maybe ... maybe ... you'll get your wish."

Like a flash they were out of their beds and standing beside me. Each took one hand and stood looking up at me with those trusting, believing eyes. Al turned about and smartly left the area. Suddenly, I felt like I should be somewhere else, also. My eyes brimmed with tears. Santa doesn't cry—does he? I smiled, weakly, trusting that the beard, bushy eyebrows, and makeup, which Laura had applied, would guard against letting them realize my emotions at that moment. I didn't want the parents to know either.

"Would you like to see my model airplane, Santa?" asked the oldest boy.

"No, come and see my rock collection," cried the younger one, who pulled me in the opposite direction.

An obvious, instant bond of affection had been established based purely upon tradition and the mythical personality of Santa Claus. They were offering warm reception and unadulterated love to this character in the red suit whom they believed to be the real thing. They were so vulnerable, adoring and trusting that it bothered me. I felt inadequate, unable to respond properly because I wasn't able to assess why my emotions were so bestirred.

"OK, OK, that's enough now, Santa has many places to visit. We can't keep him here all night," said Phil. "Give Santa a hug, then jump into bed."

Each in turn gave me a warm, loving hug. Each in turn said, "Goodnight, Santa" in such a touching manner that I felt sure that I would not be able to contain myself.

What had I got myself into? These children pulled at my heartstrings. My throat hurt, tears brimmed in my eyes. They loved innocently, without schemes, artfulness, or hope of gain. It was the pure thing. They were so trusting, so dupable, so unsophisticated, so expectant of good things to come. It was being misspent on a mythical figure and coincidentally, an impostor to boot.

On the other hand, was there an element of self-induced deception? Did these children want an entity like Santa Claus? Didn't everyone, big or small, want to have some hero, some figure who was all good, supreme, sublime, omniscient, loving, kind, and giving? Like a God?

Oh, hell! Here I was in the midst of one of the most beautiful sensations of my life and I was having a long, seasoned, debate with myself. The aura and milieu of one of the most emotionally stimulating and stirring moments I had ever experienced, was still hot in my soul and I was philosophizing. Leave it for another day, place, and time. Tonight was for the children ... if I could cope. Where the hell was Al?

"Does Santa want a drink?" asked Audrey.

"Boy—and how!" I responded. "Where did Al get to?"

"Went to the washroom I think," volunteered Phil, who gave me a signal indicating that Al had been visibly upset.

Audrey went to the washroom door and quietly asked if the Elf would like a drink.

"I'll be with you guys in a minute ... yes, I would like a drink," came a strangely muffled response. Maybe Al was catching a cold.

"It was so good of you to come, Harold, and Al. The children loved it. Are you going to other homes?" asked Phil.

"Here's your drink, Harold. I'll sit Al here ... if he ever shows up," Audrey giggled.

It was at that moment that I first realized that Santa has great difficulty drinking with his beard on. This situation was to crop up, again and again, over many years. I didn't want to move the beard. It was on just right. The fact is, that I could not drink with the beard on, period. Audrey saw my dilemma. She went to the kitchen drawer and pulled out a straw. Eureka, that was the solution!

Just as that knotty problem was being solved, Al showed up.

"Jeez, guys, I'm sorry," he said sheepishly. "I just got so wound up in the beauty of that scene that I guess I broke down, a bit."

"A bit ... you old softy," said Audrey, solicitously. "You're a darling, it's no shame to be emotional and capable of showing it. Come here, sit next to me."

"Where do you go next?" asked Phil.

"Well, it's getting a bit late, isn't it?" I asked. I had left my watch at home.

"It's only ten after eight," replied Audrey. "Why don't you go to the Tanner's next door, the Nishio's live down the block, and there's the ... ."

"Whoa there, Audrey," I cried. "That's enough! We'll be up all night otherwise."

Having visited three more homes, where we were warmly welcomed and where, as in the first instance, Al and I experienced those widely swinging and heightened emotions, we decided to stop the car and cogitate.

"Hal, I think that we might be getting a bit late to visit many other places but there is one place which I would very much like to go. Do you feel up to it?" Al asked considerately.

"I guess I am if you are, Al. What have you got in mind?"

"I'd like to go to the Baptist Mission School. You know that I spend a lot of time there, helping where I can ... I'm sure that they will be cordial. What say?"

"Oh Al, what a wonderful idea. Darn, I wish that we had thought about it sooner. There are twenty or thirty children there, aren't there?" I asked.

"Thirty-three, to be exact," replied Al.

For reasons known only to Al, he had involved a lot of his free time and money in the Mission. Many of the children were orphaned or discarded. Many had never known any other home than the Mission.

I had some reservations about going there. My emotions were already over stimulated by seldom experienced reactions. I was learning about a new me. I had kept these particular emotions in constant check during most of my life. Tonight they were all bubbling out in one session. I had been raised to believe that "females" show their emotions. Men do not.

Now here I was, voluntarily exposing myself to situations which dredged up long-capped reactions. I was experiencing wonderous sensations about humanity in its finest moment.

I was having trouble governing an open display of how I felt. Al had abandoned any pretext on that score, whatsoever.

As we entered the Mission we were met by a lady who introduced herself as the "Resident Supervisor." She knew Al by sight and greeted him in a warm, if restrained, manner. I do not now remember her name, but thank God there are people like her in the world of the innocents. She was thrilled that Santa would think to visit this cold, neglected, depressing, foreboding place.

"How kind and thoughtful of you to think of our children here, Santa. Most people don't want to acknowledge that a place like ours exists. It's tragic, but many turn their back on us and our wards. It's not that they mean to be unkind. It's just that they don't want to admit that such a place, with such a need, subsists in this day and age. I suppose that we, in some way, detract from their being able to totally enjoy their own lives. Is that being selfish or am I being critical?" she asked almost rhetorically.

I liked this lady immediately. She used the plural. She considered herself to be an integral part of this dismal place and the rejection which it attracted.

"It's a bit late, but the children will love to know that they have not been totally forgotten—that they, too, have a Santa." She gestured in the direction of two large, swinging doors. I assumed that they led into a dormitory. "Forgive me, I almost said, 'be quiet please' ... talk about becoming a creature of habit," she said, displaying a tired smile.

"God, how I wish that we had brought something which we could leave behind for your charges. I feel that we will tantalize these wretched children by playing a partial role only," I said.

"Mr. Hine," she replied, "you will leave behind the one thing that these children all need so badly ... the one thing which they have been deprived of so selfishly ... that is, a display of love, some tangible evidence that someone does in fact care about them. That is what they need. They often need caring more than they need material things. No, Mr. Hine, you will not just tantalize them, you will leave behind— for each of them individually—a possession without which no one can survive for long ... love and the willingness to share it,

140

without any thought of compensation, other than the return thereof."

Oh, boy, that was too much for me. Tears cascaded down my soggy beard like a waterfall. Al was huddled against the door jamb, gasping. Could we now go through with this? I felt that my emotions were now so undermined with truisms that I was developing a mounting resistance to the deceptions of this charade. This had started out as a harmless caper for my own children. How could I continue to subject myself to this visceral wrenching and at the same time feel good about it? There had to be a comminglement, a fusion of those various emotional resources. Boy! The human mind is a conundrum.

"Come this way gentlemen," interjected the lady. "We'll see the younger ones first."

She led us down a short passageway, then through two swinging doors. She turned on the lights and sang out in a motherly, melodious voice, "Wake up children, look who is here. Wake up now, he can't stay very long."

She picked up a child of about three or four years of age. The child rubbed sleep out of her eyes. She peered at Santa, then rubbed again; she peered, disbelievingly. She turned her head into the neck of the lady and cuddled up closely. She wrapped her arms about the supervisor's neck then pulled her legs up in to the fetal position. Slowly she turned her jaw, so that her head turned slightly. She looked cautiously around the curve of her mentor's neck. She again rubbed her eyes. Then I saw her other eye, as she turned her head partially to stare at this clown in red.

"Santa?" she whispered. "Santa Craus?" she questioned.

"Yes dear, it is Santa Claus, not 'Craus,' he has come to see you and the others. This is Christmas Eve. Someday, God willing, you will know what that is really supposed to mean," said the supervisor.

The "others," to whom she referred, were now stirring and making gestures to be picked up, protected, or otherwise attended to.

"Santa," was the universal cry.

"Santa, come over here," they cried in unison.

Slowly some of them got up from their beds. They went to the supervisor and clamored around her legs. Some crawled, too young, yet, to walk. Some made their way to my legs, which strangely felt like jelly. Others made their way to that strange elf who was semi-reclining on the floor, leaning up against one of the metal, double bunks. His arms were full of little, wiggling bodies; his eyes full of tears.

After what was probably only four or five minutes, but which felt like hours of tortuous mental anguish, we separated ourselves from these beautiful children. "Separated" is not the correct word. "Pried" ourselves away is more precise. Some of those tiny fingers refused to let go of "their Santa."

Once out into the comparative sanctuary of the corridor again, I had serious misgivings about going back into what I fully expected would be another emotional tempest. I was trembling with indelible, cloying, trauma.

"I guess I've learned a lot about myself tonight," I said to the supervisor. "I don't know that I can cope with any more of this, although it would probably be inappropriate not to see the others, now that we have commenced this scenario?"

"I'm sure that you are only being rhetorical, Mr. Hine. I understand why, of course, but not to continue to see the older children would be taken, by them, as another rejection of the worst kind," she said emphatically.

"Of course, that's true," I replied. "Are you ready Al?"

"As ready as I'm ever going to be, Hal," he said bravely, under the circumstances.

We played our roles for the children, ages seven to ten. As wards reached the age of eleven, they were sent out to another Mission, in Edmonton, I believe. They moved on to higher education "outside."

The scene with these older children was virtually a repeat of that experienced with the the younger ones. The same disbelief. The eyes which bespoke of a fleeting hope that there might be relief from anonymity. The shyness and the reticence, which is so often exhibited by people of all ages who have been the subject of gratuitous maltreatment and rejection without understandable cause.

There was one youngster who impressed me so much that the memory of the event is crystal clear in my mind, even to this day. He refused to rise from his reclined position. He merely extended his arm and stared up from his bed. When I took his hand he grasped it and would not let go. Gradually, he moved his hand onto the furry sleeve and stroked it in such a way as to make me think that he was recalling the touch of another garment, worn by someone in his bittersweet memory.

Once out into the car, both Al and I sat in silence for a long time. Neither of us seemed eager to leave. We were certainly

In most communities the mayor is the chief magistrate. The statutes (ordinances in the Yukon) which create the communities, almost invariably makes such provision. Ergo, Gordon H. Armstrong was a magistrate. He was the mayor of the city of Whitehorse.

Urgent phone calls were placed. The mayor was still abed. Get him up! It's essential that he be at the RCMP detachment office within the hour!

Fred's belongings were collected from the hotel and his bill paid. At 9 a.m. a sad lot were seen to gather at the detachment. The senior NCO paraded the prisoner before His Honor, Magistrate Armstrong. There was reluctance on the part of that NCO. He sensed that there was something irregular about these proceedings but he, too, had become familiar with the fact that the mayor, in the numerous areas in which he had been posted, was the chief magistrate.

Fred stood and faced his compatriot of yesterday. The prosecutor read the charges. The magistrate, who was not in any way familiar with such proceedings, asked what it was that he should do. The prosecutor counselled the magistrate, while Fred sagged and constantly checked his watch.

"Released on your own recognizance," pronounced the mayor. "Now let's get out to the car and get you up to that bloody plane."

The three perpetrators of this peculiar event rushed off in the prosecutor's car. Fred boarded the plane. It was taxiing to the runway in preparation for takeoff when a police car, with lights flashing, drove up to the terminal building. The roar of the plane's engines almost drowned out the NCO's yelling at the mayor and the prosecutor. He had checked into the ordinance which established Whitehorse as a city. The goddamn mayor was not the goddamn chief magistrate. The two of them had just shanghaied one of his prisoners, illegally! Goddamnit!

Chapter Fourteen

At Christmas time across the land,
The hearts of many change,
From work a day, exhausted, bored
To a more emotive range.

That little man, in beard and suit
Bright red and trimmed with fur,
Brings out the better side of man
Good will to all assured.

And yet a wistful soul still cries,
To do this once per year
Has hollow mockery at its base,
No constant views adhere.

The Great Santa Claus Saga

What happened on the eve of Christmas, 1953, started out as a private, family prank. It has repeated itself, in one form or another, for thirty-two consecutive years thereafter. The nature of the event has always been of the same intent. Only the number of persons involved and the varying locations comprise the changes in the format.

During Christmas Eve day, I had been conducting the conclusion to a long, demanding, civil trial before Mr. Justice Jack Gibben. My opponent counsel, "my learned friend," was Allan Bate. He was then, and is now, a well-respected lawyer, with a wealth of experience. He and I had gone to law school together and had formed a strong bond of friendship. Al was single and there were no special women in his life at that time. He was tall, maybe six feet two inches in height. He was well-built, not powerfully but staunchly. He was a bit gangly because of his size and lack of weight. His dark hair was always combed but it would not stay in place. It forever draped across the left side of his forehead. He was handsome, in a sad way. He smiled reluctantly, even passively. Only when Al got out with peers on a party, did he seem to become spontaneously animated. Other times he was somewhat discontented.

The judge, the court staff, the registry employees, the court reporter, Wynn Clarke, and all others involved in the court system, were eager to hear the end of the summations being made by me and Al. There was a party planned following the hearing. We were cutting into that precious time frame. Everyone, including the respective counsel, wanted to terminate the serious and get on with the festive. I'm not positive, but when the last word was said by counsel, I think I heard a faint cheer go up from outside those venerated, forensic walls. Mr. Justice Gibben, in his constant, dignified manner, thanked both counsel for the assistance which he was sure he would receive from our submissions, then adjourned court for the holidays. Then I was certain that I heard an anonymous chorus of cheers.

Within moments, long before Al and I had changed from gowns to street attire, the law library was full of people. That place had been chosen for the festivities for several reasons. It contained a large, elongated table, it was completely segregated from the rest of the federal building and it was next door to the washrooms.

A polyglot crew was in attendance: the sheriff, Robert (Bob) Friend; his deputy Cece Moser; the commissioner; the omnipresent mayor; the registrar of the court; all of the local lawyers; representatives of the military; and some clergymen.

As the group swelled, the party took on new dimensions, nuances, colors, and flavors. The strict adherence to recognition of the distinctive divisions of government, together with the usual reserve arising from the categorized identity of the "forces" and the rank involved therein, soon disappeared in the font of camaraderie, fellowship, and seasonal diplomacy.

As much as I was enjoying the party, I realized that I must break away and assume a familial role. My immediate responsibility was to Laura and the children, who waited at home. They were waiting impatiently for the arrival of "Old Saint Nick." Laura or, "the Big Chief," as she was known affectionately by many, had given Al and I direct orders that morning, to "get home early." She wanted to get the children (ages six and three) to bed at a reasonable hour. They would be up at 5 or 6 a.m., possessed by curiosity and full of anxiety. They needed their sleep.

Al, being a bachelor, had been invited by Laura to spend Christmas Eve and Christmas dinner with us. Without knowing what it was that he might be in for, he had accepted.

"Al, do you think that we should slide out of here, while we still have the ability to navigate," I suggested. "The kids will go to bed early so we can, if you want, go out and do some visiting after that, or you can stay now and I'll pick you up later."

"Jeez, Hal ... Oh, boy! Am I in trouble ... God! How could I be so damn thoughtless, so stupid?"

"Whoa, Al, hold on. What are you talking about? Don't get so worked up. Did you forget to call some gal?" I asked, giving him a friendly punch on the shoulder. "Did you overlook that delicious little school teacher?" (I had seen him out with a real cutie some weeks before, but never teased him about it. He was a bit shy where girls were concerned, that's probably why he was still a bachelor).

"No, Hal, it's much worse than that, this is serious. Oh, God! How could I? I forgot to get presents for your kids. Damn!"

As much as I knew that the children would be truly disappointed if their favorite Uncle Al failed to bring them a gift, I also knew that the same Uncle Al would suffer about it far more than they would.

"Well, all the stores are closed now. There's not much that we can do about it," I said.

"What about Rolfe Hougen, he's single, maybe he would come down and open up his department store for me. What do you think?" Al offered.

"Yeah, he just might. Let's call the store, he may still be there. If not, we can call his home," I suggested.

I caught Rolfe at the store. He had been taking a "breather," as he called it. I called it an after work drink. He had been exceptionally busy in his store. It was a popular place to shop for the entire community. Rolfe and his mother together with his younger brother "Blondie" were responsible for the management of the store. Rolfe was the moving force therein.

"Sure thing, come on over, bring that big oaf with you. I still have some toys and Christmasy items left. There aren't as many here now as there were recently. That'll cut down the period of agony and indecision," Rolfe said, laughing about one of Al's noticeable quirks.

Rolfe responded to the bell, which we rang as we arrived at the front door of the store. The main lights were out. He soon had the interior ablaze with neon lights and occulting tree bulbs. Tinsel and other decorations hung everywhere.

"Do you guys want a bit of good cheer?" asked Rolfe as we went into his private office.

"Great idea, Rolfe, you and I could have one while Al does his shopping," I said with a wink.

"To hell with that," said Al, "that invitation was for all of us, eh, Rolfe?" cried Al.

"Yeah, what both of you guys need right now is another drink, like another hole in the head. What a couple of jokers. Where have you been, at the judicial blast?" asked Rolfe.

"I didn't realize that the party had taken on the status of having a formal title," said Al. "Must remember that."

"OK, Al," said Rolfe as he handed each of us our respective drinks. "You come with me. I'll show you what we have left and give you prices. I suppose you want the discounts, too, even if it is after the sale has terminated," joshed Rolfe.

"Bloody right, man! I'm probably buying stuff that nobody wanted and that's why it's still here ... eh, Hal?" asked Al. He followed by putting an arm around Rolfe and laughing, "OK, Rolfe, let's go and get'um."

I headed to the doorway slightly behind them. I had no clear intent. I was merely wandering while sipping my drink. My attention was attracted to a large cardboard box which was tucked to the side, just outside Rolfe's office door. What had caught my eye was a flash of red, trimmed by white fur. It might be a Santa Claus suit. When I lifted the top, my suspicions were confirmed.

Maybe it was the drinks. Maybe it was because Rolfe was a friend and I, therefore, felt at liberty to try on the suit. Maybe it was fate. I'll never know the true answer, if there is one. In any event, I removed my top coat and suit jacket then put on the jacket of the Santa Claus costume. It wasn't a good, nor proper fit, but it felt good. Before I knew it, I had donned the entire outfit and was making with the "HO ... HO ... HO's."

The costume was replete with fur trimmed black leather boots, a black leather belt, from which dangled little silver bells, and a luxuriant white beard. The beard had an elastic attached at each side which went up over my ears then around my head. The substance of which the beard was made tickled my face and ears. A droopy mustache attached to the beard sent little hairs up my nostrils, giving me a tendency to want to sneeze. The precarious angle at which the elastic encompassed my head, was made more secure by the white wig, which was just a tad tight for my skull. This particular wig came down over my forehead, then applied itself, like a beanie, from there to the nape of my neck. The white tresses were shoulder length. There was no mirror, but if I looked as good as I felt, I had to be a reasonable facsimile of good old Saint Nick himself.

Succumbing to the ham in me, I picked up my drink and wandered off to find Rolfe and Al. When they saw me they burst out laughing and made rude comments about "the shortest Santa in captivity" and "you certainly don't need any padding there, Hine."

"OK, you guys, enough of the insults. With Rolfe's permission I may play one of me better roles tonight. What say, Rolfe, may I borrow this until tomorrow?"

"Going home to surprise the kids, eh?" asked Rolfe. "Sure, Harold, keep it until after the holidays are over. No need for it until next year, anyway. Hope you get good use out of it. Have fun, and a Merry Christmas to both of you guys and to your families."

"Thanks, Rolfe, I'll just do that. I'll take good care of it. I'll bring it back day after Boxing Day," I said.

"Don't worry about it—I won't. Have fun," Rolfe responded.

"OK Al, let's get out of here. What have you bought?" I asked.

"You are going to love this little item," Al said, as he pulled a small drum off of the counter and started to beat it with sticks which looked like toothpicks in his large hands.

"Yikes! Laura is going to kill you for sure, Al. She's going to have to listen to that being pounded all day long. I don't envy you her reaction Al, but get it if you must," I cajoled.

"I must!" Al insisted, as he thrust it into a large paper bag which Rolfe had supplied. "I'm not going to show you the rest of the things, Hal—you're a party pooper," he said feigning annoyance.

One could always tell when Al was starting to feel his drinks. He lost the facade of the big city attorney and became the big, loveable, teddy bear that he really was.

Al and I tried to sneak into my house through the back door. We were being "as quiet as little mice." Suddenly, the door flew open and there stood Laura, wrists on hips and with a mimicked hostility.

"It's about time you two jokers got here. Where on earth did you get that outfit, Harold? It looks great! Come on in, I want to see the reaction of the children," she said.

"Who are you calling Harold, madam," I insisted. "My name is Santa Claus."

"Yeah, and mine is going to be Lizzie Borden, if you don't get in here before the children get too tired waiting and go to sleep on me," Laura retorted.

Al had been standing directly behind me, holding that ominous huge, paper bag. He stepped (maybe staggered) forward and proferred the bag to Laura. "It's for the kids, nothing's wrapped. Could you do that for me, please?" he said shyly, even though we three had been well-acquainted for at least eight years.

"Al, you dear man, of course I'll wrap them for you ... whatever 'they' are."

"It's just a few things for you, this guy, and the kids. You'll be able to figure out which is which," he said.

"I'm sure that I will be able to figure them out, but where are you going that you won't be able to tell me yourself. Are you going out again?" Laura asked suspiciously.

"Well, I thought ... that is, Hal thought ... that we should go and visit some of the families we know which have children. I'm sure that they would love the idea of having Santa drop in on them, like a private Santa. Hal can jolly up the children, tell them about the reindeer, the sleigh, the gifts, the elves, and things like that. I think it is a great idea," Al said most seriously.

"Sure, and getting the children all excited, so that they won't go to bed or to sleep. It's truly a lovely idea and a charitable thought Al, but you two guys are already half smashed. What will you be like after visiting a few of your pals?" Laura mused aloud.

"Well, let's try it on our kids, and see what happens," I said.

"Let's try it on our kids, then talk about it further," said Laura, as she led the way into the bedroom where our daughter and her younger brother were already in bed, where they had been waiting for Daddy and Uncle Al.

Cathy had just turned six years of age on her recent birthday, which was December 3. She had long, reddish hued hair and the lovely complexion which usually goes with red hair. She was bright, healthy, and athletic. She was above average intelligence for her age and loved going to school with Wade Jorde, another six year old, who lived across the street. We had got to the point where we said that Cathy was "six going on sixteen."

Art, on the other hand, who was just three years of age, was more interested in music and being cuddled, either by his mummy or by Cathy. One might doubt that Cathy had a true mother complex for Art when one hears that she had put Art into the Bendix combination washer/dryer machine, then turned it on. Art would have been wrinkled and dizzy if Laura hadn't investigated the cause of the sound, just as the machine got started.

I suppose I should list "curiosity" as one of Cathy's characteristics, as well.

Laura opened the bedroom door and peeked in. She found that the children were, or appeared to be asleep, so she waved Santa into the room. As I entered, I flicked on a wall switch which controlled a small table lamp. The lamp went on, but the little darlings did not move a muscle. Art, as he so often did when he was tense, had crawled into Cathy's bed. Somewhat abashed by their lack of attention, I let go with a loud "HO HO HO."

In a most matter of fact way, Cathy sat up and surveyed this ersatz Santa. Art, as usual, copied her every move. Both sat there in bed, supported by their arms behind them, and blinked.

"Daddy what are you doing in that funny outfit?" inquired Cathy.

"Daddy look silly," said Art.

"What do you mean 'Daddy'? Don't you two know the real Santa, when you see him?" I inquired, using a put-on voice.

"Daddy, you are funny," said Cathy, as she and Art started to giggle. Each encouraged the other. Before we realized what had happened, the three adults were caught up in the humor

134

of the moment. We, too, were laughing with the children. It was a delightful moment.

"OK, you guys, just see if Santa brings you any toys tonight. You've hurt Santa's feelings now, so he's going to leave and take his toys back to the North Pole," Santa pouted.

At this sobering suggestion, Cathy flew out of bed, closely followed by her shadow, Art. She wrapped her arms around Santa's legs in a big hug. Art fought to find space enough for his hug too. I picked both of them up and carried them out into the living room, where we all fell into a heap on the chesterfield. Hugs and kisses abounded. Cathy investigated the beard, the wig, and the suit. Art checked out that which was nearer to his level, the boots. Then we snuggled for a few precious moments.

"OK, you chillun's, time for bed. Maybe the real Santa will show up tonight. Give Daddy another hug, then one for Uncle Al, then off to bed, quickly now," said the Big Chief.

"Goodnight, Daddy Santa," called Cathy as she pulled the covers over her head and started to giggle loudly. Of course, Art had to emulate Cathy's every move, so they were at it again.

"Thanks a lot you two," said Laura as she joined Al and me after trying, unsuccessfully, to get the children settled down. "I knew what would happen if you went in there wearing that outfit. I don't think Cathy was a believer and possibly she had told Art that there was no real Santa. Now there will be no doubt in either mind, and now you want to go around town doing the same thing to other families?"

"Well, it won't be the same thing, the other children won't know me intimately enough to see through this disguise. Anyway, they really did get a lot of pleasure out of Santa's visit didn't they? Did you ever hear such artless, carefree laughter?" I asked.

"I had to go into the living room," said Al. "I knew, that if I once got started laughing with them, I would be a basket case. A child's laughter is so guileless, spontaneous, and innocent, it becomes completely contagious to me. I'm never certain, at the time, whether I'm going to laugh with them or cry with the beauty of it all."

"You're such a big softy, Al," said Laura. She went over and gave his arm a hug.

"Well, I've decided, I'm going out to visit the children of our friends. Are you with me, Al?" I solicited.

"Well, I've gone this far with you Hal, might as well keep going. Somebody has to look after you," replied Al.

"Now there is a real case of the blind leading the blind," offered Laura.

"Should we have one more for the road, Al?" I asked.

"No you don't, you guys have had enough. If you're going, get, otherwise you won't be home 'til midnight. Scoot, get going. You'll probably be 'forced' to have a few while you're out. Try to get back early, and I mean tonight, not early tomorrow, OK?" Laura insisted.

"Jeez, Hal, what a witch you married. Now you know why I stayed single," teased Al as he and I headed for the door.

Laura held the door open for us and kissed us both good-bye. We didn't know it then, but we were off on an adventure that many of the "oldtimers" from the Yukon still talk about whenever they get together at Christmas time.

Stopping at the first home which we had selected for Santa's visit, I knocked on the door with some trepidation. Christmas Eve is, after all, an evening which is set aside for a quiet gathering of family members. Particularly, this is so if there are youngsters involved.

I was not at all prepared for the reaction which I received when Audrey opened the door.

She stood there for a moment or two, just staring. Then she cried, "It's Santa Claus! Look it really is Santa, and his helper. Come on in. Pretty big to be an elf, isn't he? Come on in, Al ... is that the name of your helper Santa? Look Phil, it's Santa!"

Phil Iverson who was a pilot for CP Air, was also a law student in our office. Audrey was his beautiful wife. She was a very practical lady. She was exactly the right woman for Phil, and was truly his helpmate. Audrey was a good and loving mother to their two young boys. Phil was industrious and ambitious. Not long after he was admitted to the Bar he was killed in a flying accident near Anchorage, Alaska.

Audrey led us into the living room, then placed her head against the window and asked, "Where are your reindeer, Santa?" Without waiting for an answer she turned and joined us. I assumed, correctly, that their sons were still awake and what might have appeared to be a rhetorical question was, in reality, being overheard by the children.

"I left them up on the airstrip," I responded. "Al, here met me and said that he knew of some children who had been good and he wanted me to meet them. Are there two children in this house who have been good, and who might like to meet me?" I asked in a stage voice.

"They're down this way, Santa," said Phil, "they're probably asleep, but you can look in on them." He shook his head in the negative and smiled, all the while he was saying this.

I poked my head into the room. Phil turned the lights on and two young heads bobbed up from the pillows. The light bothered their eyes but they were otherwise wide awake.

"Come out and say hello to Santa, dears," said Audrey.

The children didn't move. In fact, they were a bit retiring. This apparition in the red suit appeared to overwhelm them. I waited, patiently, for them to make up their minds about me.

"What is it that you want for Christmas?" I asked the youngest one.

"A bike," he responded immediately.

"And what about you?" I asked the older of the two.

"I want a bike too," he declared.

I looked outside the room and saw Audrey nod to me in the affirmative.

"Well, I've heard that you have both been very good this year, so maybe ... maybe ... you'll get your wish."

Like a flash they were out of their beds and standing beside me. Each took one hand and stood looking up at me with those trusting, believing eyes. Al turned about and smartly left the area. Suddenly, I felt like I should be somewhere else, also. My eyes brimmed with tears. Santa doesn't cry—does he? I smiled, weakly, trusting that the beard, bushy eyebrows, and makeup, which Laura had applied, would guard against letting them realize my emotions at that moment. I didn't want the parents to know either.

"Would you like to see my model airplane, Santa?" asked the oldest boy.

"No, come and see my rock collection," cried the younger one, who pulled me in the opposite direction.

An obvious, instant bond of affection had been established based purely upon tradition and the mythical personality of Santa Claus. They were offering warm reception and unadulterated love to this character in the red suit whom they believed to be the real thing. They were so vulnerable, adoring and trusting that it bothered me. I felt inadequate, unable to respond properly because I wasn't able to assess why my emotions were so bestirred.

"OK, OK, that's enough now, Santa has many places to visit. We can't keep him here all night," said Phil. "Give Santa a hug, then jump into bed."

Each in turn gave me a warm, loving hug. Each in turn said, "Goodnight, Santa" in such a touching manner that I felt sure that I would not be able to contain myself.

What had I got myself into? These children pulled at my heartstrings. My throat hurt, tears brimmed in my eyes. They loved innocently, without schemes, artfulness, or hope of gain. It was the pure thing. They were so trusting, so dupable, so unsophisticated, so expectant of good things to come. It was being misspent on a mythical figure and coincidentally, an impostor to boot.

On the other hand, was there an element of self-induced deception? Did these children want an entity like Santa Claus? Didn't everyone, big or small, want to have some hero, some figure who was all good, supreme, sublime, omniscient, loving, kind, and giving? Like a God?

Oh, hell! Here I was in the midst of one of the most beautiful sensations of my life and I was having a long, seasoned, debate with myself. The aura and milieu of one of the most emotionally stimulating and stirring moments I had ever experienced, was still hot in my soul and I was philosophizing. Leave it for another day, place, and time. Tonight was for the children ... if I could cope. Where the hell was Al?

"Does Santa want a drink?" asked Audrey.

"Boy—and how!" I responded. "Where did Al get to?"

"Went to the washroom I think," volunteered Phil, who gave me a signal indicating that Al had been visibly upset.

Audrey went to the washroom door and quietly asked if the Elf would like a drink.

"I'll be with you guys in a minute ... yes, I would like a drink," came a strangely muffled response. Maybe Al was catching a cold.

"It was so good of you to come, Harold, and Al. The children loved it. Are you going to other homes?" asked Phil.

"Here's your drink, Harold. I'll sit Al here ... if he ever shows up," Audrey giggled.

It was at that moment that I first realized that Santa has great difficulty drinking with his beard on. This situation was to crop up, again and again, over many years. I didn't want to move the beard. It was on just right. The fact is, that I could not drink with the beard on, period. Audrey saw my dilemma. She went to the kitchen drawer and pulled out a straw. Eureka, that was the solution!

Just as that knotty problem was being solved, Al showed up.

"Jeez, guys, I'm sorry," he said sheepishly. "I just got so wound up in the beauty of that scene that I guess I broke down, a bit."

"A bit ... you old softy," said Audrey, solicitously. "You're a darling, it's no shame to be emotional and capable of showing it. Come here, sit next to me."

"Where do you go next?" asked Phil.

"Well, it's getting a bit late, isn't it?" I asked. I had left my watch at home.

"It's only ten after eight," replied Audrey. "Why don't you go to the Tanner's next door, the Nishio's live down the block, and there's the ... ."

"Whoa there, Audrey," I cried. "That's enough! We'll be up all night otherwise."

Having visited three more homes, where we were warmly welcomed and where, as in the first instance, Al and I experienced those widely swinging and heightened emotions, we decided to stop the car and cogitate.

"Hal, I think that we might be getting a bit late to visit many other places but there is one place which I would very much like to go. Do you feel up to it?" Al asked considerately.

"I guess I am if you are, Al. What have you got in mind?"

"I'd like to go to the Baptist Mission School. You know that I spend a lot of time there, helping where I can ... I'm sure that they will be cordial. What say?"

"Oh Al, what a wonderful idea. Darn, I wish that we had thought about it sooner. There are twenty or thirty children there, aren't there?" I asked.

"Thirty-three, to be exact," replied Al.

For reasons known only to Al, he had involved a lot of his free time and money in the Mission. Many of the children were orphaned or discarded. Many had never known any other home than the Mission.

I had some reservations about going there. My emotions were already over stimulated by seldom experienced reactions. I was learning about a new me. I had kept these particular emotions in constant check during most of my life. Tonight they were all bubbling out in one session. I had been raised to believe that "females" show their emotions. Men do not.

139

Now here I was, voluntarily exposing myself to situations which dredged up long-capped reactions. I was experiencing wonderous sensations about humanity in its finest moment.

I was having trouble governing an open display of how I felt. Al had abandoned any pretext on that score, whatsoever.

As we entered the Mission we were met by a lady who introduced herself as the "Resident Supervisor." She knew Al by sight and greeted him in a warm, if restrained, manner. I do not now remember her name, but thank God there are people like her in the world of the innocents. She was thrilled that Santa would think to visit this cold, neglected, depressing, foreboding place.

"How kind and thoughtful of you to think of our children here, Santa. Most people don't want to acknowledge that a place like ours exists. It's tragic, but many turn their back on us and our wards. It's not that they mean to be unkind. It's just that they don't want to admit that such a place, with such a need, subsists in this day and age. I suppose that we, in some way, detract from their being able to totally enjoy their own lives. Is that being selfish or am I being critical?" she asked almost rhetorically.

I liked this lady immediately. She used the plural. She considered herself to be an integral part of this dismal place and the rejection which it attracted.

"It's a bit late, but the children will love to know that they have not been totally forgotten—that they, too, have a Santa." She gestured in the direction of two large, swinging doors. I assumed that they led into a dormitory. "Forgive me, I almost said, 'be quiet please' ... talk about becoming a creature of habit," she said, displaying a tired smile.

"God, how I wish that we had brought something which we could leave behind for your charges. I feel that we will tantalize these wretched children by playing a partial role only," I said.

"Mr. Hine," she replied, "you will leave behind the one thing that these children all need so badly ... the one thing which they have been deprived of so selfishly ... that is, a display of love, some tangible evidence that someone does in fact care about them. That is what they need. They often need caring more than they need material things. No, Mr. Hine, you will not just tantalize them, you will leave behind— for each of them individually—a possession without which no one can survive for long ... love and the willingness to share it,

140

without objectives or directions at that moment. Our thoughts were kaleidoscopic and not ready to be articulated.

Moments passed before Al said, "Hal, there is no way that I am ready to go to your house just yet. What say to a drink at the tourist's bar?"

"Great idea, Al," I said. "I have to change the taste in my mouth, all I taste is salt."

"Wow! What an experience. I don't know yet how I feel, exactly. I don't know if I want to repeat this adventure or not. Time will tell, I guess," Al responded.

"Well, Al, I have come to one definite conclusion, as a result of tonight's escapade. On balance, I think that I feel better about having played Santa than I feel emotionally drained by the experience. I intend, with your continued help and the help of others, to set up an annual Santa Claus Committee. We can gather the names of the needy, get food, presents, and whatever else appears to be appropriate. We can do a 'Santa Flight' every year. We can do it not only for the children, but for any others who are in need of love and attention; even if only for that one day. I'm confident that we can get others interested in the idea. What do you think about that proposal?" I asked enthusiastically.

"I'm all for it, Hal ... count me in. It's a great idea," said Al, as he proferred his hand to bind the deal.

Such was the beginning of an annual event in which I have been involved, in the role of Santa Claus, for the past thirty-three consecutive years. My children and their spouses are now eager participants. Many people, some unknown to me, join the "flight" each year. The transposition from Whitehorse to the lower mainland has not interrupted the "flights." Each year I have heard myself say, "This is the last year." Maybe next year will be.

Chapter Fifteen

It's New Year's Eve and auld lang syne
For police, like all the rest,
So take them up some real champagne
And wish them all the best.

The trouble was, we got involved,
In contests athletic
And when perchance the phone did ring
The results were quite pathetic.

Wrong Answering Service

On New Year's Eve day in 1954 I advanced a proposal to my friend Allan Bate. You remember him from the Great Santa Claus Caper.

"Al, what do you think about buying a case of champagne and taking it over to the RCMP detachment barracks? There are a lot of the younger constables who are new here. They probably would appreciate having a bit of a party. You and I deal with them quite a bit, so we could wish those whom we know a Happy New Year and meet those whom we don't yet know. What do you say?" I asked.

"Great idea, Hal. I don't have to be at the party I'm attending at any specific time. I'm invited to show up before midnight, that's all. What about you and Laura?" he replied.

"Well, we have a party planned up at the Air Force Officer's Mess but, like you, there is no fixed time. Let's do it, are you available now?"

"Sure, I'll leave my car here at the courthouse. We can have the 'do' with the police, then you could drop me back here on your way home, OK?" said Al.

In no time, Al and I had gone to the liquor vendor's, picked up a case of domestic champagne, (nothing cheap about us) and driven to the RCMP barracks.

The barracks were located on Fourth Avenue, south of Main Street. The building was glaring white with red or orange trim. Whatever the color, it was a ghastly combination. The detachment personnel who were single were housed in the upper portion. The lower floor was used for administrative purposes. The cells were also on this floor. Upon entering the premises one encountered to the left, a counter behind which "the watch" would perform their duties. The counter had a section which lifted up to permit a person to pass through. That section would then be returned to its resting place to complete the continuity of the counter top.

The duty watch, which was not out on the streets, would be housed behind the counter. They could answer the telephone from their various desks there. They could also look directly into the cells to keep an eye on any prisoners who might be languishing there.

When Al and I arrived we went through the doorway described. We were greeted by an individual whom neither of us recognized. We took him to be the janitor who had started the New Year celebrations a bit early. We greeted one another in the fashion of the season. Following the salutations, Al and I passed through the administrative section and went up a flight of stairs which led to the living quarters. It housed mostly constables but a few NCO's stayed in the barracks as well. There was a door at the top of the stairs. Since Al was carrying the champagne, I knocked on the door.

When it opened we were greeted by a scene of institutional life. There were two rows of metal, double-decked bunks pressed up against the outside walls. There might have been ten feet separating the rows. My recollection is that there were about twenty such bunks on each side of the dormitory. The building had a peaked roof which created downward slanted ceilings. The effect was to make the room appear to be much smaller than it was. It was not well-lighted. The room was full of cigarette smoke and the odor of beer.

There were possibly fifteen or eighteen members present, all in varying degrees of dress. Most wore boots, many wore yellow striped trousers held up by suspenders. Others were in boxer shorts, socks, and no shoes. Some were wearing shirts which were unbuttoned and hanging partly in and partly out of their pants, others were shirtless. The one thing which was uniform was the fact that, without exception, everyone held an opened bottle of beer.

The building was old. I was of the opinion that it might have been constructed prior to the war, yet it had the same styling as wartime structures. The floor in this dorm was wooden, old, stained and showing signs of wear. There were many windows; they were smaller than the regular window, narrower and shorter. They had been inserted into the wall between each set of bunks and a few at each opposite end.

The member who opened the door was a corporal who I knew well. He greeted us in such a loud voice that the attention of most, if not all, of the members present focused on our arrival.

"Hi there, Harold, and Al. Happy New Year! Come on in. What the hell have you got in the box?" cried the corporal.

"It's a gift for you guys," replied Al.

"Yeah? What is it?" asked the corporal.

"It's champagne, you joker. Can't you read?" I teased.

"Champagne! You're kidding ... what the hell ... you are kidding aren't you? Us guys don't drink champagne, we drink beer, eh, guys?" yelled the corporal.

"Yahoo!" cried one of the new recruits.

"Lay some of that stuff on me," shouted another.

In no time the bottles of beer disappeared, not that they were put aside. Everyone drank them down in gulps. It was an unannounced race to see who could empty their respective bottle the fastest.

In just as short a time, the corks from the champagne bottles were popping all over the dorm. Tumblers appeared as if by magic, bubbling liquid effervesced throughout the room. Toasts were endless. Most of the men were not much more than mere youths. At age twenty-nine, I felt like a senior member.

Well, I don't drink much of the bubbly myself so I'm no expert on the subject, but I learned that evening that one should not mix beer and champagne. Talk about getting smashed! Some of the members must have laid a foundation before Al and I got there. In no time most of them were loud, boisterous, and having a great time.

Al and I had a few drinks with the troops. I brought along a flask of Canadian Club because my stomach dislikes the acidity of champagne. I don't want to speak callously, but I think Al could drink anything.

We were all having one hell of a great time.

For some reason which I find difficult to explain I always seem to go to, or end up at, parties where displays of physical prowess take place. This party was no exception. Who could do the most consecutive push-ups? Who could stand on his head? His hands? Who could Indian wrestle? Who was the best at arm wrestling? It was endless.

Al, on the other hand was not interested in the athletics. He was more of a conversationalist. A thinker, an inquirer. He engaged some of the members in deep psychological discussions. To each his own!

After several hours of exercising either bodies or tongues, someone came up with an irresistible suggestion. Let's play knights on horseback! For those who do not immediately recognize this game, it is also called horseplay. Usually a lighter person climbs onto the back of a larger, stronger, heavier person. Two teams line up opposite one another. Someone yells "charge" and the two lines engage in combat. The idea is to tear the rider (here read knight) off the back of the "horse," or pull both horse and rider down simultaneously. The last knight and rider left standing wins the game for their side.

Just as an aside, you may find it interesting to learn that on one occasion at the Air Force Officer's Mess this game was in progress, as it so often was. My dear friend, Mr. Justice Gibbens, while playing the role of the knight (which suited his stately personage) was removed from the back of Victor Wylie, the lawyer, with such force that he fell into the fire pit and fractured his toe.

Our particular combat had been going on for possibly an hour. Everyone took turns since there wasn't sufficient room in the dorm for all of us to compete at one time. The place looked as though it had been ransacked and pillaged by the Mongols. The bunks had been turned sideways against the wall. Every piece of furniture had been either stacked in a corner or cast up upon the top bunk. Foot lockers were thrown on to the lower bunks. The walls dripped towels and heavy winter clothing all in disarray. The place looked like a drastic explosion had just occurred.

I had coaxed Al into joining the game. I was riding a large recruit. Al was carrying the corporal. One hell of a battle was going on. Torn shirts, ripped suspenders, scratched backs flowing blood, hair mussed beyond mother's recognition, and all of this intermingled with groans, verbal challenges, and thuds as bodies hit the wooden floor.

Then the door opened. Framed in the doorway was Inspector Steinhauer, the Commanding Officer of the Royal Canadian Mounted Police in the Yukon Territory.

What had been bedlam became a still picture. Have you ever seen a motion picture stopped in full flow? This was it! Bodies slid or fell to the floor as members snapped to attention. Curses in response to the abandonment were stifled by the corporal's repeated calls to "Attention!" Bloody noses just continued to drip as the recruits saw their careers going down the tube. The corporal's shirt, or the remaining shreds of it, hung down from his trouser waist. Even Al and I snapped to attention. It was a spontaneous, copycat action. The air was already rank with the combined odor of smoke, beer, sweat, and champagne. Now it had the additional factor of the stench of fear—total, unmitigated fear.

"Who is in charge here?" demanded the inspector. Then looking over at Al and concentrating upon me, he said, "I don't have to ask who is responsible."

The corporal took a pace forward and said, "I am, SIR!"

The corporal was bleeding from various visible parts of his upper body. Not profusely, but noticeably. The inspector paraded toward him with unflinching, steely eyes.

"I tried to telephone this office for twenty minutes, there was no answer. Finally, when I did get through, a sleepy, drunken voice answered. I came over to investigate. My purpose in trying to telephone this detachment was to pass on my best wishes to the members. The telephone was answered by that individual downstairs. Who is he?" demanded the CO.

There was a dramatic, protracted pause. The corporal seemed to be searching for an answer which would pass muster.

"Is he a short man with a brush cut, and a plaid shirt, Sir?" asked the corporal.

"Yes, that's him. Who is he? Is he a member? If he is, I don't recognize him, at least not in the state he is in ... and if he is, he should not be on duty, he's totally intoxicated. Who is he?" he yelled.

"He's a ... a ... prisoner, Sir," the corporal stammered.

"A PRISONER! A prisoner is answering our telephone!" screamed the inspector.

148

Well, Al and I left just about that time. There may have been a suggestion to that effect. I don't know what happened, exactly, I do know that no one received any disciplinary punishment, not of consequence anyway.

The next morning prior to noon, the commissioner of the Yukon held his annual New Year's Day soiree. Anyone wishing to attend was welcome. It was a matter of duty for some of the "establishment." The military wore their dress uniforms, their ladies added gloves and hats. Civilians wore their best "bib and tucker." Laura and I made a point of attending each year. Being one of the crown prosecutors, it was expected behavior.

During the course of these activities, a giant wearing the dress uniform of an RCMP inspector, backed up to my back and said in a stage whisper heard by all within range, "Hine, no more champagne parties at the barracks, not unless we are forewarned about your arrival. Not only did you create a shambles there but several of the members are not medically or otherwise fit for duty today. Next time you feel like having a party, go some place else ... PLEASE!"

Chapter Sixteen

Silks and jewels, white tie and tails,
Chandeliers and furs,
Shimmering drinks in crystal glass,
At Hamburg opera this occurs.

Chauffeurs and maids and butlers too,
In banker's suits each day,
In racing yachts and limousines,
Was pretty much his way.

Some inner self required much more,
To see the "Last Frontier,"
The animals, too, which still survived
Over "there" but did not, near.

To the Yukon then, a trip was planned,
To see true wilderness,
With wild life, as the quarry sought,
In a different kind of dress.

Cameras only were required,
No blood would shed this way,
Shimmering came from lakes pristine,
And furs were on to stay.

Contrasts

There is a vast difference, culturally and in scenario, between row two, center aisle, of the Hamburg State Opera House, Hamburg, West Germany, and a deserted air strip at Aishihik, Yukon Territory, Canada. However, on one occasion, the elite metropolitan upbringing of a certain individual blended easily and comfortably with the wilderness and its creatures of the north.

Pleasure and entertainment, combined with excitement, created by the happenings occurring in the immediate surroundings were a common factor shared in each event.

It was, however, the contrasts which made each of the events outstanding.

I was on a business trip to Germany, with a client. This particular client was raised among the ultra elite of post war German society. Many, if not all of his friends, were from the same caste. His home was, in fact, a castle. It was within a stone's throw of the huge wire fence which separates West and East Germany. His was an old family, with a well-established business. He and his family had long been accustomed to esoteric pleasures such as hunting, entertaining national and international figures, fast cars, fine dining places, and the opera. Being of hardy stock, they had weathered the war better than most. Being possessed of apparently unending financial resources could have been a major contributing factor.

At one of their wonderous soirees, I was introduced to a young man whom, I was told, was in the printing business. His name is Nicklaus Broschek. Everyone called him "Nikko." He was full of animated curiosity about Canada. His interest centered, primarily, around the wild animals which could still be found in Northern Canada. He decried the fact that because of the uninhibited slaughter of Germany's own wild animals, together with the lack of husbandry in the field, most of the interesting wild animals of Europe were now almost extinct. He referred chiefly to the larger animals, such as the bear, moose, large deer, and other four-legged animals, which had, at one time, been indigenous to Europe. Birds of prey also fascinated him.

He was slight of build, blond, short, and delicate in structure. He was in good trim. He sailed a sloop on the Baltic Sea. One has to be in good shape to go up there. He had a pleasant disposition. Sometimes overly polite but well-intentioned. He was good looking, with a small, clean shaven face. Intense blue eyes pierced out from small oval sockets. His interests ran principally to the arts and cultures. It was because of this that I was surprised to hear him go on, at length, about wilderness and wild animals. It was not until virtually his last sentence that I realized that he was not interested in hunting

151

these animals, he wanted to photograph them in their natural setting.

We arranged to meet for lunch, two days hence. He suggested that we should meet at the Vier Jahreszeiten Hotel in downtown Hamburg. By sheer coincidence, that was the very hotel in which I was staying. He did not seem to be the slightest bit surprised that my clients would "put me up" in that particular hotel. It is considered, amongst hotel habitue, to be amongst the four best hotels in the world.

I support that contention.

While waiting for Nikko to arrive, I sat at a dining room table and watched the patrons of this superb, quintessential restaurant. The tables were spaced in such a way as to insure that the occupants of each table could carry on a private conversation. They could rest assured that what was discussed would remain confidential. Spacious and magnificent were two words which, instantly, sprang to my mind. The silverware was of the finest quality, and in fact, was made of silver. (Like the old dining cars on the railways in Canada, prior to the war.) Each setting was immaculate and precise. The heavy linen cloth under the settings literally sparkled, such was the sheen of the embroidered edges and overall pattern. On the left of the center napkin were located three forks. Each had differing lengths and varying size of tines. On the right of the napkin laid in proper order, with great care and pride, were two knives and two spoons. One was for soup, the other for use in stirring a beverage. The bread dish on the left had laid across it, at exactly the right angle to enable a patron to reach and raise it with ease, a personal butter knife. A real crystal vase, the centerpiece of the table, contained one red carnation. If it could speak, I'm sure that it would brag about the fact that it, as opposed to another, had been chosen to grace a table in the restaurant in this particular hotel.

The waiters (it seemed so inappropriate to refer to these highly-skilled, proud professionals, in such a common term) wore crisp, well and recently pressed, trousers. They wore starched white shirts with flared collars around which was enwrapped a black bow tie. Each wore a vest of a different color, in order to indicate his status or station in the pecking order of the staff. The waitresses wore a black flared skirt over which each wore a ruffled apron tied in the back with a large ostentatious bow. Their respective ranks were likewise displayed by way of the color of the aprons. The maitre d'restaurant stood majestically at the entranceway, effortlessly directing the flow of patrons, waiters, and waitresses. The manner in which he directed the traffic with a flare and courtliness, was of such grandiloquence as would cow any lesser lights who tried to invade his sovereign domain.

One would have to watch one's manners and etiquette under these circumstances. Wouldn't one?

Such were my thoughts when Nikko appeared. He arrived exactly at the appointed time. The muted tones of a carved, marble clock located upon the mantelpiece of the fireplace in the restaurant attested to his punctuality.

"How are you today, Nikko?" I asked, as I rose and extended my hand in greeting.

He shook my hand gently, and remained standing until the maitre d'restaurant pulled back his chair, waited until he stepped in toward the table, and slid the chair under him. Then Nikko sat. One could barely perceive the nod of appreciation which Nikko gave in response to the handling of the chair.

"Just fine, Harold, did you have a good rest? How was your train trip back from the castle last night?" he inquired.

"Most interesting, Nikko," I responded. "I never fail to enjoy that trip from Werra to Hamburg. Not only is the scenery reminiscent of British Columbia's interior, but it has a far older and exciting history to stimulate my thoughts and curiosity. Just surveying the vast continuity of the Russian's fences conjures up horrendous atrocities involving the war and the human suffering on all sides."

"Yes, Harold, I'm sure that to you people from other lands the fence is a great rarity, much like the Great Wall of China. Like the Great Wall, one wonders whether its fundamental purpose was to keep the people in or to keep undesirables out. Maybe the truth is that it is neither of those but is in fact purely jurisdictional, and to hell with the human element entirely," he said with either boredom about the subject, or pure disdain for the purpose, whatever it might be.

I had noted that the fence was a matter of great curiosity to the tourist, but to the residents it had become a matter of indifferent monotony.

I dropped that subject of conversation and switched to one which I knew to be nearer to his heart; wildlife, uncaged and not surrounded by any fence or other confinement.

153

"So you think that you would like to come out to Canada and visit the Yukon, Nikko?" I asked.

"Yes, Harold, I have thought about it for years but I never met the person who could show me the Yukon, until I met you," Nikko said unabashedly. "I have friends who have emigrated to Canada, but they have settled in concrete jungles, just like the ones they left. They offer to go up there with me, but that is not what I have in mind. I want to 'see' the Yukon, inside and out. I want to go to places, the names of which are not on the tourist's tongue. I yearn not only for the sight of game in its natural surroundings, but I want to be able to feel that I'm a part of that which I photograph. I would like to see them from the air, on the ground, even touch them if it is sensible, reasonable, and possible. Does that all sound like a stupid fantasy?" he asked, almost embarrassed.

"Not in the least, Nikko," I replied. "What you reflect is an innate curiosity about wild animals, which does not require their death for you to be satisfied. This is a rare and welcome fantasy for me. I see too many itinerant hunters, who want only to add a new and different trophy head to their collection, without even the most casual acknowledgment that it was one more killing which did not have to take place. Many of that type of hunter kills, just so that he can get the guide to take his picture beside the kill. If that kill is not of international trophy size, the hunter will leave it where he dropped it. It turns my stomach," I spat, somewhat surprised at my outburst.

"Then you do understand why, until now, I have resisted taking the trip? Yes, I do want to see the places and things of historical moment, and yes, I am interested in meeting the people in that part of the world. Yes, most certainly, I feel compelled to see those huge grizzly bears, the moose and the fish which I read about. But no, not as a waddling tourist, laden down with cameras and an eagerness to tell all and sundry what it is like 'back where I come from.' I want to submerge myself in the terrain, the history, the originality, and the novelty of that pristine wilderness, which I feel sure is still there. I would like to do all those positive things with someone who shares my views. Someone who is in a position to and who will, in fact, expose it all to me," Nikko said with profound sincerity.

"Nikko, you express yourself with such intensity that I am having some reservations about whether I am qualified to do what you think I can. I would hate to disappoint you," I hedged.

"Sorry, Harold, I don't know why I felt at liberty to speak to you in such a candid, open, and frank manner. It is not like me, really. Yet from what our mutual friends tell me about you, I had formed some opinions about you of my own. I am satisfied that you are the person who I want to show to me the kaleidoscope and panorama of the Yukon. I'm satisfied that you are the one to introduce me to the folklore, history, and idiosyncrasies of the terrain and the wildlife. Will you do that for me?" he implored.

Nikko was so sincere about his desires, so eager to fulfill this particular dream, that he was almost emotional on the subject.

Intuitively he realized that he was importuning me. He must have sensed that I, too, felt that he was placing pressure upon me to do his bidding. He quickly changed the subject to the decor and the fine reputation which this restaurant had, amongst friends of his from various parts of the world, where he traveled on his printing business.

It was soon patent that Nikko was a valued customer of the hotel. From the moment that he had entered, the eyes of the maitre d'restaurant had constantly flicked over to our table. I assumed that it was to insure that his every whim was catered to properly.

"Harold, may I recommend the Lady Curzon soup? It is a specialty of the restaurant. It has a base of turtle stock and is combined with other delicacies of culinary artistry to result in what is my favorite soup. I hope that it might become yours," he said solicitously.

"Sure, Nikko, sounds intriguing to me. Let's have some," I responded.

Nikko merely raised his arm, not even to shoulder height, while he continued to look and smile at me as the senior waiter glided to our table. Upon placing the order, and receiving a smile, coupled with a knowing nod of approval from the waiter, Nikko turned to yet another subject, the opera.

"Harold, would you be interested in attending the opera this evening? It's opening night, you know. I'm a director of the Hamburg State Opera and as a result I have some tickets for some choice seats. I saved two for you, would you care to go? I would be pleased if you would attend as my guest. The performance tonight is Mozart's Don Giovanni," he said encouragingly.

"I can think of nothing I would rather do, Nikko. I may not show it but I'm a real dyed in the wool, opera buff. I don't get much chance to attend the opera personally but I attend vicariously, through recordings and the occasional radio program. When I travel, the second thing I do, after registering, is to check the entertainment guide to determine if there is an opera or operetta available to me in that particular city," I responded. "Will I be expected to 'dress?' I didn't bring my tuxedo with me."

"Don't worry about it, Harold. Some people go to the opera in order to get dressed up and join in the apres opera festivities. They sit there all evening, bored to tears, until the party begins. Others go to enjoy the poetry, music, and beauty of the opera itself. I'm from the latter group. I will see to it that some members of our group wear less than formal attire. My car will pick you up at 7:45 this evening. Is that agreed?" he asked.

"That's a deal, Nikko, I'll be ready and waiting," I responded.

At that moment the soup arrived. To this day I have never tasted soup which matches or even approximates the delicate flavor and full-bodied, savory, ambrosial delight of that Lady Curzon soup.

The opera was superb. I was absolutely enthralled with the total presentation. The lead singers were not only splendiferous, with engaging professional voices and acting talents, they obviously enjoyed performing. They did not grimace and struggle while singing, they sang openly, candidly, as though they felt good about what they were doing, unlike many of our modern, popular singers who appear to be in agony while singing the simplest notes. These performers had zest and enthusiasm for their respective roles. In summary, these performers were proud of their abilities and wanted to entertain. The audience recognized this objective and responded accordingly. There was repetitive, appreciative, voluminous applause and cheering.

True to his undertaking, Nikko had persuaded some of his party to wear informal clothing. The ultra-refined group with whom he travels would not normally have done so, not on opening night. They and I were certainly amongst the minority.

Following the performance, Nikko and his group took me on a tour of the places to which the entertainers go following their stint on the stage. It, too, was a truly exciting experience.

I met many of the troupe from Don Giovanni. Upon learning that I was from Canada, the man who sang the role of Don Ottavio launched into singing *Il Mio Tesoro Intanto* (To My Beloved). It is a great aria and is popularly known to many who do not attend the opera. I was astounded at his range and powerful volume. I stood close enough to touch him yet he sang with all the gusto which he had used upon the stage.

I was in ecstacy.

The group shared many drinks and more laughs. Nikko and I were fast becoming good friends. We appeared to have many interests in common. He was "good people" and was admired and respected by all who knew him.

When Nikko dropped me off at the hotel that evening, he reminded me that I had not given him an answer to his request that I give him a personalized flying tour of the Yukon.

"Nikko," I said, "you set up a tentative timetable for your visit to the Yukon. Give me a few options. We can then get together by telephone and confirm a mutually suitable date. When we have arrived at a firm arrangement, I would like you to come over with an open mind. I will make it my business to see to it that you will have, in the Yukon, as wonderful a time as I have had here, in Hamburg, tonight."

"Harold, I'll be seeing you soon," said Nikko as he closed the door to his limousine.

Months later I waited at the commercial airport terminal building in Whitehorse. Nikko was to arrive that particular afternoon. Despite his earnest intentions to take a long leisurely tour of the Yukon, he could spend only a few days with me before heading off to Alaska to meet with some publishers. His itinerary, thereafter, took him to Japan, then back to Germany by way of Greece, Italy, and Spain.

Soon I saw him. He was standing in the baggage lounge, waiting for his gear. He looked around inquisitively. I assumed that he was looking for me.

What on earth had happened to this epitome of sartorial elegance whom I had met in Hamburg? The man standing here in the terminal was an amazing dissemblance to that other. The dissimilarity was almost total, from the top of his tousled head to his Nike running shoes. He had a pair of sunglasses parked upon his head. He was wearing a collarless shirt, almost unbuttoned. He revealed a hirsute chest laden with gold chains. There was a cashmere sweater tied about his shoulders. It had a large, careless knot. He was not wearing a belt.

Where that would normally be, there was a colorful necktie substituting for the same. He wore faded blue dungarees. They had been tie-dyed. The cuffs to the pants were rolled up well above his ankles, revealing argyle socks.

This paragon of the cultural establishment of Germany, more accustomed to tuxedos than the average man is to blue pin-stripped suits, and who spoke five languages fluently without a trace of accent in any of them, now looked like the typical high school dropout, beach boy. He could have been from a Hollywood ghetto movie, where fractured English prevails.

Nikko leaned carelessly against a pillar, with an air of a complete lack of concern. He dripped cameras. He had at his feet an expensive aluminum attache case which I recognized as being a special container for a movie camera and complementary equipment.

My astonishment was complete when I saw Nikko pick up one, only one, back pack. This apparently constituted his entire luggage other than the attache case. He must have sent the balance of his belongings on to Japan.

As Nikko was slinging the pack onto his back, he saw me. His face split into a broad, friendly grin, exposing his white regularly spaced teeth. He waved exuberantly in my direction, then bounded out of the lounge.

"Hi, Harold, how are you? So nice to see you again!" he cried. He bounced around with excitement. "How are things going? Have you got everything organized? Where are we going first? What time do we leave?" he asked.

"Hi, Nikko, I'm just fine," I replied, infected by his youthful effusiveness. "Whoa, I'll try to keep my answers related to your questions. Yes, I'm all set, we can go tomorrow, if you wish. We can leave at any time after daylight. The earlier the better. The air is less turbulent in the early part of the day. The light is probably better for photography at that time, as well."

"Great, just great, Harold, please excuse my rambling. I'm sure that I have jet lag. I flew for nine hours to get to Vancouver. I was only there a matter of about an hour when I boarded this flight to Whitehorse. The connections were excellent, but I have had little rest for the past night and the better part of this day. Do I have a hotel room available? If so, I'll go and get some rest for an hour or two, then join you later. What are your plans for this evening?" Nikko said, possibly all in one breath.

"First, let me get you to your hotel. I'll call you in about two hours and see how you feel then. We can certainly have dinner this evening. There isn't any opera but we could go to the cabaret. I hear that there is a good female vocalist in town. How does that sound?" I asked.

"Excellent, and very accommodating, thank you," he replied, listlessly.

As we drove to the hotel, Nikko chattered endlessly about how thrilled he was to have arrived at this "last frontier." I thought that his reference to the Yukon in that way was classic. It was a cogent appraisal of what this part of the world really was. I hoped that I would be able to show off the wilderness of the last frontier in such a way as to do justice to that evaluation.

We met later and had dinner. Nikko asked to be excused early after the meal. He was just too exhausted. He felt that a full nights sleep would better prepare him for the "excursion" (as he called it), than a night on the town.

I telephoned his hotel the next morning at 7 a.m. I was astonished to learn that Nikko had wakened early and had gone for a drive along the Alaska Highway. Apparently he had arranged for the rental car before retiring. He would call me upon his return prior to 10 a.m.

My first reaction was one of disappointment. I had purposely organized the flight for early in the day. I wanted a ride which was not bumpy. Once the sun got up over the mountains and was in full flight to the west, the air got stirred up in a most uncomfortable fashion. Oh well, it was his trip. I knew that he wanted to "live" the "last frontier." There was a certain amount of challenge remaining in going out onto the Alaska Highway. Maybe he wanted to experience the sensation on his own. He could probably immerse himself in the wilderness and steep in it better alone.

I left a telephone number with the hotel clerk, as to where I could be reached later that morning. I took the opportunity to get at some work which was becoming a bit pressing.

It was just exactly ten o'clock when Nikko phoned.

"Hi, Nikko, how are you feeling today?" I asked.

"Superb, Harold. I'm sorry if I messed up the plans but I got up real early. I guess because of the time change I couldn't get back to sleep, so I got up and got a map of the area from the desk clerk. I drove out along the highway and up to Kusawa Lake. I turned off the Alaska Highway at a place called

Mendenhall Landing. I couldn't travel any further than I did. The road ended at the lake. I stayed a while, took some pictures, then came back. I had a great time," he said proudly.

"Good for you, Nikko, that is quite an undertaking for a stranger to the area," I volunteered.

"Nothing to it, Harold. The clerk first told me about the place, then drew me a map. I just followed directions. Do you have any plans which involve me?" he asked.

"Yes I do, Nikko. I thought that we might get out to the airport within the hour. The plane is ready and waiting. It has been fully serviced. I have filed a flight plan which will take us over some of the truly remote parts of the Yukon. I can activate the plan when we get to the airstrip. How does that sound to you?" I inquired.

"Fantastic, just great, Harold. Have you eaten? I have," he asked in rapid fire.

"Yes, I have already eaten. I will ask the cook at the hotel to make some sandwiches and fruit. A thermos of coffee won't do us any harm, either. Shall I pick you up within the hour?" I asked.

"I'll be ready and waiting eagerly," he said, and hung up.

I made all the necessary arrangements, concluded the business matter with which I was involved, and left for the hotel.

"Hi there, Nikko!" I said, as I strode across the hotel lobby toward him. Nikko was sitting there totally prepared for the excursion. I picked up the several paper bags of goodies and we piled into my car. We took but a few minutes to get to the airport, park the car and board the aircraft. For this trip I had arranged for a Cessna 175. It is a four seat airplane with good visibility. It has one high wing. This factor would enable Nikko to take photos without too much obstruction. Only a slender strut might intervene and it could be circumvented.

Nikko boarded the aircraft without any outward signs of trepidation. I didn't know whether he had flown in light aircraft before. In Europe, it is not as common as it is in North America. He stowed the satchels of food behind the front seat. He carefully secured his camera equipment on the seat behind us. He wanted to have his various types of cameras immediately available to his hands. I thought that it was a bit unusual that he would be anxious about his photographic items, yet exhibit no outward concerns about his personal safety. I assumed that the relationship between sailing in tempestuous water and traveling through the air were matters over which he had acquired personal control and a sense of confidence. He would probably be just as interested in the safe confinement of his cameras on his yacht.

After a few moments hesitation, during which the various methods of accessibility, as carefully weighed against the protection of the equipment, were evaluated. I suggested that the most certain way was to place them in a net which could be slung across the rear of the front seat. This we did.

Once airborne, I headed northeast toward Mayo Landing. It is about 280 miles from Whitehorse. I had planned a circle tour which would encompass some 700 to 800 miles of the most interesting, virgin, wild, and uninhabited terrain in the north. It certainly qualified for the title "last frontier."

Just north of the take off point we passed over Lake Leberge. Nikko, who was following the air map, said, "I used to be able to quote poetry about that lake. It was written by Robert Service. Are you familiar with it?" he asked.

I nodded and with mock eloquence and exaggerated gesticulations, I said:

"There are strange things done in the midnight sun
by the men who moil for gold;
The Arctic trails have their secret tales
that would make your blood run cold."

Then Nikko joined in and we said in unison:

"The Northern lights have seen queer sights
But the queerest they ever did see
Was the night on the marge of Lake Leberge
I cremated Sam McGee."

We both broke into laughter over our poetic renderings.

"How on earth would you have picked up on our national poet, and particularly enough to be able to recite his works," I asked, amazed at the breadth of his knowledge.

Talk about your "well read man," I thought.

"As a child I was often sickly, Harold. I stayed home from school a lot, so I had a private tutor who 'lived in.' He had been a world traveler who had been born in England but had gone all over the world. It was he who turned me onto Robert Service. I don't know whatever happened to him. One day he announced that he was leaving and I never heard from him

161

again. I have often wondered what turns his life took after he left," Nikko said.

I interrupted Nikko's reflective thoughts by saying, "Those are the Pelley Mountains over there, off to our right."

"I'll get some stills of them with my telescopic lens," he said. "Then I'll get a few with my wide angle lens. Let's see now, what setting should I use to ... " his voice trailed off as his attention was riveted upon his great love, photography.

"Beneath us is the Pelley River, Nikko. See over there to the left? It joins up with the Yukon River. I suppose that you know that the Yukon River travels hundreds of miles through both the Yukon Territory and the State of Alaska, finally pouring out into the Bering Sea near a community called Hamilton."

Nikko just nodded affirmatively. Yes he knew that, but he was too busy organizing his cameras.

Then suddenly, Nikko raised his head. There was a reflective, quizzical look upon his face. It was as though a thought which had been put on hold for a moment had finally got through. He turned to me and said, "Will we be able to go to Dawson? I have read and heard so much about the Klondike and the gold rush that I would love to see it, if it is possible?" he urged.

"OK with me, Nikko. We'll bypass Mayo and go right on to Dawson. I'll radio ahead and arrange for us to rent a car. We'll have time to go out to the Gugenheim tailings, see the old floating dredges, the museum, and the actual home of our mutual friend Robert Service. How's that?" I asked.

I couldn't help but smile at the way his face lit up with the prospect of it all.

Nikko was absolutely enthralled with Dawson and the surrounding historical highlights. His various cameras had a real good workout. "Incredible" was his constant word companion.

We toured the community for several hours. I pointed out to Nikko some of the features which I personally considered to be highlights. I showed him the sidewalks which were raised three or more feet off the ground. This was done to compensate for snow, permafrost action, and general leveling. We visited the old, preserved dance hall, with the huge murals of semi-nude bulging females; the thirty foot mahogany bar; the brass rails and spittoons. We toured the boat docks, to which was tied one of the original paddlewheelers with a lot of past history. We went by the gold commissioner's office, w'.n it's scales and huge safe. We met and talked with many of the townspeople, some of whom were (or said they were) remnants of the gold rush. Nikko took many, many pictures. He took them with valid reason. What we were exploring was the last vestige of what had made Canada known to the world in the 1890s. Without the gold rush there would have been no Dawson. Without the gold rush Robert Service may not have become a world class poet. Without the gold rush we would have no purpose here.

We were famished as a result of all the flurry of discovery so we decided to take a break and have something to eat. We patronized one of the old cafes, which had been built during the gold rush. After a hurried lunch we headed out for a short saunter around the town to see if there was anything of note which we had missed.

"Are we just about ready to go, Nikko?" I asked as he took several pictures of the Yukon's floral emblem, the fireweed. "We can now go back to the airport by way of the dredges, if you like. I am keeping my mind on what we want to see, and on the daylight factor. Are you just about ready?"

"Harold, this is incredible. Look at that sky. Not a single cloud. There is no pollution to destroy the beautiful blue color of it. Smell the air. It's clean! It's ... ."

"I know, Nikko, it's incredible right?" I interjected with a big smile.

"You're mocking me, Harold," he said, then joined me in a good laugh, adding, "yes I'm ready. Let's go."

After visiting the gold fields and their discarded dredges, we flew off in a southeasterly direction. I was headed for the flatlands and Aishihik. Away off in the distant south, we could make out the high peaks of the Saint Elias Mountain Range. Kluane National Park nestled at their feet. The contrast between the meadows and that soaring wall of granite would perforce, be a visual and photographic cardinal feature for Nikko.

As we flew down past Thistle Creek, we entered upon the grazing range of the large four footed animals about which Nikko spoke so passionately in Hamburg. I kept my eyes focused for any movement below which would signal the presence of his photographic quarry. Soon, while passing over a small unnamed lake with a shoreline ringed with thick, stultified bush and short trees, I saw what we were seeking.

"Nikko, get ready for some action. Look below, just where the tail of the aircraft is now passing. I'll bank to the right so that it will be on your side. There is a big bull moose wading in the shallows. He's foraging for food, he barely looked up," I said, as I put the plane into a steep, starboard turn.

"Yes, I see it! I see it! What a majestic creature. Look at him stand his ground. It's incredible! There, I got him with the telephoto lens. I'll get a few more before he moves. Can you reach the netting, can you get out my Zeiss Ikon? I'll get him in motion. There he goes! Look at the graceful movement, he's crashing down those saplings like they were match sticks. It's incredible. Do you see him, Harold?" he cried.

Of course, I could see him but my hands were full keeping the plane in a position which would enable Nikko to continue photographing.

"You bet I can, Nikko. Are you getting some good shots?" I responded.

"Fantastic shots, Harold. Look at him. He's stopped, he's looking up. I think he's challenging this bird to come down to his level and fight. This is his lake. What a beauty he is! Look at that rack. I'll bet that it is forty inches across, at least. He must weigh a ton. Harold, thank you, thank you so much. This is just incredible," he chattered.

Following the excitement engendered by finding the moose, I became somewhat complacent about the likelihood of seeing more wild game. That is until we flew over a narrow shallow river. I don't know if it has a name. There, to my utter amazement, we found a large grizzly bear. He was huge. He had been drinking or fishing, it would be hard to tell. He glanced up as we went over him.

"Harold, there was a bear. Did you see it? You just went over him, to the left. That's a grizzly, I think. Where's my Leica? Oh! Right here. Can you turn? We'll lose him. Will he run? What shall we do? Can we get down closer?" Nikko urged.

I banked the plane in as tight a turn as I thought Nikko could take. The plane was virtually standing on its wing tip. I hoped that the bear would wait, or at least not hide. When we got turned around we saw it standing on all fours, looking at us.

Nikko got his fill of pictures of that monstrous bear. It looked like it was an oldtimer who knew that airplanes were not out to harm him. Only people would. He reciprocated the curiosity. At one point he stood up on his hind legs. I thought that Nikko would faint for sure, at that point. I knew

164

that Nikko was living and breathing because he kept yelling, "Incredible! Incredible!"

We continued to fly in a southerly direction. Soon I could pick out Sekulman Lake (which is at 137.30 W and 61.36 N for those who are curious and following our course). I knew that almost due north of the lake we would find the abandoned airstrip at Aishihik. It had been built during the second war. It had been constructed as a landing strip for war planes which were being flown to Russia by the Ferry Command. I had seen it many times. The low tower stood tall out of the plains surrounding the strip. There were some other service buildings and crew quarters. The runway was of packed earth and was about 2,200 feet long. It ran roughly east and west.

At first I saw what appeared to be a dust cloud. It was narrow in scope, powdery, and motionless. It was centered in one location and that appeared to be right where I remembered the airstrip to be. It was a strange phenomenon.

Nikko was busy with his cameras. I think that he may have been reloading. It's a good thing that he was. The disturbance below was going to demand a lot of his attention in a moment.

A large portion of the runway and the surrounding grass was occupied by wild horses! There were forty or fifty of them nonchalantly chewing on the short bladed grass, or just "horsing around." It was probably the colts which were creating the dust cloud on what was to be our landing surface.

"Nikko, look what we have here," I yelled excitedly.

"Wild horses?" he cried. "My God! Look at that! Are they really wild? I've heard about them and seen movies with them in it, but not actually in the wild. Can we get down a bit so that I can get detailed pictures of them? I'd like to get a panoramic view which will show the abandoned buildings, the mountains, and the prairie. Is there any way that we could land? I would love to get pictures close up. Can we? Harold, this is the personification of the last frontier."

"Well, let me try something. It might work. Hold on to your equipment," I urged.

My plan was to try to shoo the horses off of the runway. I flew the plane to the east end of the strip, then banked into the wind. I put on about forty degrees of flap. This would give me lift and at the same time let me fly more slowly. I throttled back, so that the plane would sink toward the ground. When I was about fifty feet above the ground and two hundred feet back from the end of the runway, I pushed the throttle in and the engine roared. The sudden change from wind merely whistling past the airfoils to the thunderous roar of the engine was near deafening. It must have been horrific on the ground. I pulled up just as we went past the horses. Some merely stared at the plane. Others made tentative moves to avoid the craft. Nothing spectacular happened, generally speaking they stayed put.

I did it again. Some ambled off the strip, some younger ones bolted away. Talk about callousness. Familiarity does breed contempt.

Several more charges over the runway and the way was clear to land, but only at the easterly end.

I had barely touched down when I realized that I must turn off the engine. The horses had turned around and were coming back. The propeller had just barely stopped rotating when the first stallion led his section up to Nikko's window.

"Harold, look at this!" cried Nikko. "He's nuzzling the door. Should I open it? I can't believe this. This is incredible!"

"Well, try and open the door. Push it out gently. He might budge. Try not to alarm them, I'd hate to be caught up in a stampede," I said.

Nikko first organized his camera equipment. He took several pictures of the horses surrounding the plane. He wanted some of this giant stallion which was rubbing its nose against the window and shaking its head vigorously. This particular horse was a seasoned scrounger. He whinnied and nodded his head, he turned and nipped at a mare who was becoming too inquisitive. She shied away, but would not leave. He stomped his forelegs and constantly shook his head.

"He'll be an 'old gray mare' before you get through photographing him, Nikko," I joked.

"No way this one is ever going to fit that description, Harold. It's physically impossible," responded Nikko, showing a broad smile.

"Harold, there is no way that my friends in Hamburg would believe the tale of this event, unless I cover it with pictures. It's just too unimaginable ... too ... momentous ... too incredible. Harold, I'm going to try to get out. I want that panoramic picture. I'll try to open the door now, OK?"

"Just a minute, Nikko. I asked the chef at the hotel to give us some fruit. I think that there is an apple in the sack," I said, as I rummaged in the back seat.

"Here offer him this," I said as I handed Nikko a big, red MacIntosh apple.

Nikko was familiar with horses. He belonged to what some of the judgmental people call the "horsie set." He had some of his own. He exhibited not one whit of fear. He had but one dedicated objective, to get out of the plane and be with, touch, and be in contact with a herd of wild horses in their natural surroundings.

Having opened the door, very gingerly, he stepped out onto the airstrip. He had it half made. The horses shied a bit, and some of the younger mares ran off. The stallion stood his ground with his ears back.

Nikko extended the hand which contained the apple. The stallion first eyed Nikko, then the apple. The stallion stared into Nikko's eyes. Whatever he saw there prompted him to sense no threat to his well being as he cautiously stepped forward and smelled the apple.

"Harold, get my color movie camera. Get this quickly please. The settings should be just fine. Hurry!" Nikko cried.

The scenes which I photographed would most certainly satisfy Nikko's friends that he had, in fact, been in and amongst a herd of wild horses. They were not entirely "wild." They probably belonged to some hunting guide who would come and collect some of them annually for the hunt. He would then turn them loose again for another year. They were not tame either. They are the classic wild herd that is common to the Yukon.

What a scene I photographed. There was Nikko in his outrageous "mod" attire, standing up to his shoulders in shaggy nags. He was now completely surrounded by them. I had difficulty picking him out, from time to time. Only his bright colors kept him in view. Here he was standing alone, amongst the herd in his "last frontier." His friends knew him better as the fastidious business man who wore dark blue suits or black and white tuxedo attire. His business associates sat with him in board rooms while he aggressively hammered out multimillion dollar contracts, or while he directed the course of the opera season. Here he extended his hand to give a wild horse an apple. In Hamburg, he would extend the same hand to welcome a potential customer, or hand an olive branch to a union leader. Today, he was strolling amongst shying, unsure horses, stroking nostrils, rubbing behind ears, patting shoulders when he could, and posing for the camera. He would flash his infectious grin and tentatively slide an arm around the neck of a horse. In Hamburg he would stride majestically amongst the "first nighters" bowing gracefully to silk, lace, and pearls. There he would pose for the papperazzi. Here it was for me and his camera.

When we finally scooted the herd off the runway and got airborne again, Nikko placed his hand on my right arm in a gesture of friendship and said, "Harold, let's go home. Nothing can top what I have experienced today. I would hate to run into an unexpected, negative incident now. I have seen and lived what it was that I came to find. I can never thank you enough. You may never know what a magnificent experience I have had this day. When you come back to Germany again, I will try to measure up to the wonderful time that you have just given to me. It has been incredible. I, too, will try to expose to you the contrasts in life, such as you have done for me today."

His eyes became damp and shiny as he turned away to look out the window upon his last frontier.

Chapter Seventeen

An order from the court required,
We had to find the judge,
While flying out to hunting camp,
We feared he would not budge.

Petition dropped wrapped 'round steel,
It coursed right through his tent,
The opinion sought, we got that day,
plus curses judge did vent.

A Wrenching Experience

There were times, in the lives of many of us, when we wished that our aim was more accurate. I am sure that upon occasion each of us has heard another say in exasperation, "I could never do that again in a million years even if I really wanted to." This chapter deals with just such an event.

While in my Whitehorse law office my intercom buzzer sounded. It distracted my attention from the law book which I was studying in preparation for an upcoming trial.

"Yes, Phyllis," I said, "what is it?"

"It's Mr. Wylie on the phone. He wants to speak with you, he says that it is urgent," responded Phyllis, in her usual, efficient, no nonsense way.

"OK, I'll take it," I said, somewhat miffed at the interruption.

"Hi there, Vic. How are you today?" I asked.

"Fine, Harold, just fine, but I ... or more accurately, we, have a serious problem. We are going to have to deal with it immediately!" said Vic in a tone of urgency.

"What's the problem, Vic," I asked, hoping that it was one which could be solved quickly on the telephone.

"Your clients are still dumping their tailings into the river above my client's property. The court order, made by Mr. Justice Gibben last week, specifically prohibits them doing that! It has got to stop immediately! My client's cattle have become ill again and one more has died. Harold, have you no influence over your clients? Can't you make them stop? Why won't they obey the court order? You know that what they are doing is in contempt of court, don't you?" asked Vic, very perturbed.

"Yes, I know, Vic, I spoke to them about it when the order was made. They told me that they would behave until the trial next week ... or is it the week after next? I really don't know what to tell you except that I will telephone the head man again," I offered.

"Not good enough, Harold! I must take steps to protect my client's position and his cattle. I want to get the injunction which I did not apply for the last time. I intend to apply for it this morning. I'm giving you telephone notice as a courtesy. I'll have the actual documents served upon you within the hour, they're being typed now. I want an injunction which will include the fact that your client must pay punitive damages for having breached that first order. Those damages can be assessed later. I intend to file the documentation in support of the motion for the injunction, at about ten thirty. You could meet me at the Court Registry, if you wish. I have asked for an immediate hearing before the judge. Will you be there?" he asked, with a suggestion of a demand in the tone of his voice.

"Well, yes I can, Vic, but let me call my clients. I must have instructions, as you know. Not that there is too much that I can do to stop you under the circumstances. How about you filing your documents, then arranging for an immediate hearing and I'll be over there in about fifteen minutes, OK?" I suggested.

The moment Vic accepted, I hung up the phone and asked Phyllis to come into my office. She was there in a moment. Experience as a legal secretary had taught her well. She could sense a state of emergency and was eager to be involved and to help. She was prepared for her role in the skirmish which she knew was about to happen.

Phyllis was tall; she stood about five feet six, but in high heels she must have approached five nine. She was slender. To hear her tell it, she was dreadfully thin. She wore only

170

comfortable clothes, style being a secondary matter entirely. She had a definite conviction that the clothing manufacturers preyed upon the competitiveness and consequent susceptibility of women. She alleged that their objectives were financial gain, not genuine comfort for the wearers.

Phyllis was exceptionally skilled as a legal secretary. She knew it and was justly proud of the fact. She had two elementary grade daughters. Her husband, "Red," kept threatening to take her away from the office so that she could produce a boy. I dreaded the thought but just chided them about not knowing the proper formula, anyway.

"Phyllis, will you get me the general manager of that company on the phone. He doesn't seem to understand that he is seriously damaging our chances in court by his continuous inattention to court orders. This is the second time we will have this go 'round. No, wait a minute, I'm going to try to circumvent him. Get me the president of the company. Maybe I can convince him of the seriousness of the situation. Maybe he will appreciate how his case is being undermined by the disobedience of the management personnel. If you can't get him, get some other senior officer. I'll be drafting an affidavit for you to type when you're through there, so come back in, OK?"

"Your wish is my command, boss," she said, smiling.

"Get out of here!" I ordered with a feint 'back of my hand.'

I went to the wall library to get a particular book. Ours was a small library by big city standards, but it was adequate for quick references. It contained the Statutes of Canada, the Ordinances of the Yukon Territory, the Canadian Criminal Code (Crankshaw), and the Western Weekly Reports. The most frequently referred to books in our library were Halsbury's Laws of England. In this latter set of books there was set down, in a logical, readable, comprehensible way, all of the Civil Law of England, from whence Canada took its common law.

After about ten minutes Phyllis returned. She was patently disturbed about something.

"I have not been able to get anyone on the telephone. I'm told that they are all traveling. Not one of the senior officers will be available until Friday, day after tomorrow," she related.

"OK, get me the general manager. I'll try and get some instructions from him, notwithstanding that it is his responsibility to prevent what has happened. Phone Vic at the registry and tell him what is happening. By the way, if you happen to run into a cup of coffee ... ."

"Yeah I know, steer it in here, right?" she said.

"You're a doll, Phyllis," I said, as she retreated out the door to her bailliwick.

In just a few moments, the door to my private office opened. The junior girl in the office entered with a cup of coffee. She deposited it in front of me without uttering a sound, then turned and left. I made a mental note that she exhibited thoughtfulness and tact in not disturbing me while I was concentrating (from her observation anyway) upon my law books. Just as the door closed quietly, my telephone rang.

"It's the secretary of the company on the line. I can't reach the manager. She says that he is traveling too. Do you want to talk with her?" asked Phyllis. She resented not being able to achieve her objectives.

"OK, Phyllis, I'll talk with her. You stay on the line, it will make it easier for you to understand whatever documents I will have to draw. Have you tried to get Vic?" I asked.

"He's standing right here, waiting for you to get off the phone. He is really perturbed about something. I'll put the secretary on now."

"Hello, who am I speaking with?" I queried. I needed all the data that I could extract if I was to prepare an affidavit that would be of substance, even if it could not be of true value.

"My name is Joan Wing, (not the real name) I'm the personal secretary to the manager. I believe that I am aware of the reason for your phone call," she said, with a definite air of self-confidence.

"Good, then I won't have to go into a ream of background information. Is your boss there? I need to talk with him," I asked.

"No, Mr. Hine, he is not here. He has gone 'outside,' for a meeting in Edmonton. He just left this morning, so there is no way that I know of to contact him today. You might get him at his hotel tonight or tomorrow," she said matter of factly.

"Well, look here Joan, I'm being faced with an immediate application to the court for an injunction against your company because of the tailings which were discharged into the river yesterday, or the day before. I must talk with someone who can give me some cogent information, something which I can use in an affidavit. What on earth happened out there, anyway? Do you know?" I inquired.

"Mr. Hine, I think that your call was anticipated. The manager forgot to tell the crew in the field about the court order. They didn't know about it when they dumped on Monday. He said that he was sorry, but that's the way it is, he cannot undo the wrong. He said that if the other side complains we should stall until the trial. He said to try to get all of the problems, including this last dumping, included in the trial. I'm sorry, but that is all that I can tell you. Does it help?" she asked.

"Not an awful lot, Joan. I'm afraid that the judge is going to consider what happened to be a most contumacious act. I'm sorry, Joan, I don't mean to berate you, it certainly is not your fault. I guess I'm just frustrated at not being able to come to grips with the problem. Thank you for the information which you have given to me. I'll just have to make the best of what we have. I will draw an affidavit based upon 'information and belief.' I will be relying upon the story which you have just told me. I may have to ask you to support that data later, OK?" I asked. I didn't want any misunderstandings later. In any event, Phyllis had been on the phone and probably had made comprehensive shorthand notes.

"Yes, Mr. Hine, I have seen such affidavits before. I will stand by what I have just told you," she confirmed.

"Thanks, Joan, you've been a great help in my time of need," I said lightheartedly.

"Anytime," Joan concluded.

I walked out into the general office area to find Vic impatiently pacing the floor. Upon appraising him, I sensed that it might be more than impatience which was bothering him.

"Hi, Vic, did you get a cup of coffee. Are you all set to go before the judge?" I asked.

"I tried, Harold, but the judge is out on his annual hunt. He and a friend left on the weekend. Damn it all, anyway! I haven't needed the judge urgently for years, now that I do need him, he's gone into the wilds to God knows where," he exclaimed.

"I know how you feel. All of the people who could give me instructions are out of town. I can't get anything until tonight or tomorrow, at the earliest. I will have to prepare an affidavit on information and belief. Not the best, but what else can I do? I have no alternatives, unless you decide to wait," I hinted.

173

"No way, Harold. I'm really put off by the actions of your clients. They act like they are above the law! They were ordered to delay all dumping until the issues had been decided at a full hearing in court, and they bloody well went and did it anyway. I should have insisted upon an injunction in the first place, instead of accepting a directive, buried amongst a bunch of other matters, in that order. I want damages, PUNITIVE damages, damn it! Maybe that will make them heed the law," Vic roared.

"Well, how are we going to handle this, Vic? It's your application to the court, but the court is out there in the wilderness somewhere. We don't have any other judge available," I said, hoping that upon reflection, Vic would simmer down and wait for the trial.

"If the bloody court isn't here, then I'll go to the bloody court," cried Vic. "I'll charter a plane and fly out to where he is. I'll get my injunction out there. My client has rights and they are being trampled upon. My client wants action, and he's bloody well going to get it! Even if I have to drive out somewhere and walk in to the judge's camp," he exploded.

I admired this trait of Vic's. He was tenacious on behalf of his clients. Right or wrong, if he believed in what he was doing, he posed a formidable opponent in the courts. Right now, he was not only his unyielding self, but that trait was compounded by the frustration brought on by the judge's absence.

Vic was a short man. He had a bit of a stoop. Not pronounced, but noticeable. He was in his mid-forties. His hair was graying and he wore thick glasses—they might have been bifocals. He didn't smile much. His wife was deathly ill with cancer, and it was only a matter of time. They had never had children. Newfoundland was his birthplace and it showed in his pattern of speech. He was a bit overweight but nothing significant. Smoking was a constant with Vic. I can't remember a time, except when he was in court, that he didn't have a cigarette going. He drank in moderation. Once in a long while he would let loose, but not often. He had been a close friend to the judge, probably still was. When the judge had been the commissioner of the Territory, Vic had been his legal advisor. Except for the patent integrity of the judge, and Vic, one might wonder about objectivity.

"Well, there is an off chance that you will be able to locate a charter aircraft which has not been spoken for. You know how busy they are at this time of the year. The season is

174

coming to a close. Everyone is either going out for one last check on a property, or the planes are busy picking up the prospectors and others whom they took out earlier in the year. Just in case you get lucky, I'll start dictating an affidavit. You can use that office there, it'll give you a bit of privacy. Phyllis, will you come in now?" I said.

When I had finished dictating the lame excuse provided by my client and Phyllis had started to type it into proper form, I went over to talk further with Vic.

"Damn it all to hell, Harold. There isn't a plane available in town. They're all out on charter, there won't be one for a week. Damn it all, anyway! What will I tell my client? That was a purebred that just died. God, what a predicament," he spat. He was dejected, and with good cause. Yet, no one would begrudge the judge his entitlement to an annual holiday.

Vic sat looking down and scratching his wrist. He lit up a cigarette and watched the smoke with far away eyes. Occasionally, his eyes would close for a moment and he would intertwine his fingers, squeezing them tightly. Slowly he raised his eyes to meet mine. I could almost read his mind. He stared at me, or through me. He was formulating the words which he wanted to use, to con me into flying him out to meet with the judge.

"Hold it, Vic, I think I know what you have on your mind. Please don't concoct some scheme which will prove to be awkward for both of us, and particularly our respective clients. Why don't you just wait until the trial? I'm sure that my client will toe the line, once I get a chance to talk to the proper officers," I stated, without too much conviction.

"I don't want to wait until the trial! I CAN'T wait until the trial! I just cannot stand by and let some more first class cattle die, needlessly, on the off chance that your client will start doing something right. Those cattle are not just scrubs, they are very expensive and in many cases, irreplaceable. The bloodlines are all important. Some cattlemen search for years to get the precise bloodline that they want. That precision is what costs the money. Those cattle are precious, just as precious as your bloody client's product. God damn it, Harold, I want some protection from your rotten clients!" he yelled. His voice had been ascending in pitch all during this last dissertation.

"Hold it, Vic, you'll blow a gasket," I said with a smile. That outburst was typical of Vic. His doggedness was a strong part of his makeup. "Let's get a coffee and see if there isn't some sensible solution that we can arrive at quietly."

"I don't think I'm going to like this, Harold. I've heard those 'let's talk quietly' suggestions come from you before. I don't want quiet talk. I want action!" he snapped.

I called in Phyllis. She was just about finished with the affidavit. She would "steer" some coffee our way.

"Harold, why don't you just consent to an injunction? No, hell that's no good, not unless it's signed or at least authorized by the judge. Your consent wouldn't make it enforceable. I might as well ask your clients to behave, as I have. I think that you probably would consent 'cause I sense that you don't approve of what your clients have done, any more than I do. They might agree to act less imperiously, but if they didn't, I'd be back to square one again. No, by God! It's got to be a proper injunction," he concluded.

Vic's reasoning was sound. I took it that he was just thinking out loud and coming to all the right decisions. However, the fact was that he was no further ahead than when he entered the office. He also knew that I couldn't consent to the injunction. I had no instructions to do so and consequently no authority to consent.

"Harold, I have a request to make of you," Vic said, as he rose from his chair and circled it.

I knew, or least I suspected, what was about to come forth. I had been expecting to hear Vic's next statement ever since he discovered that all of the charterable aircraft were unavailable. The proposition which I thought I was about to receive could be viable but it had to have some proper balances. I might well be faced with juggling the protection of my client and the ethics of the legal profession against the obvious rights and the justice which rested on Vic's side of the ledger. I hoped that it would not come down to unpleasantness.

The one feature about the practice of law which disturbed me then, and has throughout my career, was that some lawyers ignore the "justice" which rests with those on the opposite side to their case. They are the lawyers who consider themselves to be paid minions, who function for hire, regardless of the balance of rights. It is money, in the form of fees, which is to be pursued, not justice.

I was not, and never have been, one in that category, neither was Vic.

176

"Harold, you know how to fly and have a plane at your disposal," Vic continued. "How will it be if we fly out to where the judge is, make our submissions to him out there and, of course, be governed by the result?"

"I had a feeling that you were going to end your mental gymnastics by making that suggestion, Vic," I responded, "but I may have some conflicts that I need to resolve, before doing anything along those lines. I'm sure that you appreciate that if I fly us out there and the judge grants you an injunction, which includes a provision for punitive damages, because my client has disobeyed that previous court order, then my client would have grounds to complain about my actions. Right now, you can't get out there and consequently my client is safe from that threat, at this stage, anyway. You must remember that my client claims that your client doesn't have all the rights on his side, either. On the other hand, if you get lucky and find a plane, you might get an ex parte injunction (one which is acquired unilaterally by one of the parties to the case, without the need for the other one to be present). Alternatively, if you find a plane in the next day or two and we both go out there together in that plane, then I have not become involved in a potential conflict of interests. I will not have been the means by which you got there. I am sympathetic to your client's complaint about the tailings poisoning his cows, but on the other hand, my client was there long before your client arrived and your client went into that area with the full knowledge of the water problems. I agree that two wrongs do not make a right, but you do agree that those are the bare facts, don't you?" I argued.

Vic nodded his head in accord, but immediately leapt to the attack.

"Yes, but your client can take measures to reduce, or even nullify, the toxicity of the tailings and hasn't done it!" he asserted.

"OK, Vic, let's not you and I try to decide the problem here. There is valid substance for debate, but we need an impartial referee. Maybe there is a way out of this mess," I suggested.

Vic smiled. He saw that I was trying to skirt the main issue with a diversionary tactic. He had been expecting this. He sat and waited.

"OK, Harold, I'm prepared to listen to your proposition, but only if Phyllis gets me another cup of that delicious coffee," he said whimsically.

Once we had some freshly-brewed coffee and Vic had started his umpteenth cigarette, we settled in to try to solve the dilemma. As usual, Phyllis had anticipated the need for more coffee and it had been made and waiting.

"Look, Vic, I'm sure that you see the quandary that I am in. I'm certain that you will get your injunction. It's just a matter of when. However, I don't want to be placed in the position of having 'assisted' you in getting it, unless I can show that by doing so I thereby achieved some lasting or even temporary advantage for my client. If you obtained a provision for punitive damages at this stage and I was a party to you doing so, that would be a conflict of the worst kind. Can't we have a compromise of some kind?"

"Of some kind, eh? That's a good one. You've got me over a barrel and you have the nerve to use that term?"

"Now, just a minute, Vic," I interjected. "I have already acknowledged that you might find a plane in the next day or two or more, but in that case, I know that I am likely to go with you to present my client's side of the argument. If I fly you out, and you get the injunction AND punitive damages, AND the costs, might it not look like I was your pawn?"

"I guess that you could definitely expect someone to think that, Harold."

"So what is it that we can agree upon which will make our appearance before the judge, if we find him, not look as though I am consenting to the entire application? That's the question."

"You sly bastard, Hine. Oh, boy, that's cute. You're trying to con me out of the punitive damages, aren't you? Jeez, what a tricky maneuver that was. Wow, that's a dandy!" cried Vic, as he got up and paced the floor. He was shaking his head, in a negative way and making unintelligible comments and wild gesticulations with his cigarette.

I said nothing. This was the balance for which I had been struggling. Knowing Vic, I had to first get him to calm down, then present a logical argument, which he would, by himself, find palatable.

Time started to drag. Vic was obviously assessing the pros and cons of the proposal. He stood at the rear windows to our office looking out. He stayed there a long time.

"Excuse me, Vic, I'm going for some more coffee and to check on the affidavit. I'll be back in a few minutes," I said softly, as I removed myself from the aura of his thoughts.

While I was in my private office, I quickly dictated an injunction containing the provisions that I desired. I asked Phyllis to type the same as quickly as she could. Finally, I asked her to check with Gordie Cameron, the aircraft engineer at the airstrip, to see if the Cornell was serviced and ready. Gordie Cameron was an excellent mechanic. He loved aircraft and was associated in business with Whitehorse Flying Service, which was a client of our firm. He was well-liked by all who knew him. He went on to become the mayor of Whitehorse and thereafter, the commissioner of the Yukon Territory. He had a major distinction in that particular regard. All commissioners, prior to him, had been federal government appointees. Gordie was the first person, being a resident of the Yukon, to be selected and so appointed by his peers in the Yukon.

Gordie was about six feet tall, big build, broad smile, and a tremendous sense of humor. I'm sure that he must have kept a diary of jokes because he had a new, good one, every day of the year. He was then, and still is, married to a lovely girl named Bonnie. They had four sons, I believe. One of them still lives and works in Whitehorse, his name is Robert. Another son, was, by coincidence, the pilot of a Beaver which I chartered some ten or more years ago. His name is Scott, and he is now a pilot for a large commercial airline. I don't know about the other two sons.

Anyway, back to the story.

I telephoned "Musty" Thompson, the clerk of the court, and asked her to tell me, if she could, the exact location of the judge's hunting party.

"Well, Harold, as I told Vic Wylie, I'm not exactly certain where they went this year. It appears that you guys are serious, so let me phone around. I'll call the judge's wife and others. Someone will know. I'll call you back. Do you think that he will be annoyed by the interruption of you two showing up?" she asked.

"No, Musty, (her maiden name had been Mustard) I don't think so. He is very good about fulfilling his judicial responsibilities. See what you can do, then call me back. Thanks."

Having been away from Vic for about twenty minutes, I thought I had better join him. I had barely got my hand upon the door knob of my office door, when the door opened. It was Vic.

Without so much as a "howdy do" he said, "OK, Harold, this is the only deal to which I will agree. I've just talked to my client. He didn't like the idea but I explained my predicament. I will apply for the injunction. You will fly us out. You will not object to the injunction. That's different from consenting to it. I will not ask for punitive damages, damn it! At trial, I'll ask for only provable and general damages, which I'm sure that I will be able to get. So the deal is, you fly us out at your cost, I get the bloody injunction and wait for the trial when I will prove the actual losses suffered by my client. It will be up to the judge to assess the general damages, and to determine what should be done about your client ignoring the last order. But, if your client disobeys the injunction, then any agreement which we have made today, about damages of any kind, is negated. Is it a deal?" he insisted.

The way I saw this, I couldn't make a better deal; particularly with no ammunition, no hard information. Vic, in the name of all justice, was entitled to an injunction which would carry its own damages if my client goofed again. If Vic won his case, then he would also win the provable loss to his client. That, also, was only just and proper. Punitive damages, on the other hand, could be a severe penalty for my client. I had to avoid them, at all costs, including the cost of the flight. Vic had got his pound of flesh there.

"God, Vic you sure don't leave a guy much bargaining room. You want me to agree to all that AND pay for the flight as well?" I replied.

"Don't mock me, Hine," said Vic in an aggressive voice, tempered with good will born out of friendship. "You had this all figured out before you left me, didn't you?"

"In a way, yes, but I saw it as the only solution from your side, so I figured that's where you would arrive. I've got the plane all organized. Musty is trying to locate the whereabouts of the judge, and I've taken the liberty of drafting the injunction for your perusal, Vic," I said, with what might have been a twinkle in my eye.

"God, Harold, did you leave anything to chance? Suppose I hadn't arrived at the conclusion you expected ... what then?" Vic said, shaking his head and smiling.

"Vic, I've come to understand you pretty well. I know what will turn your crank. You'll get the injunction today for sure, the battle for the damages can be for another day. You might not get any general damages at all, only special damages, those that you can prove, so I figured that you wouldn't hold out for the punitives. Logical, isn't it? That's what I felt you would think too," I said.

"Smart ass!" quipped Vic. "We're wasting time, let's get going."

As soon as Musty phoned back, we were off for the airport. She gave us a fairly precise area in which we should find the judge. Once at the airport, I drove up alongside the hangar, near to where we were to pick up the plane. Keeping the car close to a large building was one way of reducing the congestion of obstacles for taxiing aircraft.

We walked around the corner of the hangar and saw that the plane was out on the apron, apparently ready for use. The plane that we were going to use today was a Cornell (a Fleet built P.T.26A). She was a fighter trainer which had been used extensively during the second war. She had one low wing and landing gear affixed to that wing. She was yellow in color, as were most of the training aircraft. She had two seats; tandem, i.e. one behind the other, instead of side by side. There was a sliding canopy which both the pilot and the rear passenger could slide independently of one another, over their head, once they were inside the plane. This permitted great visibility and protection from the elements. The power plant was an inverted Ranger engine. It was really insufficient power for the size of the plane, but it was adequate.

"Hi there, Gordie! How are you today?" I inquired of the aircraft engineer. I had to yell to make myself heard. Gordie was machining something and making an awful racket. He turned off the machine and walked over to greet us.

"Hi you two, what's up today. How are you, Vic? Don't see you up here very often. I understand that you are going flying with this kook here," he said, gesturing at me. "Have you got your insurance premiums paid?"

"Thanks a bunch, Gordie," I said. "You're cut off the guest list for the next office party."

"You would never get away with it, Harold, the women wouldn't stand for it," responded Gordie, good naturedly.

"I haven't got time to listen to the stories about your latest conquests, Gordie, I have to phone the tower and file the flight plan. See if you can get Vic to listen," I joshed, as I headed for his office phone.

181

The weather was what is called CAVU (ceiling and visibility unlimited). I knew the area in which we were to locate the judge, I had been up that way many times. Unfortunately, there was no landing strip nor clearing near where he was and there were no lakes large enough to accommodate a float plane; hence the Cornell. This presented one last problem. How to get the documentation into the hands of the judge. I had an idea. I had to confirm it with Vic.

"OK, Vic, we're all set. There is just one more problem to solve," I said.

"Christ, Hine, you're not going to start the negotiations all over again are you?"

"No, Vic, I'll wait until we are flying upside down, then I'll advance the new proposals," I replied.

"Yeah, that would be just like you. Alright, what's the problem then?" he inquired, smiling.

"Well, we have to see to it that the judge can read our material. How do we get it into his hands, if we can't land and do it personally?" I asked rhetorically.

"Hell, there has to be some way. I'm getting put off with all these bloody hitches," snapped Vic.

"My suggestion is that we write a note right now, then put all of the documentation into a large envelope, weight it down with some ample weight, and drop it into their camp. How does that sound?"

"Great, you find the envelope and the weight, I'll write the note. I'll ask him to nod for yes and shake his head for no. Agreed?" asked Vic.

"Agreed," I replied.

The manila envelope into which Phyllis had inserted my documents should suffice for Vic's too. I went to my car to get a wrench. This should do as the guiding influence. We jointly read and signed the note for the judge, so that he would know that we would accept the motion of his head as his judgment. The note went into the envelope with the wrench, it was a hefty package. We pulled Vic's manila envelope over the whole thing. This should be adequate; but was it a bit heavy?

"Jeez, Harold do you think that this is too heavy? Maybe the envelope will burst when it hits the ground," said Vic, as he hefted it a few times.

"I agree that it is a bit heavy, but it's all that I've got that will fit into the envelope. We haven't got time for an extensive search. This game is going to be called on account of darkness, if we don't get going," I replied.

"No way, Hine, you get this bird into the air. I want that bloody injunction. I'll drop this package right onto his feet. I used to be pretty good at dropping marbles into the neck of milk bottles," boasted Vic.

"Yeah, I know, Vic, you were called 'Bomber Wylie,' right? Was that a favorite pastime in Newfoundland, way back when?" I joked.

"Smart ass! How do I get into this kite? I've never seen one like this before. What did you call it, a Cornell? Looks like a fighter plane. Are you sure you know how to fly this thing?"

"Sure Vic, I'll give you an exhibition of stunts on the way out, OK ?" I asked.

"You just fly this thing straight and level and I'll be happy, agreed?" he insisted.

"Righto. Now listen, Vic, there is an intercom in this plane. When you get into the rear seat, you'll see some earphones and a small boom mike. Put them on and when you see my hand waving, that's when we'll test the equipment, OK?"

In no time, we were airborne and flying due north. We had checked the intercom, it was fine. Vic got himself strapped in with the shoulder harness and appeared to be at ease. He held the envelope free from obstacles. It had been agreed that I would make one, maybe two, passes over the camp before the drop was to occur. He would not drop the envelope until I gave the word "now."

"How is the weather, Harold? Will we have any trouble. Looks like pretty heavy weather further north," asked Vic.

"Yes, there is going to be a rain squall. We should be able to reach the camp and be on our way back before it hits the area of the judge's camp. I'm not anticipating any weather problems at all," I replied over the intercom.

We flew for about an hour or so, then we reached the hunting area in which we were to find the judge. We soon saw two white dots off to our right. These would be the two tents, one for sleeping accommodation and the other for storage and eating. White stood out like a beacon in all the surroundings, which were assuming their fall mantle. The hunters had located the camp in a small, sandy clearing, beside a small lake. The bush had not grown on this particular spot; it might have been about 1,600 square feet of clearing. I could see someone working at the propane stove. It wasn't the judge, I couldn't see him yet. A wisp of smoke from whatever was being cooked became my flight sock. I made my first test run over the camp. Just as I was about to make my turn for the run, I saw the judge come out of a tent. The way he was rubbing himself I assumed that he had been lying down for a nap. The sound of the plane must have awakened him. He waved up at the plane, it was not an enthusiastic wave. Maybe he wasn't fully awake, yet. There was only this one Cornell in the Yukon at the time, so I assumed that he knew that it was flown by someone that he knew.

I waggled the wings of the plane to acknowledge the greeting. I flew the plane in over the camp at treetop level. The sound on the ground must have been deafening. My purpose was to insure that the drop could be made precisely on target. If we had encountered cross winds or turbulence, then I would have had to revise the flight path. Fortunately, the air was smooth and stable. The heavy, unsettled air, from the rain clouds, had not yet reached this point but they were certainly imminent.

"OK, Vic, we are going over again. This time you make the drop. Remember now, when I wave my arm, you have to pull back on the canopy. There will be a lot of air rushing about you and it will be noisy. Don't let that bother you, there will be nothing wrong with the plane. Get the package ready in your right hand. The camp will be on our right side. Don't heave it out until you hear me yell NOW! Understood?"

"Roger, and shouldn't I say Wilco, or something like that? This will be a perfect drop, trust me," said Vic.

I turned the Cornell into the wind, put down twenty degrees of flap, throttled back so that the plane would start to sink, as though we were about to land, then aimed at the left side of the camp. Just as we reached about seventy-five feet above the ground, I gave her more throttle in order to get her to fly level, then waved my arm. I could feel the sudden rush of cold air. Vic had gotten the canopy open, alright. Just as the first portion of the clearing disappeared under the nose, I yelled "NOW!"

I gunned the plane in order to get her up into the air again. I wanted more space between me and the ground. As we climbed, I made a gradual turn to go back over to the camp area. I wanted to see how well "Bomber Wylie" had done.

Why was the judge standing in the clearing shaking his

fist at us? Why was his companion doubled over as though he was overcome with laughter? Why did the judge raise both arms above his head and shake them at us? It was an act of total exasperation. Why?

As we flew downwind, I slowed up our air speed in order to get a better look at what was happening in the camp.

"Holy Christ, Harold. Do you see what happened? The bloody envelope went right through the side of the judge's tent. Christ what a hole! You could drive a bloody truck through it. Talk about good aim. Jeez, is the judge ever mad! Look at him shaking his fist. I'm bloody glad that we're up here and not down there. Wow! Look at him stomp those feet. Jeez, is he furious!"

"Boy, will he tear a strip off us when he gets back into town. We'll have to offer to get the tent repaired," I suggested.

"Repaired! Are you kidding? They couldn't repair that damage. Christ, look at that, the judge just threw something onto the ground. Jeez, it's our envelope. What a mess it is. That bloody wrench was too big, Harold. Oh, hell I wonder what he'll do now? I've never seen him so angry," said Vic despondently.

Vic and I flew around the area in wide circles for about ten minutes. We could see the camp off in the distance. I thought that the further away we were the better off things would be, under the circumstances.

Soon the judge walked out of the storage tent and over to look at the demolished tent. Then he stood in the center of the clearing with his hands at his sides. We took this to be the signal that we had been waiting for, so I flew back toward the camp. As we neared the clearing, the judge nodded his head in the affirmative.

Vic had his injunction. My client had escaped the threat of punitive damages.

Having delivered himself of his judgment, the judge again started to shake his fist at us. More vigorously this time. Then he pointed to the north. Oh boy! Those storm clouds were coming up fast.

Chapter Eighteen

A simple flight to drop off gear,
Prospectors and their dog,
Became a frigid, glacial hell,
In pain my body throbbed.

Wading in that liquid ice,
So they'd stay warm and dry,
Was torment in its terminal form,
I was sure that I would die.

On the Cold Side of Hell

The paramount obligation of every pilot who transports passengers whether for hire or not, is to insure the safety of that passenger and his belongings. Sometimes this responsibility reaches absurd proportions. Yet, if you take on the job, you must honor that which comes with it; be it comfortable or agonizing. As one United States President said, "If you can't bear the heat; don't stand near the stove."

One day, in Whitehorse, I was to be faced with a Hobson's choice of no mean dimensions. To this day I shiver, just thinking about it.

It was early June, 1955. The air had not yet warmed up, although there was a promise of it in the wind. The ice on the Yukon River had broken up and was on its way to St. Helena on the west coast of Alaska. Possibly the ice pack would thaw before it reached that destination. After all, the chunks of ice would have to survive some 1,600 miles of tortuous turns and twists in the river before reaching tidewater.

What this breakup meant for the collective economy of the Yukon was easy to see with the naked, unskilled eye. Prospectors were in the stores acquiring their supplies for the short summer's work. The whole period would encompass about three months, at the best of it. Winter at those latitudes is never really gone; it's only on leave. Its specter merely retreats on a temporary hiatus until the sun fails to reach its northernmost flight above the equator, whereupon its icy grip returns for another pregnancy term.

Such was the situation on the particular day in question. I was waiting on the aircraft float dock for what I understood to be a passenger and his gear. I had never met this potential passenger and I had no idea of what his "gear" consisted. If it was like the others who had been getting out to the mountain ranges in the past few weeks, it could consist of a tent, one or two rifles with shot, a heavy parka with hood attached, heavy work boots, a few plaid, wool shirts, a bed roll, ropes of varying circumferences and lengths, a hatchet, a large hunting knife, a prospector's pick with several replacement heads, several duffel bags of clothing and blankets, some pots and pans, and the inevitable coffee pot. Somewhere there would be wooden matches dipped in wax to make sure that they would be dry when needed. It was still quite cold at some of the altitudes reached by these intrepid sourdoughs and when a fire was needed it might be urgently required. They could not risk the fact that their match might not work.

The gear varied somewhat, but not enough to quarrel about. A metal or hard wood back pack was an invariable. Heavy gloves, mostly fully lined, were popular. Add to this what the passenger was wearing: a Mackinaw coat; heavy hiker's boots made of substantial leather and probably with a steel toe, laced with leather thongs; heavy woolen socks, which usually peeked over the top of the high boots or were folded down over the top so that the red or blue line, which was universally woven into the socks, would show; and there was usually a down vest under the Mackinaw and over the plaid shirt. In most cases, they wore thermal underwear under all of what I have itemized. Heavy twill or denim jeans were popular. Oftentimes a prospector had a pistol and holster somewhere in his pack. He would slide a belt through the holster on the opposite side to a scabbard, in which he carried the long bladed knife.

My reason for outlining all of these items is not only that the reader will have an intimate knowledge of what it is that makes up a prospector, but another reason, more pertinent to the story, will become evident later.

Soon a jeep drove up. It contained a driver, two other men, a huge malamute dog, and a pile of gear. There was so much gear that portions of it draped over the rear and sides of the vehicle.

"Hi ya, Harold!" barked the driver. "I've got your load here. Have you met Gordie Rutledge and Mike Waters, his partner?" (not the real names)

"No, I haven't. How are you gentlemen?" I said as I thrust out my hand in greeting.

"God! I hope you're better at flying than you are at judging people. We ain't no gentlemen, we're just plain folk," said Gordie, who leapt out of the jeep like a gymnast. "I'm Gordie and this little guy here is Mike. Great to know ya!"

He wrapped his huge hand around mine and shook violently. He wasn't really paying attention to what he was doing. He was waving at someone up the street. He almost wrenched my arm off, so violent was his greeting.

He was a huge man. I guessed that he stood about six feet four and weighed, easily, two hundred and twenty pounds. He wore a heavy black beard, sprouted bushy, thick, black eyebrows, above which he sported a fur cap. In some way, I'm not sure how, he looked like a grizzly bear. Maybe it was his size and the way he ambled instead of walked.

"Whoops there ... hold on Gordie ... I may need that arm for flying ... man ... I hope you never decide to get angry at me. How much do you weigh?" I asked.

"Well, I think I'm away down to 235 this week," he responded.

"Do you think that your plane is going to have trouble getting all of this gear and Mike and me into the air?" Gordie asked as he started to unload the jeep.

"Well, we'll soon know. We will have to weigh everything that goes aboard to make sure that she will get into the air. We have to determine how much fuel will be needed for the distance of the trip and return. Then we have to calculate its weight, too. The plane is pretty powerful but, of course, she has her limitations," I said pleasantly.

Up to this point, Mike had said absolutely nothing. He had just sat in the jeep, watching the action. I turned to proffer my hand to him and the dog let loose an ominous growl. My hand returned to my side as though it had been on an overstretched elastic band. This would be a most unwelcome event

188

if it turned out that this huge mutt was unruly, vicious, or disobedient. Nature posed enough threats to flying without voluntarily adopting some unusual menace in the form of a wild dog.

"You don't have to be concerned about him, Harold," said Mike. "I think you might have just startled him, you being a stranger and all."

"I certainly hope that was the case, Mike. We just can't hazard having an animal which is the slightest bit obstreperous. Has she flown in a small plane before?" I asked with obvious concern.

"Sure she has, many times, hasn't she, Gordie? She's been flying with us for years, you don't have to worry about her. I guarantee it!" Mike asserted.

"Well, OK then. It's understood that if the dog gives us, and in particular me, any trouble at all, I will immediately turn back, no matter where we are. Is that understood and agreed between all of us?" I asked, pointedly.

"Ya got yourself a deal, Harold," said Gordie with a broad smile.

"Sure thing, Harold ... you have a deal ... you really don't have to worry about her. She'll be just fine ... you'll see," Mike stated, encouragingly.

I made a point of going over toward the dog again. As I stepped toward her I said, "What's her name?"

"Tammy," replied Mike, whereupon the dog reacted to her name and looked attentively at Mike.

Tammy was still sitting in the Jeep behind Mike. He had not made any patent move to get out of the vehicle.

"Come Tammy, come here, come Tammy," I called, as I stood several feet away from the Jeep.

To my surprise the dog leapt out of the Jeep and came to my side. She circled me, sniffing all the way.

"You must have a dog, Harold," suggested Gordie, "that's the way she behaves toward people who smell of dog."

"You're right, Gordie, I do have a family dog. The peculiar thing is that her name is also Tammy. She is a miniature boxer. She is just great with the children."

I felt myself relaxing. I had really been concerned for a few moments. I had heard stories about pilots having to contend with unruly creatures which run amok in the cabin, while in flight. I wanted no part of that. I didn't intend to become a statistic over someone's vanity about his dog's idiosyncrasies.

"OK, let's get going. That sun is racing us to your drop off point. I'd like to get back here in daylight. Let's form a chain and get everything stowed. Hand me that duffle bag. I'll start with it," I shouted, hoping that any tension engendered by the dog episode would soon be forgotten in the loading activity.

All of us got involved in the careful loading of the gear. Tammy found a spot in the sun and lay there, watching every move. I took great care about where and how the equipment was located. Weight and balance would be crucial factors on this flight to a high level lake.

The plane was the Beechcraft S.17 D., about which I have previously written. She was a gorgeous plane. I suppose that some may find that term peculiar, when applied to an aircraft. My dictionary defines gorgeous, in part, as "strikingly beautiful, fine, extremely pleasing, good ... " Well, my plane was all of those things, and more. With that powerful 450 Junior Wasp engine, she could get a large load off the water quickly and carry it comfortably, for about 700 miles before needing more fuel. She was not a "forgiving aircraft," one had to devote undivided attention to her at all times. Maybe that's why they refer to aircraft in the female gender.

This Beechcraft 17 is considered by many to have been the forerunner of the famous Canadian built De Havilland Beaver aircraft. The Beaver is noted for its ability to lift heavy loads out of the water in short take-off runs. There are many former Beaver "bush-pilots" who have gone on to become airline captains, including my nephew, Wally Davis. The disciplines learned as a bush pilot, in small powerful aircraft, is considered to be a proper grounding for advancement to huge commercial planes. Such disciplines translate into that pilot's acceptance of the necessary responsibilities, which are exigent, when a pilot has the obligation to take care of so many precious lives.

As we neared the completion of our loading task, I noticed that Mike had slacked off early in that program. He was sitting with Tammy, leaning up against a wall, basking in the sun. He seemed to be in some discomfort or was otherwise lacking in energy. When we had finished the loading, I moseyed over to Gordie and raised the issue. Gordie drew me further away from the scene and said, "You've noticed it too, eh? I tried to get him to rest for a few more days. He's had a bad bout with pneumonia. He was in hospital for three weeks. He sure isn't the spry old Mike that I have known. I'm worried about him going into the hills so soon. I've spoken to him and to his

doctor, but here he is. What else can I do? It's his life."

"Or his death," I countered.

"Ya, that too, Harold, but I just can't do anything about it. He says he's my partner, and where I go, he goes. We have been prowlin' those hills for about twelve years together. He would most certainly resent your intrusion, so don't bring it up OK?" he cautioned.

"OK, so be it. We'll just leave it in the hands of fate," I philosophized.

"Ain't we all?" replied Gordie.

"If you guys want to get that last cup of coffee, which is made by someone else, you'd better do it now; after that, it's coffee in the wilds for three months. I have to file the flight plan which will give you time," I suggested.

I knew that once they got into the mountains, they might have to chop ice for water. They'd climb up to higher levels where the sun had not yet worked its magic. I had even heard of prospectors who took a thermos flask of water to bed with them so that they would have water, not ice, for the morning's coffee.

After the coffee and following my filing the flight plan, we boarded the plane. (A flight plan is a detailed report of the type of aircraft in use, its registration letters, the intended course, time of travel, destination, your proposed air speed, altitude of flight, amount of fuel on board, number of passengers and crew, their names and addresses, next of kin, ETA, expected time of arrival, at your destination, and the same information covering your return flight to base).

Tammy shinned her way up onto the soft packs which had been placed on top for her comfort. These were stowed in the compartment behind the rear seat, which would hold three persons. In this case, Mike commandeered the back seat, along with some knapsacks and other "junk," as he called it. Gordie climbed into the right front seat and would sit alongside me during the trip.

This flight was not going to be of long duration so it was not necessary to carry a full load of fuel. The lighter we were, the easier it would be to get off the water. Having satisfied myself that the plane was properly fueled for this flight, I boarded the plane through the special door for the pilot. This door is located just ahead of the larger, wider, passenger's door.

"Is everybody strapped in, including Tammy?" I asked generally. I received an affirmative response from Gordie and

191

a grunt from Mike, which I took to be a positive response. I inserted the ignition key but didn't turn it yet. I had to feed the engine with some primer fuel first. Three blasts and she should be ready. I turned the key and she coughed a few times and whined a bit, but did not start. She was cold. The propeller had rotated a couple of times but it was obviously a struggle. I gave her three more shots of primer and turned the key again. She coughed, whined, the prop turned, then she roared into activity. The sound was deafening. The morning quiet was shattered for that day. A small volume of smoke puffed out of the exhaust, and we were just about ready to taxi out into the Yukon River. I signaled the dock hand to let go of the lines which held us to the dock. He tossed the ropes up onto the top of the float. They would trail there, safely, until they were needed again upon landing.

The Yukon River has a reputation as an unusually swift river. The current passing the float dock traveled at about four to five knots, when it wasn't frozen solid. Once untied, the floats got caught up in the flow. I had dropped the water rudders, which were attached to the heel of the floats, so that I could steer the craft much in the same way as one steers a boat, which is just about all that the plane was, at this moment. We were out into the main stream in moments, heading north. I let her drift with the flow so that I could get a clear, straight run to the south, into the wind. I let the plane glide a mile or so downstream then turned her into the wind by using a combination of water rudder, tail rudder, and a bit more throttle.

Once into the wind I pushed the throttle in, to bring the rpm's up to about 1250. The opposing speed of the river would have taken us downstream backwards otherwise. Once stationary in the center of the river, I was able to wrench up on the cable which in turn pulled up the water rudders. There was a metal hook under the instrument panel onto which the ring at the end of the cable connected. Now the craft would be "steered" by the rudder on the tail, and by the thrust of the engine forward as far as it would go. The sudden and powerful forward thrust accelerated our momentum forward through the water. The plane got "lighter" in the water as the plane was obtaining lift from the air. The faster the plane goes the less surface of the floats touches the water and therefore the less surface friction. On aircraft floats there is an upward indentation, about half way back on the float, where it starts to taper up to the tail or back end. The point at which this tapering starts is called the "step." A float plane must get up on the step before it can take off.

Soon, within seconds, we were skimming over the surface of the water instead of wallowing in it like a log. The control column, which had been pressed against my stomach, insisted on moving forward. This is a welcomed sign so I cooperated with a bit of a frontward shove, not too much, I didn't want her to porpoise, i.e., dig the nose of the floats into the water. Soon the air speed built up to a safe, take off speed. I pulled back, gently, on the column and we were airborne, we were flying!

I flew past the float dock, where I started my gradual climbing bank to the right. The lake we were headed for was almost due west, which meant getting above the high mountains. We had to gain altitude as quickly as the plane could properly climb. I adjusted the throttle, the propeller pitch, and the mixture control, then let the plane do the job for which it was designed.

"Everything OK?" I yelled, in order to be heard above the din.

"Just great with me, Harold," replied Gordie.

I turned to see why Mike had not responded. He was fast asleep. Either he was a seasoned traveler, in small planes, or he was fatigued from the strain of the recent activity, close on his prolonged illness; or a combination of both. In any event, both he and Tammy appeared to be well into the arms of Morpheus.

Anyone who has been up in this part of the world would not dispute the statement that, in the Yukon, Mother Nature outdid herself with beauty and majesty. Whitehorse is nestled in one of the many crooks of the Yukon River. Vast plains rise up gently from the river, gradually forming rolling foothills on each side, then emanating into mountains. Lakes abound in that region. Each with a different hue of blue-green. Each peak has its own distinctive characteristics. Some were snow-capped; others had deep crevices which looked like they had split into several units centuries before; others had long, sloping meadows of green pastures; others were surrounded from base to peak by rotting rocks and boulders. Some humps were dark blues and purples. Others showed the gray-brown of ancient granite. The sun treated our eyes to a continuously changing spectrum of colors as we traversed the eastern edge of the coastal mountains.

We spotted mobile specks of white, the Dall sheep for which the Yukon is famous. The world's largest remaining herds of such sheep live in these mountains. There was one huge moose below who, startled by the sound of the aircraft, charged across the meadow, first in one direction, then another.

The highlight of our nature study was to see a monstrous grizzly bear and her cub. I'm sure it was my imagination but did she really sit back on her haunches and shake a defiant paw at us?

"There's the lake, Harold," cried Gordie. "See it over to the left?"

"You bet," I replied. "It's exactly where it's supposed to be, according to my flight map."

He smiled at me and said, stoically, "Thank God for that."

"In just a minute we should see the glacier which feeds that lake. It's over to our left, just out of sight beyond that mountain wall," I said.

"Yes, I know, Harold. I was up in this area several years ago. It's that damned glacier which keeps this whole area so cold. The water is frigid and there is always a breeze blowing off that ice," Gordie replied.

Just at that moment we passed the edge of the mountain which formed the obstruction to our view of the ice field. It was an immense sheet of discolored ice. It was as though a wrinkled, unclean flannel sheet had been carelessly cast over a sea of great rocks. It looked sterile, out of place, lying there. It had one peculiarity for me. It looked man made. It was a ski ramp or a wide, white highway which tapered, through skilled engineering, into the lake.

The glacier, as it moved inexorably down the valley which it had created for its resting place, ground the rocks and granite beneath it, depositing the silt into the lake. Glacial morain was everywhere down the valley. From our altitude we could see ripples of sand benches under the surface of the lake. From here they looked like close-spaced, rolling hills.

Having determined the direction of the wind by watching the wave action and confirming this by looking at the vegetation for motion, I trimmed the plane for landing. From the air, it was difficult to be certain as to the depth of the lake near the shoreline. There was nothing against which to measure the depth. There appeared to be nothing but sand upon the lake bottom. The undulating striations stretched from shore to shore. The center of the lake was too dark to allow any depth conclusions.

To be safe and sure I decided to land well into the middle of the lake. It was about five miles long, and possibly three miles wide. Plenty of room for a safe landing. What was more important; it was large enough to permit take off at that altitude. Have you heard about planes which have landed at high altitudes and then tried to get off again? It could only be a story of frustration and possibly of tragedy.

Once down on the water, I pulled back, fully, on the control column in order to have the heels of the floats dig in. In this way a pilot has a crude form of "braking." The forward motion is slowed dramatically. I released the cable holding the water rudders up. They dropped into place, and we were then ready to taxi to shore and disembark.

At least that was the plan. That was the norm. That is the way it had always happened in the past. Shouldn't I have been entitled to expect the customary to repeat itself? WRONG!

Suddenly, while we were about one hundred feet from shore, the floats caught on something. The nose of the plane pitched forward, just slightly, and we came to a complete halt.

I pulled back on the throttle to let the engine idle. I opened my special door and looked down into the water. There were dusty swirls of water just beneath the floats. I didn't need an engineer to tell me what had happened. My heart sank and my blood pressure rose. The sand waves, to which I previously referred, rippled out from the shoreline to the center of the lake. We were caught on the crest of one of those waves. I could easily see others which crested up between us and the shoreline.

We were in the grip of a prehistoric phenomenon. Glacial silt.

"What the hell do we do now, Harold?" said Gordie, not aggressively, but in a tone which exhibited frustration and disappointment. So near and yet so far?

"Can we paddle to shore?" drawled Mike from the back seat, without enthusiasm.

"Good thought, Mike, but the weight will be the same whether we paddle or try using the engine," I retorted.

I shut the engine down. All that could now be heard was the whining of the gyros; soon to be superseded by the whistle of the wind outside.

Tammy started to stir. I guessed that her logic was that, once stopped, it was time for her to get out and romp.

"I know what has to be done. I sure as hell don't like the prospects, but there is nothing else to be done, except go back, and that is absurd." I said rhetorically. I received no response or other comment. I was sure that they, too, saw the obvious solution and didn't care for it either.

Here we were, hundreds of miles from nowhere. They planned to stay here, in the wilds, for about three months. Mike had just had pneumonia and was still weak. There was no way that they could get wet now and hope to survive that cold weather, without encountering possible complications. Frost was still to be found in the shaded areas, and a ridge of ice clung to the shore. There was enough breeze to make the plane bob on its unwelcome anchor.

"Will Tammy be able to make it to shore from here? I assume that she can swim?" I asked. "The water is only three, maybe four feet deep, at the most. It's difficult to judge the depth of water at the best of times, but when it is as crystal clear as this water it is almost impossible without a measuring stick. I'll check it with the paddle."

"I see what ya have in mind, Harold. I don't like it one bit. Maybe we should go back," Gordie said dejectedly.

I knew that a prospector doesn't choose his area for examination lightly. They sometimes chase an outcropping for miles and years. Some "grid" and "cross-grid" an area in which they "sense" mineralization. It's a fever with many of them, like addiction to gambling. After all, they are the true dreamers, the seekers of treasures hidden by nature. To some, the wilds of the north are what the bottle is to the alcoholic. It is their way to escape the tedious, mundane existence of the modern, nine to five, concrete jungle.

"Let's not talk about turning back just yet, Gordie," I replied. "Let's try lightening the load a bit, then see if we can get her free of the bottom. I might be able to drive her in closer then."

"Yuv got a helluva lot of 'ifs,' 'maybes,' and 'mights' there, Harold," Gordie responded without enthusiasm.

"I'll grant you that, Gordie, but our options are very limited. I know that you two don't want to go back, any more than I want you to. I know how you guys plan right down to your last nickel and hour of time. Trust me, I know this plan will work," I lied.

I took the paddle out of its catch on the strut. The water on the concavity side of the mound measured about thirty inches deep, no more ... thank God!

"Mike, you get into a sleeping bag and wrap yourself up well," I ordered. "Just sitting there without any movement in this cold will make you a prime candidate for recurring pneumonia, unless you stay warm and dry."

Tammy was hesitant about getting out of the nice warm plane and into the frigid glacier water. I couldn't blame her for that.

"Ice cold water," I repeated to myself, "Christ, if there is anything I hate more than snakes, it's cold water to swim in."

Gordie handed, no, pushed Tammy down to me. I was standing on the port float. She came reluctantly. I still had the sound of that growl in my ears. I was balancing myself on that float without a handhold. My hands were full of a big, shaggy, dog which struggled and bucked, trying to get her feet onto something solid. She slid through my arms to the float. Her coat of hair must have contained some lanolin like substance because she was impossible to hold onto. Once on the narrow float, she circled uncertainly, constantly looking up to Gordie for support and direction. He encouraged her to get into the water, but she wasn't going. She weighed about one hundred pounds and a push from me met with stubborn resistance. Gordie clambered down the ladder to join the two of us on the float. Gordie said, "Sorry, Tammy," gave her a monstrous shove, and into the water she went, splashing both of us in the process.

"Damn dog," muttered Gordie.

I appraised the lightening effect that Tammy's departure had on the floats. There was little to none.

"Hell, we still aren't light enough, Gordie. I'm going to jump into the water and try towing us in. We're committed now anyway, unless you want to leave your dog up there on the beach," I said, with far more bravado than I felt.

I surveyed myself to determine if there was anything on my person which I did not want to get wet. I removed my leather flight jacket. I would want that to put on when I got back into the plane to fly home. I tossed it to Gordie who put it in on the front seat.

"OK, here I go," I yelled, as I gingerly lowered myself over the side of the float. The water was agonizingly cold. What else could it be? It had just run off the glacier over there. I thought that my body was accepting this torture fairly well, right up until I felt that icy grip on my private parts.

"Hooolllyyyy Kkkeeeriiissst!" I exclaimed, "I wasn't ready for that!"

Just then, my feet struck bottom. The water was just up to about my belt line. Christ it was cold! I had already started to shiver. My teeth chattered uncontrollably. I had heard and read about this, now it was happening to me. I worried about hypothermia before accomplishing the objective. I'd better hurry!

The plane started to float. I pulled it for maybe forty feet. I was walking up and down on those underwater hills of sand. About fifty to sixty feet from shore she stuck again. After all, it was getting shallower and the weight was the same.

"Gordie hand me some of the heavier stuff. Be quick, I'm getting numb!" I cried.

Gordie handed me heavy items and I ran to the beach, dumped them and ran back into the water. I made several trips this way but the plane stayed stuck.

I couldn't stop my body from making erratic movements. Parts of my body jerked or flayed about spontaneously. I shivered in spasms. My head twitched. I felt nauseous, yet somehow calm. I had heard stories about people who had almost frozen to death. They all said that, just as they passed out, they were overcome by a peaceful calm.

"Gordie, you've got to get on my shoulders and let me carry you to shore—don't argue, hurry up, get on ... and for Chris' sake don't fall or it will mean I have suffered all of this pain for nothing," I ordered.

"Jeez, Harold, I weigh almost twice what you do, we'll never make it," responded Gordie, as he climbed onto my shoulders.

My God he was heavy! I had noticed that before, but then I had not been required to heft him. I walked with great caution. Those mounds were treacherous and invisible in the now murky water. Gordie was hunched over my head, but the balance was good. We reached shore and fell in a heap. He was there and he was dry. Thank God for small mercies!

The bloody dog was running back and forth barking and circling. She thought this was a huge frolic. She picked up sticks and brought them to us to throw them for her. Damn dog, indeed, but what did she know of our exasperation?

When Gordie climbed on my shoulders, I had let go of the rope connected to the floats. The breeze was blowing in the right direction to force the plane towards shore, if she could float.

Something had to be right.

I turned and headed into the water again. I heard a voice in my head saying, "Once more into the breach, dear friend ...." It was like a stranger's voice, not mine. I was trembling constantly. I felt miserable. In fact, I was turning blue.

As I reached the water's edge, about to plunge into the surf again, I almost ran into the wing of the plane. What the hell? Sure enough she had floated in. She was on the beach. She was where we had hoped to be an hour earlier. I grabbed the float and started to turn her tail in so that the end of the float could be pulled up onto the beach. Gordie helped.

In very short order, Mike was out of the plane and onto the beach. Gordie got back into the craft and started to hand out the gear.

"For Christ sake, Gordie, hurry. I can't take this cold much more, I'm freezing to death!" I cried.

"You're sweating, Harold, that's the problem. You've got ice on your hair and ears. I'll build a fire, a big fire, right away," said Mike.

After what seemed to be an eternity, we got the plane unloaded. Mike wanted me to go to the fire. It was a small fire, and consequently it gave off almost no heat. Maybe to a pot, in direct contact, there was heat but not to me standing there in that breeze, soaking wet. While carrying Gordie, I had stooped over with his weight and I was now wet up to my armpits.

"Sorry, you guys, but I can't take it here. I must get out to the plane and into the cabin. The engine will warm up in no time and give off heat. I think I stand a better chance there, in the cabin, out of the breeze, than here."

I hobbled to the float. Gordie was right behind me. My clothes were going rigid. They were freezing solid!

"Gordie, the minute I'm in the cabin, give the floats a big shove out into the water, OK?" I urged.

I staggered along the float alright but I couldn't get my knee to bend enough to enable me to get up the steps into the cabin. I stood like a frozen statue with one hand on the wing strut and the other reaching up to the door handle. My legs refused to respond to my mind's signal to step up. I bent over and lifted my left leg. The pain occasioned by this maneuver was beyond description. A commonly known word which might approach the sensation is "excruciating." My foot slipped off the rung. It had jerked away on its own accord.

Gordie ran along the float and came up behind me. He opened the special door with one hand and with the other lifted me as though I was a small child. He shoved me into the cabin and pushed me along the seat. I tried to sit up but couldn't make it. I curled into the fetal position. My eyes were closed. My arms were wrapped about myself. I was going to sleep! I heard my name being called, as though from a great distance. Gordie appeared again and levered me into a sitting position facing the controls.

"Harold, start the engine ... wake up, Harold ... do you hear me?" the voice demanded.

Gordie was shaking me violently trying to get response. I felt that I had been down a deep tube, out of which I was now floating towards a rim of light where I saw Gordie's face.

"Come on, Harold, that's it. Get this thing started. I'll shove her off," he said sympathetically.

He stood at the open door, as I tried, unsuccessfully, to insert the ignition key into its slot. My trembling hands would not cooperate. Why had I taken that damn key out of the plane anyway. Just habit?

"Let me do it," ordered Gordie as he shoved his huge body into the cabin. "There, it's in now. All you have to do is turn it, I guess. See ya, Harold. I'll never forget this, thanks a lot. I'm sorry that you froze your butt off but it sure helped us a helluva lot. See ya in three months, right here."

Gordie disappeared down the float as I cranked over the engine. She started up just fine. I still trembled uncontrollably, but managed to get her out into the center of the lake. The passage of air caused by the propeller was agonizingly cold. The heater was not yet producing any appreciably warm air. I taxied around for a short period of time until I felt my senses returning to normal. I managed to get my flight jacket back on. What might not have been warm air for some, in that cabin, was like a blast furnace to me.

I wanted to get home. I wanted a hot drink of any type, preferably a hot rye or two. I turned her squarely into the wind and gunned her. She jumped off that lake like a scared rabbit. She was light. We had discarded the people, the luggage, and that dog. We had also burned up some fuel.

200

Whenever I hear, read, or think about torment, my mind invariably slips back to that trip. If hell has a cold side, I've already been there. If the other side is even half as bad, I don't want to go there.

Chapter Nineteen

The scourge of man is daylight lost
When a path must yet be seen,
From unheralded source, the aid may come
When man's inner light doth beam.

A Guiding Light

In late August of 1955, just after our son Larry had been born on the seventh of that month, I was sitting in the living room reading a transcript of a preliminary hearing. I was preparing for a trial which was to start in a few days. The phone rang, and as Laura was in the kitchen doing dishes, I called to let her know that I would take it.

That phone call was the precursor of an incident which manifested the spontaneous compassion which humanity possesses, but does not often get a clear opportunity to demonstrate.

"Hello," I said, in the voice which I used when I wanted the person at the calling end to realize that I do not wish to be disturbed.

"Harry, don't let on that you know who is calling. It's to be a surprise for Laura and Mom, and you, of course," said the voice which I instantly recognized to be that of Laura's sister Belle.

"Well, I really am kind of busy at the moment," I responded, hoping to make it sound as though I had just received a business call, in the event that Laura or her mother could hear me.

"Do you know who this is?" queried Belle.

"Of course, I do," I said, without further commitment.

"I gather that Mom or Laura might overhear you?" she asked.

"Well, maybe ... I'm just not sure. Why don't you just explain the problem and I'll see if there is anything that I can do to help," I offered.

"I'm down at the Whitehorse Inn. Can you come down and pick me up right away?" she inquired.

"Well, I guess so. I have a trial that I am preparing for, but I suppose that I could spare a few minutes," I responded, hopefully getting my message across.

"OK, then I'll wait for you here. Hurry up, I can't wait!" Belle said excitedly.

"OK, but not for long," I replied.

"What was that all about?" asked Laura, as she came out from the kitchen, wiping her hands on a towel. "Surely no one would expect you to go out at this time of night?"

"Oh, yes they do," I replied. "But I shouldn't be gone for very long. I'll be back soon."

I was out the front door and headed for the car before Laura could advance any objections.

Whenever any one calls me "Harry," I can immediately identify the era during which that person knew me. I was called by that name only when I lived in Regina and while I was in the navy. I had adopted using my actual, formal name when I went to law school.

Belle is the type of person referred to when someone uses the term "old fashioned girl." She was then, and is now, a person to whom most people react in a friendly manner. Her aura is that of a sociable person, so long as you behave properly. She was attractive in appearance, without the need to be made up to be so. She and Laura looked very much alike. Belle is a few years older than Laura. Both sisters had learned, from their mother, to be well groomed. Her hair, like Laura's, always looked like she had just stepped out of a beauty salon. Yet she too, did it herself. Her smile would light up a room. Belle was always totally open and candid with everybody. She was jolly, loved a good party, and had many friends. She had married Ken Charlton, whom many readers will recall as a professional Canadian football player of exceptional ability. He was inducted into the Saskatchewan Football Hall of Fame just months before this book was published.

Ken and Belle lived in Regina, Saskatchewan, at the time of this particular event.

When I entered the Whitehorse Inn, I wondered if Belle had yet learned of the historical legacy of this building. I also wondered how on earth she got up here.

The hotel, at the time, was owned by T. C. Richards. He was a bigger than life character. I probably knew his proper given names, but like everyone else I called him by his initials, T. C. He was a large man, well over 240 pounds, and stood about six feet two in stocking feet. He consistently wore a white Stetson hat. Some say he even wore it to bed. He certainly wore it in his, and other bars. His capacity to imbibe and hold his liquor was a legend in the north. My own personal experience with him was that I had sued the Inn, on behalf of some disgruntled employees. They claimed that they were due additional funds for services rendered. Following the trial, which T. C. lost, he invited me to share a drink with him to show that there was "no hard feelins." We went to the Inn. He led me to his favorite table and beckoned the waiter over. "Wadlyahave, Harold," he asked. I told him that I seldom drank anything but Canadian Club and water, no ice. "You heard him, bring him a bottle of C.C. and a bottle of gin for me," he ordered. That is exactly what the waiter brought us.

The legend, about the chronology of the hotel, has it that it was built about the time of the gold rush. T. C. was a teamster and then a "cat" driver. He hauled freight from "outside" into Whitehorse. During one sojourn he is alleged to have won the hotel, as a result of being involved with the preceding owner in a crap game. True or not, he ran it with panache. He stood high in the local folklore.

"Hi, Belle," I said to the shortish, slender lady, who was reading the items on the notice board in the lobby of the inn.

She whirled around and gave me one of her famous smiles. She ran up and gave me a big hug.

"Hi, Harry. How are you? How's Laura? How's Mom? How's the baby?"

"Whoa ... Belle," I said, laughing about her enthusiasm. "Which question do you want me to answer first?"

"All of them, you clot," she cried, as she gave me another big hug.

"What on earth are you doing here?" I asked. "We didn't know that you were coming up for a visit."

"Neither did I, until I heard that Harold and 'Stevie' were coming up here. Their last name is Reid. They are friends of ours from Regina. He is in the furrier business and he is going to have a big, fur coat sale; getting all the ladies prepared for winter." (I will refer to him as Reid, in this story, for obvious reasons.)

She grasped me by the hand and led me toward the bar.

"My friends are in here, having a drink with their business contacts. I'll introduce you, then we can go and surprise Laura and Mom. OK?"

"Sounds fine with me, Belle," I said, as I followed closely behind her.

After meeting her friends and discussing Reid's strong desire to go on a fishing trip, if it could be arranged after their fur coat sale, he and I transferred Belle's luggage into my car. I told Reid that some others in town had been talking about taking a fishing trip, in the plane, up to some virgin lakes. I'd let him know how it worked out.

"How would you like to handle this surprise, Belle?" I asked, as we drove to our house.

"How'll it be if I just go up and knock on the door alone? You wait outside."

"OK with me. I just hope that nobody has a heart attack," I joshed.

At the house, Belle got out of the car and carefully prevented the door from slamming shut. She pointed, then looked at me to confirm which house it was, and hurried up the walk. She reached the door, checked her attire, brushed both sides of her hair, moved from one foot to the other, turned and looked at me again, then knocked on the door.

She was just about to knock again when the outside lights came on. The door opened and there were two sisters staring at each other. One had a large expectant smile and the other had a mouth agape. Suddenly they both squealed. Laura's eyes were still unbelieving. She flung open the door totally and reached out to embrace her sister.

"Belle," she screamed. "Mom, it's Belle. Belle's here!"

"Who is it?" cried Mom. "Did you say Belle? How could Belle be here?"

Mom came to the door and joined in the squealing and excitement.

I just sat in the car. I knew, from many past experiences, how emotional the Davis family can be. First, there would be the excitable squeals, laughter, continuous babble, then a flood of tears.

I elected to wait until the sequence had run its course.

"You've just missed Harold," I heard Laura say to Belle, as she started to shut the front door. "He'll be annoyed that he wasn't here when you arrived, but ... ."

"He's outside there, in the car," said Belle, both laughing and crying as she wiped away the tears.

"You mean to tell me that fink knew about you coming up here, and kept it a secret. Wait'll I get my hands on him," cried Laura, who was also letting her tear ducts have some exercise.

"No, he didn't know. Not until I telephoned a few minutes ago," Belle explained.

"Was that YOU on the phone? I thought it was a client. I resented him having to go out at night when he works so hard all day," replied Laura. "Where is he?" she asked, peering out into the darkness.

"I'm here in the car, listening and watching you guys," I yelled, "Is it safe to come in yet?"

"Sure it is, it's safe now. We're past the tears stage," laughed Belle. "Do you need any help with the luggage?"

"No thanks. I'll get it and be with you guys in a minute," I replied.

It was great having Belle as a visitor. She is inclined to be curious about things and wanted to see all that the area had to offer a tourist. We showed her the three story log house which was used by Robert Service when he lived in Whitehorse. It was only two blocks from our house. We walked over and examined it in detail. We went out to Lake Leberge, which was the focal point of one of his famous poems. We visited the Whitehorse Rapids from which the city got its name. The crashing, dashing, foaming white water, cascading over the rocks, was said to look like the heads of charging white horses, with bobbing heads and flicking manes.

Laura, Belle, and their Mom spent several days touring and shopping. In the interim, the fur sale ended. Not, however, without me having fallen prey to the salesmanship of the furrier. Laura acquired a beautiful, full length, muskrat coat. Anything shorter in the freezing temperatures, experienced in this part of Canada, would not make sense. Laura wasn't in the market for a fur coat, so she said. She tried it on. That was the fatal mistake. It happened to be a perfect fit. Coincidence?

Following the sale, talk centered upon a fishing trip. I had spoken to two friends who had often talked about flying to a nearby lake. They had heard about it from prospectors, so had I. It was a high lake, about 3,700 feet above sea level, and resting in a crater or natural bowl. These two were both ardent fishermen and believed the lake to be virgin territory. Aside from flying in, the only other way to get there would be to walk in. There were no roads leading to the lake.

One of the twosome, a local dentist, Doctor Nori Nishio, was a particularly close friend of mine with whom I had flown often. He and his lovely wife, June, a school teacher, now live in Nanaimo, B. C. The other was also a friend, and our family doctor. He and I had gone bear hunting together. We had floated down the Pelley River on a "house raft." He was then a medical doctor, name of Desmond (Des) Morrow. He is now a pathologist resident with his charming wife Ruth, in Kelowna, B. C. The third member, Harold Reid, has since passed away, as did his wife, "Stevie."

We all met over a beer and discussed the trip. It was agreed that we would leave early the following morning in order to get in a full day's fishing. It was imperative that we all get back early tomorrow evening. The various reasons were exigent. Reid had to leave to return to his business in Regina. Des had scheduled a particularly sensitive surgical operation for early on the day after tomorrow. I, on the other hand, was to conduct a trial, about which I spoke earlier. It, too, was to commence the morning after the trip.

When our entourage arrived at the float dock, the Staggerwing Beechcraft was being serviced. There were fifteen people in our group. Only four of us were going fishing. The others were wives, children, or friends of the families.

Luggage, fishing rods, thermos bottles, and sandwiches were checked for the last time and stowed in a picnic suitcase aboard the plane. We posed again for "one last picture." Kisses were plenteous. It was like a scene from "Gilbert and Sullivan." We passed children back and forth while a chorus sang, "goodbye-goodbye," repeatedly.

Little did we know at that moment that we were about to have a most unusual, exciting, and soul inspiring experience.

The aircraft could accommodate five adults and a lot of gear. On this trip we had only four people and not a lot of heavy equipment.

Nori sat up front with me. Reid and Des sat together in the rear.

"Will this crate be able to carry home all of the fish?" asked Reid, in a jocular mood.

"My fish, maybe, but not everyone else's," asserted Nori.

I am sure that no one aboard the plane or in the whole of Whitehorse, for that matter, would dispute the fact that Nori was by far the most skilled fisherman of the lot of us.

"You guys catch them, I'll bring them home," I said in defense of the plane.

The others had been comparative strangers before boarding the plane. Now the camaraderie, commonplace amongst fisherman, was dispelling all reserves and inhibitions.

Once airborne, I withdrew from the bantering and concentrated on the instruments and flight path. It was second nature now, although the casual observer may not recognize it's happening.

The others kept chattering away about where they had gone fishing, who knew of the best fishing "hole," the largest fish caught on what weight of line, etc., etc. They compared notes to see if they could locate any common waters.

The activity on the dock had consumed more time than had been planned. It was important that we arrive on the site early in the day. There were two very good reasons. One, so that we would all have ample fishing time, and two, that we get off the water and back to Whitehorse in daylight. The days were getting shorter already, and there were no night landing lights for float equipped aircraft. All such landings had to be made one half hour before sundown. If it got dark, one could not clearly see the river to land on. Obviously, one would not be able to see the many natural and other obstructions, such as the smoke stacks of the paddlewheelers. The aircraft had a landing light, but its use was intended for landing the aircraft when on wheels and then only on a flat, hard surfaced runway which had other lighting available.

The flight plan, which I had filed, stated that we would return to the river by 4:30 p.m.

We had soon climbed to 5,000 feet. We had only about 1,500 feet more to climb in order to clear the crater like rim surrounding the lake.

During the time that it took to reach the lake, everybody carried on animated conversation and repartee. Many landmarks were noted and the attention of Reid drawn thereto.

"Look you guys, there is the lake," cried Nori.

"I already see mine, the one which is going to win our bet," yelled Des, over the din and roar.

We made a smooth landing. I taxied up to the shoreline near the mouth of a small stream. I shut down the engine. We clambered out on to the floats, with our respective gear in hand. They helped me turn the plane around so that the heels of the floats were on the sandy beach. I tied a strong rope from the tail ring to a nearby tree. She was safe and secure, save and except, from unusually stormy weather. The sky did not indicate anything but fine weather, just as the aeronautical weather bureau in Whitehorse had advised me. There was a slight breeze blowing but it did not auger poor weather.

The fishing that day was superb. Everyone caught their limit within the first few hours. Many fish were returned to the lake unharmed. Not necessarily because they were under the legal size, but because there had to be larger ones in the lake. Nori had caught a whopper. It was a trout weighing maybe twelve pounds. Anything smaller, after that, was considered inconsequential. We all sought something to beat Nori's catch. Those which were close we kept. Smaller ones were restored, live, to the water.

After the second hour or so, we were using lures without barbs. Only the hook remained. This way of fishing is the ultimate test of the fisherman's abilities. To hold that battling, struggling quarry, which is resolutely determined to escape, demands a certain skill and temperament. Removing the barb is a challenge many sports fishermen find worth waiting for. Each of the piscators was this day dramatically displaying his individual skill at the art of angling.

The fish were so plentiful and the sport so exhilarating that it was a natural emotional "high." Cries of, "yahoo," "look at this one fly," or, "I got him," were commonplace. Each patently ignored the other; yet esoterically, each shared with the other the thrills of each differing moment.

The breeze which had been blowing when we arrived had disappeared. There was nothing but serene calm. Dry flies could float and be seen easily. The fly barely bobbed at all, so placid was the water. While this was excellent for the fisherman, it was a matter of concern to me. We were at a rather high altitude. An aircraft is exactly that. It depends upon the support of air to fly. Air must pass over its foils in order to create the lift to get up into the air, to "fly." Without forward thrust and uplifting air, the plane is a beautiful but useless tool.

At the risk of boring the reader, I will restate that air at higher altitudes is thinner than at sea level. Thinner air gives less lift. Surface tension of water sucks the floats down and it is only thrust, combined with lift, which will enable the plane to break free of the surface and "fly."

Here we had two of the threatening factors. There was no wind (the surface of the water was unrippled) and we had altitude. No matter what amount of thrust the engine produced we would have trouble getting off the water.

In a nutshell, I smelled a problem. Not serious or life threatening, thank God, but with the above referred to factors coupled with the urgent need to get back early, (and tonight for sure), yes, we had a problem.

I hated to do it, but somebody had to be the party pooper.

"OK, you guys, time to wind it up. Last cast for all," I yelled. My voice echoed and reechoed around the bowl housing the lake. There were but two valleys breaking the continuity of this concavity, in which the lake rested. Through each of them meandered a small river. One valley led to the northeast and out to Whitehorse. The other led in the opposite direction, to the southwest. The lake was at about 3,800 feet, but the surrounding mountains were up to approximately 6,000 feet.

Slowly we assembled at the heels of the floats.

"Look fellows, I've got some things to tell you, so can I have your undivided attention. We're losing our light and I would like to explain the situation clearly and quickly," I said in a composed way. I did not want to alarm any of them. Not yet.

There was a look of dismay on the face of one, a flicker of concern on another, curiosity registered on Nori's otherwise constantly serene face.

A strange silence settled around us. With no movement, no talking and no breeze, there was an eerie hush which seemed to forecast the coming of some unique, uncommon event.

"Look fellows," I said calmly but with strength. (It was now imperative that I maintain control of this expedition.) "We have to face up to some hard realities. We may not have enough time to have a long, drawn out debate on the subject, unless everyone is prepared to accept the possibility of a delay in our departure until tomorrow."

"No way, Harold," asserted Reid. "I must leave tomorrow, and early at that. It's a helluva long drive back to Regina. I've got to be at a pelt sale ... can't afford to miss that."

"I absolutely must get back, Harold," said Des. "I've got an operation scheduled. You know that!" He exhibited a bit of anxiety and disappointment. Awful to end a great fishing trip with anxieties.

"What's the problem, Harold?" asked Nori, who was noted for his directness.

"Well, let me outline quickly the factors which have prompted me to say what I have," I said, as I sat down on a float heel.

Taking my action as an indication that we were going to have a general pow wow, the others found a place to sit as well.

I outlined to them the aerodynamic problem facing us. They all surveyed the water as though really looking at it, per se, for the first time today. Nori, who had flown with me many times, nodded his comprehension of the situation. The others were not sure but were prepared to listen to more detail. I hastened to repeat that we were in no danger if we stayed put. We might get a bit cold but we could build a fire. We had fish to eat and water to drink. There might be plenty of wind in the morning. Once again, there was obstinate, verbalized, rejection of waiting until morning.

"OK then, this is what we do. We get on board and taxi out to the center of the lake. I'll gun her and travel in circles. This way we will make some waves of our own. Then I'll race down the lake, turn around, and hope that the ripples are sufficient for us to break free. OK?" I asked, really rhetorically, under the circumstances.

So we did it, several times. We made ripples much like throwing a stone into a pond. They were entirely insufficient. It was getting nearer and nearer to sunset.

"I'd better try to contact Whitehorse by radio," I said. I turned the radio on to let it warm up a bit, then pushed the throttle in until the tachometer showed 1,000 rpm's. Doing this would thereby supply the necessary power to the radio to enable it to transmit signals.

"CF-HSK calling Whitehorse Tower. Do you read? Over," I called, then paused, waiting for a response.

None came.

I fiddled with the dial in an effort to insure that it was properly and finely set, then I repeated, "CF-HSK calling Whitehorse Tower. Do you read? Over."

There was still no response.

I was not really surprised. There was a solid granite and probably, highly mineralized, wall between us and the tower. Not to mention the span of miles. The improved technology in today's radios would have achieved this objective with ease, I'm sure.

Concern registered upon the faces which I could see.

"What's the problem, Harry?" asked Reid, who leaned up from the rear seat where he sat alongside Des.

I throttled back just above an idle. Just enough to keep her going west.

"It's the ore in these mountains, I believe, coupled with the fact that we are some distance away and below the rim," I explained.

"Look you guys, we now have another problem. When I filed my flight plan I recorded that we would be back at 4:30, it's now approaching 3:30. The alarm will be up if we don't at least radio that we are coming in, even if we are a bit late. I'm afraid that natural forces have screwed us up this time. I have nothing more to offer but to taxi back to the shore and tie her down for the night," I said dejectedly.

"Harold, there is a good chance that my patient won't last another day. Circumstances are such that I must operate tomorrow morning, period. We have to do something!" cried Des from the back seat.

"Yeah, and I have all those ruddy witnesses showing up from all over the country. RCMP experts from the Regina laboratory, a witness from Vancouver who has probably already arrived. Boy, will that defense counsel be angry, and the judge, Christ! What a dilemma, what a screwed up trip," I seethed.

"Well we don't blame you, Harold. It's not you who creates the wind," offered Des.

"Well, not often," interjected Nori.

This broke the tension and we all enjoyed a good laugh.

Suddenly Nori said, "Harold, isn't that a breeze freshening? Up there, see, coming out of that valley."

"Yeah, see that ripple over there Harry," said Reid, pointing toward the west wall.

"You're right, it is!" I exclaimed.

I had been on this lake before, several times. Each time a breeze had been blowing out of that valley and across the width of the lake. I had expected it but it was almost too late, it was getting dusk.

"OK you guys, I have to put something to a vote. What I am about to propose is a bit unusual but not at all impossible or treacherous. It may be a bit uncomfortable. I've met other pilots who have done it under similar circumstances. The maneuver is done all the time in aerobatics. Most planes are designed to perform this particular stunt. Ours is. It's no big deal," I stated with as much conviviality as I could, but without diminishing my air of confidence.

"Maneuver? Stunt?" asked Reid suspiciously.

"Yeah, what the hell have you got in mind there, Harold?" asked Des.

I suspected that Nori had already guessed what I had in mind and that is why he had said nothing.

"OK, let me get one thing firmly established. Do you guys insist that you must, absolutely must, get home tonight provided that the odds are not too challenging?" I asked. I looked at each man individually in order to assess the several reactions to my question.

"Harold, I have already told you and the others that my patient is in extremus. I can't put the operation off another day. What the hell have you got in mind? The suspense is beginning to get to me," urged Des.

"Sure thing, Harry. I sure want to go if what you have in mind isn't too hazardous. What the hell is it?" insisted Reid.

"And you Nori?" I asked.

"I have a feeling that I already know what you intend to do. You and I have been up flying many times—I have a pretty good idea of the way things are," he responded.

"Yeah, I thought that you had already figured it out, Nori. Now for the rest of you, I'll give you a quick resume of what I plan. Then you tell me if you're for it, or not. It's no big deal," I stated.

"There you go with the 'it's no big deal' again. What the hell is it?" insisted Reid.

"Well, OK, here is what I propose. We taxi back out into the center of the lake. We wait for those ripples to get out to the right spot for a take off. Because of the direction of the wind, or breeze to be more accurate, we will have to take off toward that valley out of which the breeze is coming," I explained.

"Hell, so what's the big deal then?" asked Des. "Let's do it."

"I didn't finish, Des. Once we get airborne, IF WE DO, then I will have to fly into that valley. Depending upon the altitude which we get after we are airborne, of course, I will have to either turn around in a tight turn, because the valley narrows very quickly or ... ."

"You'll have to perform a hammer head stall," interjected Nori.

"A what?" asked Des, curiosity written all over his face.

"What the hell is that?" asked Reid. "And don't tell me again that it's no big deal," he chuckled reticently.

"Well, let me explain quickly. We are fast running out of light. If we get off the water and are airborne long before we reach the shoreline, then we can go into the valley and turn before the valley peters out. If it appears that we are not going to get airborne, I'll cut the throttle to stop safely before reaching the shoreline. I'll be able to tell by the sensation of the control column. If, however, we do get airborne, but later than desired, then I will not be able to turn inside the valley. I've been over the valley many times and I know its configurations. So, if to say it finally, IF we get airborne late, but get airborne, then I will fly into the valley, getting as much altitude as I can. We'll only need about 1,000 feet above the ground, then I will do the hammer head stall," I explained, running out of breath.

"Jesus what is this thing you're talking about, anyway," asked Reid once again.

"Watch my hand as I explain the maneuver. We climb as high and as quickly as we can. I know that there is height available, there may not be width. If we can't turn then I will pull the nose up like this, up, up, up, until she won't go anymore. Then she will hump over and head for the ground. While she is doing that, I will twist her around and then pull her out of the dive. Then we'll be flying out of, instead of into, the valley. Got it? It's no big deal," I said emphatically.

The silence in that cabin was deafening. Only the purring of the motor could be heard. Eyes stared at me in disbelief. That look of incredulity flashed from one to the other. Heads shook in disbelief.

"Holy Christ, Harry, are you kidding?" asked Reid. He had a look of total skepticism on his face.

"Jeez, Harold, when the hell did you dream that one up? Are you kidding us?" asked Des.

Nori jumped in and gave his two cents worth. He said, "I've done many of them with Harold, but not in these exact circumstances. We were just doing aerobatics, but we've done it."

"Look you guys, it was just an idea. It's not carved in stone. Forget it, it's almost getting too dark now, anyhow. The sun is racing to the edge of that rim. It'll be dark in this cavity even if it isn't dark elsewhere. I'll taxi over to where we had her tied down. We could get in a bit more fishing, then we can try to get off early in the morning. We may have as good a breeze as when we had when we landed," I concluded.

"Yeah, and if we don't we're stuck here the same as we are now," said Reid.

" ... and we will have the whole ruddy air force and civilian volunteers out looking for us," I commented.

Having said this, and not having heard anything from my fishing buddies, I pushed in the throttle and started to taxi over to the stream again.

"No! Wait a minute! I didn't say that I wouldn't agree. I'm thinking it over. I was a bit taken aback by your description and watching your bloody hand whip around like that. What do you guys say?" asked Des.

There was a general hubbub in the back seat. Nori had leaned over to join in. There was much palavering and gesticulation, even outbursts of laughter.

"OK, Harold, we've decided," said Des, as he tapped my right shoulder to emphasize his point. "We are going to do it. For God's sake do it right."

"And so say you all?" I asked jokingly.

"Yeah, for God's sake do it right now before I change my mind," yelled Reid.

"Everyone check your safety belts. Are they on, and tight?" I cried.

I pushed the throttle in and fast taxied to the east side the of the lake. I turned her into what was becoming a breeze, then pushed the throttle "full bore." It would now be too late to change minds.

There was definitely enough distance for us to get off and airborne before the shoreline. The plane roared her determination to perform well. We hit the ripples, they sounded like a kettle drum on the floats. We broke free! We leapt into the air and passed over the edge of the lake at about 200 feet. Into the valley we raced. There was not a lot of lift. I couldn't force it, of course. I had to accept the elevation the air would give me. Up we climbed. So far so good, but we were well into the valley now at about 800 feet.

Real good.

Those valley walls were closing in on us fast.

At 1,500 feet above the ground I knew that the jig was up. We were going to have to do it.

I yelled, "Make sure your seat belt is secure. Is everyone O.K.?"

I looked around at each man to insure that they had checked their belts again. We had done it before but I wanted to check again. I saw two masks of uncertainty and one of stoicism.

"Hold on you guys, this is it!" I yelled.

I pulled back on the control column. Instead of continuing on her headlong rush into that granite wall, she was flying straight up toward the blue but darkening sky. She started to slow up. I had withdrawn the throttle so she had no impetus except her own momentum. She was losing this to gravity. She started to shudder and hesitate. The plane had altered her attack on the air, from horizontal to almost vertical. She was trying to fly straight upwards. Her pace slowed, she had reached her point of ultimate forward thrust. She shuddered and vibrated. Then, inevitably, she was stalled. No air passed over her airfoils. She was no longer a sleek, beautiful kite, she had become a lump of machinery suspended temporarily in the air.

There was a momentary hiatus when she may actually have been completely stationary; hanging like a toy plane with a string attached to her nose. The propeller was barely turning, or so it seemed. The engine idled, waiting for a command.

Suddenly we were wrenched out of that cocoon. She pitched forward. The fulcrum concept was at work. She was heavier in the nose, and therefore, that is what would go down first. The maneuver is not entirely unlike that of being in a roller coaster. At one moment we were resting up against the back of our seats, looking up to the heavens; then suddenly we were cast forward onto our seat belts, looking directly down to the ground. We had been weightless for a moment. All of this breathtaking change had taken place in a fraction of a moment. She had gone "over the hump," so to speak. She literally fell out of the sky. Downwards she tumbled, diving at the river below. She started to twist into a spiral. Had I not applied opposite rudder she would have screwed herself into a tight spin. As the air started to pass over the airfoils she, in turn, started reacting to her commands.

Down she plummeted.

There were sounds coming from my friends but I would not want to write them here verbatim.

When I applied pressure on the rudder pedal she had turned around half a turn. What had been before us, was now behind us. I pulled back on the control column. She responded beautifully. We stopped the menacing plummeting. She raised her head obediently. With plenty of room to spare, we were flying straight and level.

"Jesus Christ, Harold don't ever talk me into something like that again," gasped Des.

"Holy Mother of God! I've wet myself!" cried Reid.

"Now that was a beautifully executed maneuver, Harold," said Nori. "I really enjoyed that."

"Enjoyed it! You bloody sadist!" exclaimed Des. "You must have ice in your veins. I think you actually did enjoy it. Jesus, no one will ever believe me. I'm not sure that I believe it myself. Man oh man, now that was something!"

"I'll never stop trembling, look at these hands go. Christ, it's a good thing that I'm not the one performing that operation tomorrow, I'd cut the bitch to ribbons!" cried Reid. "Boy, look at 'em go."

Reid started to laugh. He was somewhat reluctantly joined by the others, then we all let go. The release of tension took over. Soon they were all talking about the event as though they were old hands at the stunt.

I had turned the radio on. I wanted to contact Whitehorse just as soon as possible. We were now technically "overdue." We had solved the one problem and were now faced with another crisis. We would have to land in the Yukon River in less than prime conditions. Darkness was imminent. Indecision had consumed too much precious time. While I was totally familiar with the landing pattern and the standard obstacles in or near the river, I was still concerned. My concern was not only about the regulations but about the fact that someone without visible markings might be out on the river, on our landing path.

"CF-HSK calling Whitehorse Tower. Do you read? Over," I called.

"Whitehorse Tower, HSK. We read. What is your position? Are you alright? Over."

At this altitude and free of obstruction the radio worked perfectly.

"HSK, Tower. Yes, we are OK. We had some problems but we overcame them."

"Overcame my ass," snorted Reid. "Or did he say insane?"

" ... we are now on course 36 zero, at 8,000 feet. We are headed for the river at your point. We may be a bit late, about one hour. It will be after sunset and it may be a bit dark to land on the river. Can you help? Over," I concluded.

"We read and understand, HSK. Leave it with us for a few minutes. We will get back to you. You are the only reported traffic. Maintain heading and altitude until contacted again. Glad to learn you are alright. Over."

"HSK, thanks. Will stand by," I said.

I felt a great sense of relief that we had been able to contact the tower before the authorities launched the "overdue plane" procedures. The pressure which this would place on our loved ones, friends, and business associates, would not now occur. Any stress which might have been starting to build would now be relieved.

We were, nonetheless, facing a growing obstacle. The lack of daylight. I had no specific "ace" maneuver up my sleeve for this situation. I had only to rely upon my familiarity with the terrain and the river, coupled with what flying skills I could bring to bear.

The engine droned on. My fishing friends were quiet, somber, and thoughtful. It had been a long, exciting day, in diverse ways. The adrenalin which had rushed up during the maneuver, was now having the reverse effect. The passengers had nothing specific upon which to concentrate, other than their thoughts. I had the aircraft and the instruments. Also, I had the concern about the landing.

"Whitehorse tower. HSK, come in please."

This call interrupted the thoughts of all of us.

"HSK, tower. Go ahead. Over," I responded.

"HSK, we think that we have found a satisfactory solution to the problem. You played a role in making this possible last year. Proceed on your present course. Let me know when you are three miles out. Over," said the tower operator.

"Roger, Wilco, HSK," I replied.

"What did he say about your role? In what?" asked Reid.

218

"I'm not sure that I understood what he meant. Anyway he has a solution, you can stop worrying ... if you were," I replied.

"I don't think I am going to worry again, not after what I just went through and survived, uh, slightly damp," said Reid.

Once again, the release of tension brought on laughter in the cabin.

We were now close enough to see the lights of the community. Larger buildings began to become visible.

"Well, at least my clinic didn't burn down while I was away," said Des, laconically.

"I hope my pants are dry," said Reid.

Once again, we all joined him in a good laugh.

"Jeez, Harry, you sure know how to show us Prairie guys an exciting time, but please don't include me in on your next fishing trip, OK?" said Reid, as he punched me on the shoulder and burst out laughing again. Great sense of humor, this guy had.

I had now reached the point where I was to report to the tower.

"HSK, tower, reporting ... three miles from base," I called.

"Roger, HSK, tower ... continue normal landing pattern for a right base to the river. Call on downwind leg. Over," ordered the tower operator.

"Call downwind for a right base to the river," I repeated.

"Look at all those cars down there, Harold," said Nori. "Looks like they are all heading downtown."

As I adjusted the throttle setting as well as the pitch and mixture controls, I glanced down at the city which we were now passing over. We were at about 1,000 feet, so everything was distinctive. There was a lot of vehicular traffic, but I couldn't concentrate on what was happening. I had now reached my reporting position.

"Whitehorse tower, HSK, downwind for a right base to the river. Over."

"HSK, tower, continue to base and call," replied the tower operator.

Nori was right, there was an inordinate number of vehicles on the roads, all headed for the river.

"HSK, tower, on right base for the river. What solution do you have for me? Over," I asked.

"Tower, HSK, continue to final ... you are number one, and are cleared to land. You'll soon see the solution, you and your 'radio week.' Over and out," he concluded. I thought I heard him giggle.

As I turned, for my approach to land, I saw his solution. There, lined up all along the river bank, were vehicles of every type and description, WITH THEIR HEADLIGHTS ON! The river below looked like an elongated, silver, shimmering promenade.

I couldn't help myself. Tears welled up in my eyes and rolled down my cheeks, not the best of moments for this to happen. I had to see clearly to land properly. Embarrassing though it was, I had to get out my handkerchief immediately.

As we touched down, amidst a chorus of cheers from the crowd, I glanced around at my fishing buddies. Apparently, I was not alone in the way I felt about this display of community compassion which we had just witnessed.

Author's Farewell

Well, there you have it, the tale is told,
About the Yukon raw and bold,
You've read about the Yukon zest
The last frontier when at its best.

I've told you of the wonderous things
Which happened at the dark hot springs
Naked specter's streak to car
Which in the light was much too far.

You've read about judicial times
When brain was used instead of fines,
The Solomon touch of that fine judge
Who wondered why we'd backhouse budge.

Then there was that special day
With regal pomp the judge did say
"Harold here who came from far
Is now a member of Yukon's bar."

When Laura took that breathless flight
When toilet rolls were cast from height
Another time the plane was late
And guiding lights outlined our fate.

And what about that glacial silt?
Which brought about a thermal tilt,
Of radio week and all those folks
With songs or dance or tired old jokes.

I told you of the Klondike inch
A party to make a parson flinch
About the mayor's old buffalo coat
And the mobile backhouse which seemed to float.

The fishing trip which had a twist
The kind that some might wish they'd missed
The wings parade which capped my life
Incised my heart as with a knife.

The Christmas saga started there
Has been my shadow everywhere
That old red suit with beard and wig
Has been my constant annual gig.

The pranks we played which meant no harm
Like stethoscope and rules be darned
A magistrate whose phantom powers
Had come and gone within few hours.

The champagne party with police and guest
The judicial wrench which tore with zest
Those contrasts with the pin striped blue
A moose, a bear, and horses too.

In Alaska twice I found strange things
Once a jet with angry wings
Another time a horrific fight
Capped off with shrimp, a ghastly sight.

And so I close by saying thanks
I hope you enjoyed our Yukon pranks
And if by chance you journey near
Please do not miss our "Last Frontier."